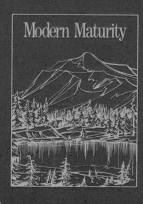

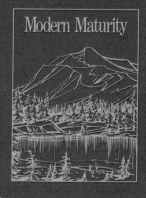

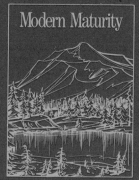

The Wisdom of
Ethel Percy Andrus

2

The Wisdom of
ETHEL PERCY ANDRUS

Compiled by:
Dorothy Crippen, Ruth Lana, Jean Libman Block,
Thomas E. Zetkov, Gordon Elliott

Published by
National Retired Teachers Association
and
American Association of Retired Persons
Andrus Building   Long Beach, California 90802

3

PREFACE

Gathered here are the 49 best editorials among the hundreds Dr. Ethel Percy Andrus wrote for *NRTA Journal,* official publication of the National Retired Teachers Association, and *Modern Maturity* magazine, official publication of the American Association of Retired Persons. Founder and first president of both organizations for retired persons, Dr. Andrus also was editor of both magazines.

It is with great pride that we present to members and friends of our organizations the wise and inspiring words of Dr. Andrus. These editorials reflect her incomparable wisdom, philosophy, inspiration and humor. They allow us to share the noble thoughts she lived by and which guided her two immediate successors and longtime associates, Cecilia O'Neil and George Schluderberg, in continuing her work. Covering the span of human ideals and progress through the ages, the rich legacy of her writings will continue to inspire millions with her self-renewing message of dynamic maturity.

TABLE OF CONTENTS

7

BIOGRAPHY

The remarkable Dr. Ethel Percy Andrus played four major roles in her lifetime.

As a *Useful Citizen* she performed at the local, the state and the national level to demonstrate her deep sense of the individual's responsibility and potential for effecting worthwhile social change in a democratic society.

As a *Practical Idealist* she instigated important legislation in the retirement and social welfare field, fought for nursing home reform and for higher standards of service in every area concerning the elderly and their struggle for dignity and recognition.

As a *Social Innovator* she founded the National Retired Teachers Association and the American Association of Retired Persons and pioneered the health insurance, travel plans, low-cost drug distribution, educational facilities and other services now available to the organizations' combined membership of nearly two million persons past age 55.

As an *Educator* she served as high school teacher and principal, shaper of young minds and older ones, too, and founded the Institute of Lifetime Learning with its totally new approach to the educational needs of the nation's older citizens.

Ethel Percy Andrus was born in San Francisco in 1884 and received her early education in Chicago. She attended the University of Chicago and received her Ph.B. in 1903. She was awarded a B.S. in 1918 by Lewis Institute in Chicago and during her teaching years in Los Angeles earned her M.A. in 1928 and her Ph.D. in 1930 from the University of Southern California.

She taught first at Lewis Institute in Chicago, then at Santa Paula High School in California and later at Manual Arts High School in Los Angeles, where she served for one year as acting principal. She went to Abraham Lincoln High School in Los Angeles as vice principal in February 1916 and that June was named principal, the first woman high school principal in the state. She served as principal at Lincoln for 28 years.

At her retirement in 1944 after 41 years in teaching, she became volunteer Director of Welfare for the California Retired Teachers Association. This first hand experience with older persons' needs led her to formulate her philosophy that the aging can attain goals of personal dignity and social usefulness by recognizing their own individual worth in a crusade for service.

In 1947 she founded the National Retired Teachers Association and in 1950 launched the NRTA Journal which she edited. In 1954 she brought to reality Grey Gables, the first and only national teachers' retirement residence, and in 1959 the Acacias Nursing Home, both located in Ojai, California. In 1967 the Andrus Apartments for convalescents were added, a new concept providing a transition between independent living and nursing home care.

To change the climate of retirement for millions of Americans outside the teaching profession, she established the American Association of Retired Persons in 1958 and became its first President. She also founded and edited its magazine, Modern Maturity. Later she founded and edited the Journal of the Association of Retired Persons International and Dynamic Maturity, a magazine directed to the problems of pre-retirement. As a natural outgrowth of NRTA and AARP, Dr. Andrus founded the Retirement Research and Welfare Association in 1961; the Association of Retired Persons International in 1963; and the Institute of Lifetime Learning, also in 1963.

From 1920–1933, Ethel Percy Andrus served as Executive Secretary of the American School for Girls, Damascus, Syria; from 1927–1937, she was a member of the Advisory Board of the Los Angeles County General Hospital. She was one of the organizers, and later served as Vice President and President of the California Secondary School Principals' Association. Dr. Andrus was a member of the Board of the National Council for Accreditation of Nursing Homes, the American Nursing Home Association, and a member of the Board of Directors of the American Association of Homes for the Aging.

Dr. Andrus was the first teacher to receive the Golden Apple Award when she was named National Teacher of the Year on Teacher Remembrance Day by the International Senior League in 1954. She was appointed by President Eisenhower as a member of the National Advisory Committee for the 1961 White House Conference on Aging and served as a delegate to that Conference.

To illustrate what older people can accomplish, Dr. Andrus planned, as a showcase, the Dynamic Maturity Pavilion at the New York World's Fair, 1964–1965, the first Pavilion in the history of World's Fairs, dedicated to older persons.

Ethel Percy Andrus was already a seasoned leader when she set out to restore to retired teachers their faith in themselves and their stature in the community. Now on a national scale she exercised her power of persuasion, her executive ability, her eloquence to bring older teachers and, later, older persons from other spheres of activity back into the mainstream of American life. When she mounted a platform, first her presence—a handsome, stately woman with compelling eyes and yet a twinkle—and then her words—a golden flow of eloquence, often spontaneous, always richly interlaced with learned references to history and mythology and with evocative quotations from Shakespeare, the Bible, the Greeks, Browning, Tennyson, Lincoln—commanded the audience's closest attention.

In person-to-person dialog she was witty, sparkling and, when occasion demanded, a rapier-sharp adversary. She loved laughter, both to join in it and to elicit it. Beauty was important in her life. She brought home beautiful objects and art from her many trips. She chose her clothes with great care. She decorated her own homes and those of her organizations with the expertise of a professional. She would tolerate nothing around her that was shoddy or second-rate. She planned the gardens of Grey Gables to bring beauty to the surroundings.

When the responsibility fell upon her, she proved an extraordinary business woman and administrator. In a calm and ordered way she directed the far-flung affairs of her million-member organizations, concerning herself with all details—hiring of personnel, purchase of buildings, development of policies, investment of funds, enlargement of benefits. While she always loved to travel, in the last decade of her life, when she was past 70, she learned literally to live out of a suitcase as she hastened to meetings, conventions, speaking engagements, legislative hearings, and international conferences.

Ethel Andrus was always an appreciative woman. She thanked her friends for their courtesies, continuously gave credit to the leaders of NRTA and AARP for their valued contributions, distributed scores of citations to fellow citizens for excellence and achievement. She believed in the value of remembrance. She remembered her own family heritage and beseeched others to respect the struggles and accomplishments of their forebears. She was ever loyal to her friends, her country, her ideals. The love and devotion that her parents had given her and that she had returned to them in full measure during their lifetime, she bestowed later on her fellow men—men and women everywhere who shared her longing for purpose, independence, dignity. Her finest epitaph was spoken by one of her long-time associates, "If such a person as Ethel Percy Andrus is given to this world, mankind is fortunate."

Her death occurred in California in July 1967.

CALL TO SERVICE

When I have food, oh God –
Help me to remember the hungry;
When I have work, help me to
remember the jobless; When I
have a warm home, help me to
remember those who have no home
at all; When I am without pain,
help me to remember those who
suffer – and remembering, Help me
to destroy my complacency, and bestir
my compassion – and be concerned
enough to help, By word and deed,
those who cry out for what we
take for granted. Amen. *Samuel F. Pugh*

"We have demonstrated that old age is not a defeat
but a victory, not a punishment but a privilege.
We have held ourselves instinctively responsive to the needs
of our people. We have become successful social innovators.
We have proved that the leisure of the elderly
can be a many-splendored thing."

Thankfulness,
of all else, we have

hat delightful oldster, Anita Day Hubbard, star reporter for the San Francisco Examiner liked to tell the story of the amazed surprise of the little nine-year old who was hearing for the first time the thrilling tale of the San Francisco Earthquake.

Anita was picturing the rugged difficulty of walking because of the cobble stones and the wooden blocks that had erupted from the pavement. The lad sympathetically queried, "Wasn't that awfully hard on the auto tires?" And, upon being told, then there were no autos, in embarrassment he covered his mistake by saying, "Of course, you'd use jeeps!"

Anita continued in her recital recalling the uneasy concern that one's dear ones far away could not be reassured of one's safety. Telegraph and telephone lines were down, but the lad protested, "But there were radios and TVs."

Anita reported the utter bewilderment of the lad at a world without the auto and the radio and its descendants. Such a world was unthinkable, and yet you and I lived in that world, a crowed, happy, busy life.

It would be hard for any lad of today to believe that we who are old are the fortunate ones. We were reared in homes where Father's and Mother's word was law. Father in our eyes was wise and farseeing. Mother's love comforted us and made our hurts whole. It was a world of security, peace, neighborliness and well-being. We were proud to be Americans, glad that all the world loved and respected us. We knew, too, if we worked hard, did the "right thing," we could count upon a contented old age.

We oldsters are the ones who have bridged the great gap between the surrey with the fringe on top and the jet streamliner, from the early telephone with the ring of its bell to the telestar with its clear contact with Europe. The one constant we older ones have experienced has been change; to it we are geared. We who live in the present are still looking hopefully toward the changes of the future. In truth, we still consider that the future is our business!

The young folks of today on the other hand, have been born and reared in a world of the atom, of a world of unrest, uncertainty, of the threat of World War and even of fear of annihilation. The young folk's home may be more urban than ours probably was—have fewer pets, probably less parental control and guidance, fewer chores . . . less obligation for giving expected services. And sadly, too, the youngster of today hears Uncle Sam often accused by those whom he has helped, as self-serving, imperialistic and hostile to the interests of the under-privileged of the world.

We who are retired have much to share with these young people—else where will they know the kaleidoscope of change? Should we not share with them the luminous faith in the American dream, the dream that made us great as a nation? In their search for security can we not inject the spirit of daring and adventure into the unknown—the re-vivifying for them of the "passion of idealism."

If our business is the future then we must scrutinize the make-up of our aged. In spite of contradictory reports, we find these persons zestful, energetic, well-integrated with a positive attitude toward the business of living; folks with a maturing wisdom.

16

We older ones are a vast and a complex group yet we demonstrate mutual understanding and good will—a wholesome human ripening. Should we not seriously, as socially conscious people, take part on a national, state and local basis in the design and development of a dynamic program in the values of the democratic way of life? Can we not help our young folk who are so eager to think us outmoded and needing their solicitous care? Can we not share with them our aims of restoring a sense of community? Can we not, as an organization and as individuals, do something significant in reducing civic apathy, and that sense of isolation, frustration and helplessness which so often haunts the city dweller? Can we not actively participate in the teaching of young people about things for which men shall live?

While values will vary from community to community, still everywhere the broader values hold true. The respect for the importance and the worth of each individual: 1) to be given the right to achieve a feeling of belonging on the basis of merit, 2) to be encouraged to participate up to his full capacity and 3) to be recognized for the value of that contribution.

This is a sizeable challenge—If it seems overwhelming, let us remember Carlyle's statement, "Every noble work is at first impossible." It isn't as if we did not know the *what* we are trying to do. That we do know. It is the *how* to do it! *We* are trying to transmit the dedication we have to the democratic way of life. We are trying, too, to transmit these values: 1) the dignity of the individual, 2) the challenge of responsibility, and 3) the understanding that in democratic groups, men equal in the eyes of each other can solve their mutual problems for the betterment of the environment—the environment in which we and our younger may proudly live.

Nor do we need to consider the *why*. We often see with dismay the tendency on the part of younger folk to "let George do it," not realizing that they are *George*. Really beyond the problem of *"how"* is perhaps that of "Why we?" Why not experts in sociology, government, etc.? We're just ordinary folk.

But is it not true that what we are discussing is the *life* of our nation? And is it not also true that, if our people need some such thing as a mechanical material or scientific product or innovation, they turn to the expert in that specialized field? But is it not also true if *life* is in jeopardy, the most precious irreplaceable possession in all the world, then our people turn, not to the experts, but to a round dozen of average folks, persons just like you and me. And was not this too the technique used by the Founder of Christianity?

Of course we know the doubts that *arise* as to our fitness, our competency, but, if we pass the essential test that *we care,* then our planning will quiet our fears.

The planning requires a clear and definite goal. Just what are the specifics that will challenge you? They must be something very near your heart, something about which you *care* and for the good of some one or some ones for whom you also care.

It may be a very personal contribution such as sharing with the young of your family the family traditions of pioneer hardship where survival depended on mutual helpfulness. We all know tales of the courageous surmounting of dangers and the thrill of planning and working together to found the family. The mutual study of genealogy with the young of your family can be not only an absorbing cooperative venture but also a very rewarding experience to you and to them, and to their children-to-be.

Your interest may extend to the neighborhood. You may be living in a city environment with people living next door and down the street —and yet strangers to you. Do you recall the President's message which included these words: "We must begin now to lay the foundations for livable, efficient, and attractive communities of the future."

What to do? to do first? Well, first of all comes your realization that you have free time and that you can make that free time enjoyable and fruitful and perhaps that the easiest way to begin is by making happy relationships with the folks next door and down the street, helping build a sense of neighborliness. You may have to become a "self-stimulator" to begin. To still the jitters you might need to add to your daily diet those intangible spiritual supplements—"A" for vision—to see the job; "B" for nervous vigor—the courage to make the first break-through; and "C" to build strength to convert that acquaintance-making

18

into friendship-building.

Try it; you will find understanding and acceptance. You will develop new friends and so replace the loss of old ones. You will build for yourself and those others, status and recognition. You may uncover, also, the vehicle for planning and working together for a mutual good, becoming partners of various ages and various cultures and backgrounds.

What might be the specifics that might weld your separate individuals into such a cohesive constructive group?

Are there irritants in your home and in those of the folks nearby that might be relieved by individual or group action? Are your street numbers easily seen? Would numbering on a curb be of help? Is the curb too high for older people to easily manage? Can that curbing be lowered and yet protect from drains? What about street names? Are they well placed? easily distinguished? And talking of names, does the town well display its own name to the traveler passing through it?

What about parkways? What about tree planting? Would the idea of decorating the curbing and the parkway act as an incentive? Are the sidewalks safe? adequate? or broken and potentially dangerous?

What about the time alloted a person crossing the street where the lights are part of town planning? Are the lights so spaced as to permit older folks' passage? Can they cross completely and safely, if they start at the beginning of the green light period and do not dawdle?

Are there enough street lights, night-time, for safety? Are there, on the walk to the trading center, facilities available such as adequate street benches? Should they not be provided? If so, where? how?

How about litter on the sidewalks, the parkway 'or the street? Are there litter cans conveniently placed? Are they themselves an aesthetic asset to the town?

And what about the communal dump? Can it be made less of a nuisance to eye and nose? If so, how?

What about engaging youth in a self-service "Clean up Day" by paper gathering, the sale to go toward a Youth Center? or prizes at a Community Athletic Festival? or a Pet Show? or a Gymkhana?

And that leads us to consider the park. It there one? Is it like the front parlor of yesteryear—something fine to have but too fine for daily use?

What about bill boards and advertising signs? Do they clutter up the highway? destroy its beauty? What can be done about them? Many towns make entrance to them things of beauty. How did they do it? Can we?

Is there anything being done to preserve the history of your community? Is there on file in City Hall, Library or County Building, tales and pictures of its growth and development?

Is our locality conscious of its own uniqueness? Some towns in California have unofficial Mayors of an informally formed neighborhood, with lots of fun and fun fare at installation times and occasional "Town Hall" gatherings and dances and community sings.

Does the history of your town lend itself to the establishment of a festival, based on a legend, a tale of derring-do, of love lost or won? something dramatic that would be pictured and sung and danced, the germ of a community festival? one that would enlist the diverse interests and skills from the poster artist in the high school to the oldest sage in the county who remembers "when"?

There are a lot of *isms* in the world—optimism and pessimism; capitalism, socialism, communism, conservatism, liberalism and radicalism. They all tend to separate groups. But there is one ism that unites everyone—*heroism*. Let's stress heroism and do honors to our local heroes. And what about arranging for plaques in places of historical significance? Such an action group can do much to help the youth of the town develop a sense of grateful pride in it.

And speaking of community programs, what about your being on the planning committee to stimulate appropriate civic celebrations on Arbor Day (June 14), and Citizenship Day (September 17), when you could do honor to those of your town just acquiring their majority and those to whom citizenship is an honor being worthily bestowed; Then there's the challenge of Halloween! Think how you can keep the fun of yesteryear and save its wreckage!

There are a hundred and one challenges about us. We must keep our imagination alert to see them and our sense of mission to do some-

20

thing about them. We'll need all our powers of persuasion at times, for we'll meet many like the old Yankee captain. "Now, my hearties," he said, "you've got a tough battle before you. Fight like heroes until your powder is gone, then run. I'm a little lame, so I'll start now."

You are asking your fellows to choose to help, spending time and energy for the future and placing upon the future and your present your own image and your own individual stamp of value.

We know too many that are suffering from apathy and indifference. You must make them see that all you are asking of them is their time? Of course you have to tell because you are honest, that time is truly the essence of life. Each day is a gift. It comes to us unbidden but it is ours to do with as we will. Reassure them with this message I came across in my reading:

> The first strategy of many
> who are faced with a problem is to quit.
> But a man who suffered such severe burns on his legs
> that he faced amputation—he didn't quit.
> He became the most successful
> distance runner of his time.
> And a man with less than one year
> of formal education didn't quit.
> He became the most revered
> president we ever had.
> And a fragile boy in Scotland,
> bedridden most of his childhood, didn't quit.
> He became such a masterful story-teller
> your great grandchildren
> Will cherish his books as you did.
> Now, if you had *all three*
> of those strikes against you,
> Nobody would blame you for quitting.
> But unless your legs are
> severely burned,
> And you're so fragile you have
> to stay in bed,

And you never graduated from
　　second grade,
Why don't you turn around
　　and get back to work?
Maybe we'll be writing
　　about *you* someday!

Yes, the future is our business, just as the past has been. We take courage from the preachment of Isaiah, "Enlarge the place of your tent; hold not back, lengthen your cords and strengthen your stakes."

We know that, in this age of atomic energy and outer space with its enormous concentration of power, physical, economic, political and psychological, we have not mastered the science of inner space human relationships. Yet we as individuals know ourselves as independent in spirit, versatile in achievement and self-reliant in mind and body. We have demonstrated the truth we hold that old age is not a defeat but a victory, not a punishment but a privilege. We have held ourselves instinctively responsive to the needs of our people. We have faithfully encouraged the American tradition of self-help and of humane service. We have successfully built a sense of togetherness. We have striven for excellence. We have in these ways become successful social innovators; we have demonstrated that the leisure of the elderly can be a many-splendored thing.

Our aims in service are definite and attainable; we will do our best to make our retirement responsible and devoted; we will try to the level of our abilities to help make the world of the future richer and happier because we are living in the world of today, working with plans and purposes for tomorrow, in the perspective of their ultimate meaning.

"Hold high the torch!
We did not light the glow
'Twas given us by other hands, you know
'Tis ours to keep it burning bright
Ours to pass on, when we no more need the light."

22

"Whether or not the public demands, what do we demand of ourselves, in enforcing common decency, common humanity, the urge and the immediate answer to the call for help?"

The Good Samaritan

ne morning recently on the steps of the country courthouse at Santa Ana, California, a house, valued at $20,000, was sold at public auction; its owner, just released from a prison term, and still on probation, could not meet the payments. His car, his boat and all his savings had gone to pay his trial costs.

This former top-flight salesman of electrical components has found no steady employment because upon their learning of his being on parole, prospective employers discover they have "no openings at present."

Friends scraped together more than $1,000 to bring the home payments up-to-date, but, they report, the investment firm that holds the mortgage refused the payment, claiming that the former owner would not be able to maintain future monthly payments since he was unemployed.

The background story is that this man who drew state-wide headlines as the "Good Samaritan," accidentally killed a man, outside a bar in his home town, in his attempt to protect a woman the man was beating.

Described by his friends as a "sweet, lovable guy who wouldn't hurt a fly," the day before the shooting, he has become hard and cynical and feels he was unjustly convicted and sentenced.

23

Be that as it may, his story is one often repeated when someone morally obeying a mandate of his own conscience comes to the help of a man attacked or a woman assaulted.

The killing was accidental and unintentional, but a man was dead, and the law prescribed the penalty. Barring the tragedy of the accident that caused the death, should the man have so acted? You might say he could have called the police at no risk to himself. The law has said he had no obligation to be a Good Samaritan. Yet our moral teachings say otherwise. But even if we grant that there is at times a necessity for involvement, in such a happenstance, are there degrees of involvement to be observed? How deeply should we involve ourselves? At what point should we allow ourselves to become involved? How about what the law classifies as the "officious intermeddler"?

The public is concerned with this problem. Often we read or hear about cases of licensed physicians or surgeons who voluntarily administer emergency care, in good-faith at the scene of the emergency, being held liable for their efforts, even where the care is rendered either without remuneration or with the expectation of remuneration. We hear, too, of qualified medical practitioners being reluctant to render aid to helpless persons in emergencies because of the fear of becoming defendants in malpractice suits in consequence, or liability for civil damages, or of facing the charge that there was no immediacy to the situation, so that the rendering of services could have been postponed until the patient was hospitalized.

Then there is the story of bystanders who, fearing to become involved, like the Levite, "passed by on the other side." The case of this type most often cited was that of Kitty Genovese of New York, where 38 witnesses failed to come to her help, even though she was being brutally attacked.

Should they have acted? Could they not at least have called the police? Should the man in Santa Ana have so acted? If he had not, he today might have saved home, boat, savings, his job, his future, and his good repute.

Recently the Sentry Insurance Society in co-sponsorship with the Law School of the University of Chicago held a symposium on the

24

Good Samaritan to consider state legislative proposals intended to offer broader immunity to would-be rescuers. For those who agree with this broader immunity, but do not feel that social inequities need be solved by governmental action, the discussion is of prime interest.

Our common law has always confined itself to legal matters and legal duties; it does not transmute moral obligations into legal obligations. Our law does not demand that, seeing some one in trouble, which is not of our making, we must come to his or her relief, but it does require that having engaged in some measure of aid that we be not negligent in our performances. Because of this stipulation, some people do nothing.

What we do becomes a question of one's manners and morals and one's emotional make-up, plus one's empathy that finally determines our reaction—whether coming to the rescue or ignoring the situation as an unpleasant nuisance. Considering the situation as we see it, we face the problem of our possibly giving or refusing aid from the standpoint of the strength or the weakness of the obligations we feel to help someone in distress. Ordinarily, unless the shock is so great that we panic, we will give aid. There is an initial assumption that we owe to ourselves to yield to our inner emotions and so pay our debt to the community, for a community becomes one only when its members commit themselves to each other to make some common sacrifice of energy, finances, privacy and comfort to preserve the community and to enjoy its advantages. There is, included in this, at least a sacrifice to maintain, existent in the community, public order and safety.

Margaret Mead, the anthropologist, explains this avoidance of becoming involved, where such is the case, springs from our drive for privacy which kills in us the spirit of a concerned neighborliness. Many years ago, when the majority of people lived on farms and in villages, they were close to one another. The population was spread thin over great distances. Those were "the good old days." Now we live in the "better new days" of cities, crowds, subways, noise, violence and people, people, people—a lonely crowd. The word neighbor, once a heartening word, of sharing our mutual helpfulness, today too often we use the word with our lips, and not with our hearts, in deed and truth. Perhaps a simple answer, for our guidance, we are told by the Sentry—University of Chicago Conference—might be the formation of a "Cowards carry a dime-card" to use in notifying the police and so call for help and protect one's anonymity. There's much to be said about minding one's own business, but today anybody's business becomes increasingly everyone's business. We cannot however require people to be of great courage, of compassionate heart and of a feeling of human kinship. We cannot punish them for lack of showing moral tenderness and pity in situations not of their making, into which they are propelled by casual circumstance. We can however consider reimbursing them when they incur loss or damage when rescuing those whose lives are endangered by a third person. Some countries do have Good Samaritan laws.

France, Germany, Italy and the Soviet Union all have such statutes. France's experience covers twenty years. It provides that if a person abstains from giving aid, either by personal action or the alerted help of others, when aid is needed and can be rendered without danger or damage to the person, he becomes liable to punishment of three months to five years imprisonment and a fine from 360 to 15,000 francs.

The situation requires: (1) that the person must be in danger; (2) that there is a possibility of rescue; (3) that there be no risk in the rescue, either for the person who denies his aid or any third party; and (4) that the refusal to render aid is voluntary; if the person, although he possibly could have been a witness to the emergency, actually was not, he is not considered guilty of failing to relieve the victim or to prevent damage or catastrophy.

In brief, the French law acts as an incentive to the Good Samaritan.

Is Good Samaritanship only an expression of a person's sense of brotherhood, or does it also have social facets?

Take the problem of a child whose life medical science predicts can be saved by an operation, and the parents, because of their religious faith, refuse to authorize it. Does Good Samaritanship become a factor in the case? Australian law permits, in such an emergency, that society can become the child's guardian, releasing the surgeons from liability and the parents from their authority to deny relief needed by and offered to their offspring.

Does the Veterans Administration qualify as a Good Samaritan to help compensate socially for damage and disability and pain gained in the service of one's country? The question arises: Is this a problem of morals or of law? Is there not a difference between the moral ideal of one's individual conscience, which is not a problem of law but of personal idealism and practice, and a moral duty, which is expected of us all as members of the community and is, when realized in practice, so taken for granted by the community that it does not become a matter of social admiration but rather one of social expectation? While our law does not concern itself with a person's moral idealism, does not the failure to perform one's moral duty become a matter of social concern and action? Society cannot enforce our coming to the rescue of a victim of personal violence, but is there no obligation for society to recognize the need of some sort of protection, immunity, restitution or compensation to the Good Samaritan who may suffer a tangible loss in his deeds of rescue?

Dr. Freedman, Professor of Psychiatry of the University of Chicago, explains the sequence of the thinking stages of the Bad Samaritan: "Apathy and indifference" he surmises, "may be the least likely primary factors in abstinence on the part of the individual to give aid." The sequence, as he sees it, is: (1) the extreme emotional shock, (2) the awareness of what has happened, (3) the paralysis of reaction, while negative in fact is positive in its result, (4) the realization of one's own reaction, followed by (5) a sense of guilt and later a type of social self-justification.

Dr. Freedman further expresses his belief that the current concern over the so-called Bad Samaritan is not because he has increased in number, but because society has increased in sensibility of our responsibility to each other.

Dr. Herman Goldstein, Assistant Professor of Law of the University of Wisconsin, believes the greatest significance of the failure of citizens to aid victims of crime is their failure to report the act to the authorities, either feeling that there can be no purpose gained, or that the reporter would be held in contempt as an innocent or a weakling or that reporting might be followed by an act of personal revenge.

Secondly, the position in men's minds that the authorities responsible for the keeping of order, the courts, the prosecution and the police should be reviewed and strengthened with the hope of a more respectful and supportive attitude on the part of the members of the community.

Such is the problem of the Good Samaritan in America. We know of no practical way of requiring people in general to render aid to someone in distress. We know that there are in Europe countries that do have such protective and constructive legislation. Perhaps the answer lies in the hope that someday people will realize that they live in a community where each helps the other, realizing that tomorrow he or one of his family might be the victim in need of help.

It is interesting to note that some 40 states already have adopted Good Samaritan legislation directed mainly at the protection of those of the licensed health practitioners who in an emergency volunteer their services.

Alabama, Arizona, Hawaii, Kentucky, Minnesota, Missouri, Oregon, Vermont, Washington and West Virginia have none. California, in 1959, enacted the first so-called "Good Samaritan" Law. Since then 40 other states have followed. The existing laws are not all uniform:

4 cover only physicians
20 cover anyone who renders emergency first-aid
20 require that the services be rendered gratuitously
4 cover only roadside accidents
4 cover only physicians licensed in state
18 cover outside-of-state physicians
18 cover physicians and other health personnel
14 cover everyone, but do not cover acts of gross negligence or wilful misconduct
40 cover only gratuitous services

In consideration of the passage of so many laws of this kind largely affecting the medical profession, passed in the four legislative sessions since the passage of the first in California, the question arises "Is such a law essential?" Governor Kerner of Illinois and Governor Nelson

28

Rockefeller of New York believe not. Both failed to approve such a measure even after legislative approval.

Governor Kerner of Illinois questions as true to facts the danger facing a physician's humanitarian act in rendering emergency roadside care to an injured party and further expresses a doubt that court would not take into consideration attendant circumstances; further would not permit unfair treatment, if such an action came to court.

The American Medical Association also agrees that there are no records to substantiate the facts of need. The answer, then, why the case for such legislation with the probable answer of "fear." Governor Rockefeller disapproved "an act to amend the education law, in relation to exemption from liability of physicians and surgeons rendering gratuitous emergency treatment," stating as his objections: "(1) Our undesirable lowering of standard accepted conduct of physicians which has prevailed for many years. (2) The present law permits in emergencies a lesser standard of performance but does not permit 'wilful neglect, or gross negligence,' which appear to be 'unnecessarily low.' (3) The exemption would apply only to physicians who rendered 'gratuitous' treatment. (4) If principle is sound why restrict exemptions only to physicians and surgeons.

If there is no discoverable legal justification why the mounting pressure and concern? Again, the answer seems to be "fear."

A study in 1961, by the Law-Medicine Research of Boston University reports findings from a 10% survey of practicing physicians in Massachusetts. If the physician were attending an evening performance at the theater and a call for a doctor was given, would the doctor answer the call? The answers showed:

21% Yes, if no other doctor answered (fear of a malpractice suit)
27% Yes
14% Would want to know what was the trouble
15% No (fear of malpractice suit)
2% No answer

What has caused this fear? Perhaps the answer is: (1) The continuing general increase in malpractice liability claims, (2) Careless stories and scare rumors and nonfactual TV tales, (3) Increase in news media about marvelous results in medical practice, "with the result that the public expects of physicians not merely perfection but miracles."

If there is insistence on the passage of "Good Samaritan" laws, it is suggested that the moderate phrasing of the laws of Mississippi and South Dakota be used as models. They provide that no physician or nurse, "who, in good faith and the exercise of reasonable care to any person at the scene of an emergency, or in transporting any injured person to a point where medical assistance can be reasonably expected, shall be liable to any civil damages as a result of any acts or ommissions by such person in rendering the emergency care."

A great many people—I suppose you and I are included—wonder what we would do if we met such an emergency. Will we realize ourselves in act and deed? Or are we likely to be in our own thinking a Walter Mitty, imaginatively alert, active, courageous and heroic, but really scared to death? Or are we, in spite of ourselves, likely to panic and do nothing? Or are we becoming afraid and running away? Are we to be a Sir Galahad, seeking the Holy Grail, or a Don Quixote fighting windmills?

One thing of course we can do is to call the police. That is sensible and certainly indicated, but the question arises: will the clerks at the receiving desk at police headquarters take us seriously? Will they be prompt enough to save the situation? The law does not require us to do anything, but what kind of persons are we making of ourselves? These are the questions that determine our personal self-respect or our personal self-contempt. Whether or not the public demands, what do we demand of ourselves, in enforcing common decency, common humanity, the urge and the immediate answer to the call for help?

John Donne reminds us: *"No man is an island entire of itself;*
Every man is a piece of the continent, a part of the main.

If a clod be washed away by the sea, Europe is the less, as well as if a promontory were, as well as if a manor of thy friends or thine own were;

Any man's death diminishes me, because I am involved in mankind; and therefore never send to know for whom the bell tolls, it tolls for thee."

30

*"If you want to raise the standards of taste,
of morals, of manners, you are the ones to do it.
You are the 'they' that must speak out."*

May our torches of enthusiasm inspire others to play a vital role

The battle of Thermopylae was over. Leonidas, the Greek chieftain, had been slain. His body was borne before Xerxes, his victor, and Xerxes, honoring his dead rival, who had been so valiant and true, and had held the power of Persia so weak, honored him by spreading over the body of Leonidas his own royal cloak. But Leonidas, from the land of the beyond, in disdain cast aside the garment of the tyrant. "But thou are dead, Leonidas," pled the victor, "do you so hate the Persian even in your death?" To the query Leonidas proudly answered. "The spirit of freedom dieth not."

And just so our spirit of freedom—and of dedication—lives in us—still impels us to go on serving its cause. This is my greeting to you and my prayer for you all. May this year be for all of us a year of renewed commitment to service—a year that will demand of us something more rare than sound intelligence—demand of us decision and resolution. Let us feel that each of us had a charge to keep dynamically alive the great dream of faith in our country as that of a free folk sharing with all other lands the ideas we hold dear—national independence, political liberty, self-determination, social equal-

31

ity and moral decency.

In this great crusade of man's development each of us has met the challenge to do the best we can. We have always realized that man's most potent weapons of both offense and defense are an idea—an ideal—a faith—and our faith in the ultimate worth, the usefulness, and the dignity of man, the individual.

We realize today that man—his freedom or his subjugation—is the crux of the battle not only for today but perhaps for all the days of our lives. The struggle is for man's mind and his emotion and his soul. In such a conflict our dynamic faith in man's worth is a potent and a mighty weapon.

All our lives we have fought the good fight—the eternal fight between good and evil, between inertia and purpose, between apathy and the growth of a social concern. All our professional years we have seriously accepted these responsibilities.

As retired folk, we find ourselves somehow relieved of the heavy tangible pressures involved in our former work. We are told that we have earned the right to rest and, without limitations, to play any role we like in advancing our own interests. As no other segment in America's adult population, we retired folk have leisure, that precious treasure of free time that grants us the opportunity for such personal satisfactions and for our own meaningful growth.

As we recognize these personal advantages we know that we must go on utilizing them in doing our share in creating in our communities an affirmative climate of opinion, to the best of our ability helping our communities build toward more beauty, less prejudice, better schools, and a more sustained sense of public responsibility.

You may recall what Francis Bacon in the quaint phraseology of his day said about professions. "I hold every man a debtor to his profession, from which, as men of course do seek to receive countenance and profit, so ought they of duty to endeavor themselves by way of amends to be a help and ornament thereto."

This is a magnificent mandate to us. Let us show to the world about us the truth that Plato once said, "Those having torches will pass them on to others." May our torches of enthusiasm and dedication help others play a vital role in the American drama of today, a day when America needs its creative leaders, needs again to put to work its social innovators. For is it not a profound and moving thought that many of us, as teachers, were such innovators, participants in one of the greatest experiments of history—an experiment that is a success. For the first time the world as we know it used education as a force to level class distinctions instead of widening them, the first time to open to all the gates of opportunity rather than to seal them shut except for a chosen few.

The *PTA Magazine* in one of its fine numbers makes this cryptic comment: "We give our schools awesome assignments. From the most diverse materials—malleable, refractory, explosive—we expect them to fashion uniformly superior products. We ask them to tame the rebellious, embolden the timid, spur the laggard, sharpen the dull, burnish the bright. We ask them to make every child good, healthy, competent, happy, useful."

It would seem that people think children are educated only when they are in school. When you see the films, when you hear the radio, when you watch television, when you see the advertisements on the billboards, do you not wonder how ever could we have such moral and upright young people as you and I know and see about us? The schools take the best that civilization has produced and show it to the children, but this world about us then presents a world of dreadful temptation; the picture the films frequently show is one of brute violence—sometimes of lewd and purposeless living and often of bestial crime. The children live their lives in two cultures widely divergent. Somehow the two cultures need to be fused into one, the lower raised—not the higher lowered. Who cares more than you? Who has more free time to give the gift of yourself, your faith, your hopes to raising for America the standards of life? If you want to raise the standards of taste, of morals, or manners, you are the ones to do it—you are the "they" that must speak out—decry mediocrity—call junk junk and trash trash, deplore the lewd and the cheap. Counter stories in the news of juvenile delinquency with reports from that great group of fine youngsters you know.

If you wish culture for America, you can help advance its cause. You with your treasure of empathy and with your wide acquaintance, your enthusiasm and your spirit of dedication can find in this service, the reward of knowing that you have helped the coming generation become a trumpeter that "summons and excites men not to cut each other to pieces with mutual contradictions, or to quarrel and fight with one another; but rather to make peace among themselves, and turning with united force against the Nature of Things, to storm and occupy her castles and strongholds and extend the bounds of human empire, so far as God Almighty in His goodness may permit."

*"The causes that can engage your leisure hours
to the betterment of society are as numberless as
the sands of the desert. Just what your choice is,
only you can tell and only you can do the job."*

Exploring new ways
of coping with old problems

ll of us are the children of immigrants—no matter how many generations back. Our ancestors came for many reasons: some fled from religious persecution, some hoped to better their living and the prospects for their children, some expected great success, and some were lured by the charm of new and novel places; but all came because of a dream of a better, fuller, freer life. And what did they find—those early forebears of ours?

Hidden forays of Indians fearful of the white man, the ever-present danger of sudden attack, of scalping, of ambuscades and wanton destruction; the terrors of Nature in tempest and in droughts, in plagues destroying their labors and their means of livelihood. No matter how simple and primitive their former lives may have been, the new land offered none of the amenities of the former days—no houses built, no roads set out, no form of communal protection or services—just land. Beautiful and awe-inspiring as it may have been, still there lurked in that land fear and dangers, hardship and often famine and illness. But our forefathers didn't go back. The Mayflower and her sister ships brought others but took back none. Those are our forebears; these are the stalwarts who won for us the rights we do proudly enjoy and the weak and vicious among us claim as a shield for their dishonor.

The seacoasts conquered, these ancestors of ours pressed onward, ever pushing back the known horizons, but always at the price of fearlessly meeting dangers and hardships. Thousands died in the effort. Some survived, but even when the survivors reached their goal, still there was the wilderness to conquer, food to be won, security to be sought. They, however, had one asset we do not share today—the untiring effort of all toward that same end.

Today it often seems that our people—good, sturdy folk, too—are divided among those who believe that America owes them a living and who search ever for security and ease by minimizing the old economic virtues of prudence, thrift and sturdy and honorable independence, and the manlier ones of effort, adventure and freedom. The second group realizes the blood, the sacrifice and the effort that has gained for America those rights; furthermore, these people have a sense of obligation to keep alive and victorious those qualities of mind, of body, and of spirit that saw the vision and tried everywhere to strengthen and to share it.

The problem is: What can we as older responsible folk do to help realize these goals?

The first, and the crucial decision, is whether or not we, as individuals, feel it incumbent upon ourselves to do something about it. Then comes the test: is your resolve one of duty only—can you put into it your zest, your verve, your sense of humor and your every resource. Then you must determine in just what area you can do your best in helping make the world about you better because you are a part of it. That will be your best forte—to do something about the situation that most seriously affects you now.

Perhaps your concern is the callousness of impersonal living—the loss of a sense of neighborliness — of sharing oneself with the lonely and the forgotten—broadening the horizons of one's personal relationships and bringing into the lives of others a sense of being sought and prized—of filling for both of need and use, the two touchstones to successful living.

36

Or perhaps you feel a drive to awake the apathetic and the inert to a sense of their wider possibility in life's hidden satisfactions—a kind of personal evangelism to move the machinery out of its dead center and forward on the move. It can be rejuvenation, or even resurrection for your protege.

Or perhaps you share a sense of history. You may have fire, imagination and conviction and can revivify the story of America's dramatic pageant of faith and effort and sacrifice so that your hearers live again that century-long struggle against the terrors of the unknown, of enemies both human and of Nature's making, of bloodshed, plagues and famine. Perhaps you can spread the sense of destiny and our individual obligation to see in history the lesson of how to handle these same terrors still with us but in other dress: crime, ignorance, suspicion, intolerance, poverty and fear.

Or perhaps you may find your challenge in your wrath at the selfish and cruel tragedy we see in film, in print, in the theatre, of selling America short by portraying a land of the indulged, the depraved and the licentious; so that the world beyond our borders comes to think of us as lawless folk, ruled by gangsters, moved by only the most primitive drives. Not pictured is the great America we see about us, the dedicated men and women whom we know, and the fine, upstanding youth who remain untouched by the temptations offered by the adult for youth's undoing. Perhaps that may be your share in stopping this erosion of the bulwarks of pride and faith that are essentially American, and which both youth—and age—need to love and share.

Or perhaps your best contribution will be toward making our land as beautiful and as clean as it can be, given the goals of orderliness and beauty. The billboards on the roads, the litter on vacant lots, the areas barren of greenery are only some of the places where a town can be transformed to bloom in beauty like the festooned baskets of flowers held aloft on the sidewalks of a western city, or with landscaping, consisting often only of annuals costing little in money but yielding rich rewards in pride and uplift.

Or perhaps your gift is more of husbandly nature; you sense the hidden dangers of uneven curbs, of the absence of a welcoming bench for the weary shopper; the lack of uniformity of street marking; the lack of proper street lighting; the absence of the sign identifying the town's name for the travelers' information. With persistent, crusading effort, yours can be a town, clean and attractive, and proud of itself.

Or perhaps you can find the end of your rainbow in helping the academically underprivileged, or in promoting beneficent causes by running a thrift shop, or in maintaining an information and counseling service.

Or, your contribution could be of a more aggressive civic nature— an informed interest and alert vigilance in helping fine, dedicated persons.

Or your finest donation can be the winning to the ranks of our two Associations those eligible to our membership, who are as yet unknowing of their very existence and the services and the challenges they offer.

The causes that can engage your leisure hours to the betterment of society are as numberless as the sands of the desert. Just what your choice is, only you can tell and only you can do the job.

*"We all have a responsibility to remain active
in retirement, to keep ourselves well informed, to
cooperate with responsible public and private agencies
concerned with programs and activities that will
make our nation strong morally, spiritually and
materially for the benefit of all Americans."*

A call for service

n institution," we are told, "is defined by what it can do alone or better than any other institution." Our two Associations maintain their uniqueness by defining accepted goals and achievements as: (1) economically, by helping stretch the purchasing power of the depreciating retirement dollar, (2) socially, by stimulating the personal and associational participation of members in community life and progress, (3) personally, by respecting the individuality of each member and helping him attain the realization of his growth, hopes, independence and self-esteem.

Accepting as our slogan, "To serve and not to be served," through publications, chapters, and the dedicated service of thousands of volunteers, we are developing challenges and opportunities for constructive community action; nourishing a mounting concern, care and capacity for the welfare of others and helping in myriad of ways those who need and are lacking in love, self-confidence, and faith in their future.

Our leadership, too, explores opportunities to hasten the general acceptance of the emerging profile of the older American, as that of a person using his expertness and experience in assuming responsibility, not only for self, but, with equal status with that of the younger American, continuing to be a master workman in the vanguard of the American tradition as a builder and a curator of American standards and values. Our nation needs the accumulated experience, knowledge, wisdom and skills of all older adults.

Our members have responsibility to remain active in retirement, to keep themselves well-informed, to cooperate with responsible public and private agencies and organizations concerned with programs and activities that will help to make our nation strong morally, spiritually, and materially for the benefit of all Americans.

We have a stewardship of influence and an obligation to assume an increasing responsibility for dynamic leadership on a national, state and community level.

David Cort in his book, *Social Astonishments,* says that more demonstrated love is shown to 26,000,000 dogs in the United States today than to any other single group, including babies and male singers. Since each dog has successful relationships with several people, it would seem that we might consider how imaginatively we could draw from this fact some serious thinking. Is this not a confession of the need of folk for something to love, to serve, and by which to be needed?

We, who are now retired, have the time; should we not emphasize the inclination and strengthen our dedication toward making every Chapter of our Association a distinguished one, presenting a stimulating and constructive program of excellence, that we can envision for ourselves.

We realize people follow a normal curve in distribution, the extremes accounting for our standard bearers on the one end of the curve and our determined dissidents on the other, to accept leadership of courage and clarity. Our membership, itself, comes from the upper brackets of older persons. In proportion as we can identify leaders and are fortunate in challenging them, so will grow our Association in power and prestige, in service and in worth.

There is an infectious quality in the man or woman who leads, affecting not only the quality of the message shared, but also its intensity and its breadth. The "so-called" leader only mirrors his constituents. The real leader is to his constituency a beacon, pointing the way to higher ground, to a wider horizon; he shares a vision of the wide spectrum of life, not only a self-centered segment, round about.

We all realize that society usually accepts a person at that person's own evaluation. Our respect and dignity are not given us. Status is not conferred upon us; it is won, and won first through our conviction of the need of others, then through our action for service to those others, and then, at long last, by others because of our cooperation and commitment.

To effect the desired changes in elevating the role of the aged person, greater opportunities are demanded for leadership. More volunteer and staff members are wanted to provide field service. An expanded communication system must be established that will be a two-way system, one between headquarters and the grassroots and one between the chapters and the grassroots and their neighbors.

We hope to transmit to our people a zest for more striking meaning and purpose in their lives; we can, by developing our skill as creative leaders. Doing so will involve a balance between the time which we can allot to this goal and the time we individually need for writing, for travel, and our own demanding personal interests and those of our modern life. Doing so, we renew our interest in and our respect for the job we have undertaken. In addition, we must keep in closer personal relationship with our groups. There can be no substitute for eye-to-eye interaction and the nurturing of a genuine respect, one for the other. We must cultivate the personal traits that would make us effective as mediators—arouse eagerness, and we must be alert and alive, if we would hope enthusiasm and love of people. We must be eager, if we desire to expand in other varied areas of interests. We must be sensitive to the great variety of human talent we shall encounter; and, above all, we must learn to appreciate people's intriguing individual differences in interests and capabilities and potentialities. A very wise philosopher describes the variety of human ability in this way:

"Vigor of imagination, depth of feeling, of sympathy and love for men, sagacity in judging character, intuitive perception of the controlling factors of complex situations (a quality I do not find singled out by psychologists, but central in the genius of leadership), planning ability, eloquence itself as skilled communication of emotion, powers of loyalty and endurance—all of these and various other unmeasurable and unexaminable dimensions of the self go to make up human magnitude."

Our leaders, because of their empathy, realize that a high degree of independence is valued by older people, as by their younger friends, nearly as highly as life itself. Dignity and self-respect that a sense of independence generate are essential; they are one's psychic wealth and emotional capital. Our leaders must constantly keep in mind that the adjustments many of our members met when they retired were cruelly drastic—harsher than any they may have ever before been forced to meet. Income cut, regularity of work gone, personal contacts with fellow workers disrupted, and no expected responsibility or work or its complexities to engage one's idle moments —here are the shortages that yield opportunities where our leaders may help; by personalized counseling, by broadening interests and widening horizons.

I like to recall the story about a general who when he was instructing his young men on leadership, would take a string—or if at table a piece of spaghetti—place it on the table and try pushing it. You know what happened.

That is what I mean. Are we among those who say, "Why ask me?" Are we content to being led or pushed; so to become bored and unhappy; censorians and even cynical? Are we willing to be beggars at the chapter's banquet; taking, not giving? I warn those who refuse to share themselves of being weakened by the thought of their lacking significance, of convincing themselves of their relative unimportance. Have they not forgotten that they are a contributing member in a society dedicated to democratic rights and privileges?

Remember each of us has the responsibility to work with our fellow members in straightforward cooperative partnership in our chapter and its community enterprises. We can serve our fellows— only as we care for them and feel with them and mingle with them.

I am reminded of an old German jingle I used to know. This is a garbled version as I dimly recall it:

A parish priest in Wittelsbach

Climbed up to his high church steeple
To be near to God so that he could
Send His word down to his people.
In Bible script he duly wrote
What he thought he got from Heaven
And he dropped it down on the people's heads
Two times each day in seven.
When came the time for him to die
He cried from out his steeple
"Where art Thou, God?" and God replied,
"Down here among thy people."

The distinguished expert on urban problems, Jean Gottman, tells us the interesting story of the problem that Nestles of chocolate and baby food fame faced in its development of an utopia of work conditions. Nestles, one of the world's great corporations, built in a village in the Swiss Riviera, an ideal work facility in the form of a skyscraper. This super work center was so equipped that any worker need never move from his desk in the transaction of his task. The result was catastrophic. From a harmonious and effective situation, even as high as among management itself, disruption occurred. Directions by telephone or television were interrupted or misinterpreted. Finally an expert was called in to study the problem, because of the vast sums of money outlayed. His report was that the place was over-tooled, over-gadgeted. And the remedy? Well, perhaps two coffee breaks in the morning and another double one in the afternoon might help; it would permit again the eye-to-eye direct human communication so essential to fine performance. Nothing—yes nothing, takes the place of personal contact and the need of constant intercommunication.

"Each of us has powers of which we are unaware, each of us has a circle of influence. Our limitations are the product of our own thinking and self evaluation. If only we think we can!"

To make life worthwhile—
a challenge
to leadership and service

Entering the land of retirement requires no passport but the border line between active and retired status is definitely there, and strange things often happen to the newcomer on passing it, about which he is at times disenchanted. Particularly is this true if he has viewed his future life with dread and has not prepared himself for the emotional reaction which such a radical change in many of the aspects retirement living is likely to produce.

Work-oriented he has been, and there is now no work arranged for him. Living on a schedule and with definitely outlined responsibilities, he faces his new life on his own terms, with no minimum obligations to meet, no required or expected outcomes to produce. Socially adjusted to comradeship in shared projects, he finds himself alone, a possible prey to loneliness; growing old, but not otherwise growing. He feels that his illusions of leisure are not the answer to the problem. Indeed, he is becoming to himself a problem, and he is not yet ready to search for a solution.

For a space, he can luxuriate in just loafing. Travel can be a

44

sheer delight, reading a solace, but soon he faces the question, to be content, how can he achieve balance and perspective? How can he live up to his intellectual level and like it? The answer no one can give him; he himself must find it, but we can give friendliness and suggestion, and, if he is ready for them, he can learn valuable and human ideas, sometimes even lifesaving ones, but his is the choice and the decision.

He, at long last, finds that retirement has not changed him or altered his situation; it has only intensified all his inner drives. If he would be content, he must realize, as never before, that he must be awake to life, be alert and active. He begins to see life as a whole. He still wants to live long and be free to order his own life as reasonably well as he can, and to make his own decisions. He still longs for affection, to love someone with a reciprocating regard for him. He knows that he must be reconciled to the fact that necessarily he will have fewer long-time friends, and that a few friendly smiles will be preferable to long faces viewing a casket. He must realize that there is no such thing as sharing happiness—alone, and so it behooves him to take time for building new friendships and keeping in repair his old ones. He is convinced, as never before, that he wants to belong — to be desired and desirable. He appreciates the value of the word *member*.

He realizes that he desires to be worthy of a reasonable share of approval by his fellows, and respect by himself, and far from last, he has a yearning for something to live *for* and to live *by,* beyond the here and now, something more compelling and challenging than his own welfare and well-being.

And so he takes his stance. Retirement to him has become "Opportunity-Unlimited." He is now aware that "no one can live to himself alone.

> *"And each one's work, whether great or small,*
> *If done with care, for the good of all—*
> *Whether one works with multitudes or few,*
> *Or in the silence of some lovely spot,*
> *A separate path that one can pursue*
> *We work together though we know it not."*

Wherever he now looks, he can discover a need, something that intelligence and energy can supply; a place congenial and useful, and a challenge. He knows that he can help, if he will. The gift of Time, which retirement brings, offers him the chance to do as he would for others, to volunteer, to participate and to contribute, to be emotionally concerned and involved, to stimulate the sluggish and the indolent lonely—the rare opportunities of service—and the treasured side-benefits of retirement living. He hopes to show them a world where nobody gets old and sad, where nobody gets godly and grave, where nobody gets crafty and wise, where nobody gets bitter of tongue.

Today's retiree is a pioneer, exploring the potentialities or a new social frontier. In our grandparents' youth, life expectancy was 33 years, 25% died before reaching the age of 6; 50% before the age of 16, and only one in a hundred survived to see his 65th birthday. The baby boy of today can expect to fill out his 3 score years and ten of Biblical report. How he is doing so makes social history.

Our generation of older folks is a pilot one. How it will be reported is a matter both of conjecture and interest. Shall we, pioneers in retirement living as a group, be portrayed as needing special assistance because we are needy, dependent or otherwise at a disadvantage? Or, can we live such rewarding and interesting lives that the report on our generation will stress the importance—to ourselves and to society—of our value to society in personal growth and community participation? Current social welfare often is found stressing isolation and rejection because of age, the inadequate income that some aged people live upon, insufficient to solve satisfactorily many of their economic, social or medical problems. Shall we, as the pilot generation, have so underscored the value we place on the individuality of each of us, a person with hopes, aspirations and capacities? Will it tell of the older Americans who try to "make do," on a tragically escalating inflationary spiral, still proudly seeking to stretch their retirement dollar, not whining but limiting themselves to pity in minutely small doses; and, to their level best, finding satisfying answers in the complex of ideas, events, and emotions that make our world a fascinating place?

We hope the picture to be considered a typical one will present

46

us facing confidently an entirely new present and an unknown future —our problem, a highly individualized one and a social one as well, trying to continue in the full stream of life. Hopefully we will not be referred to as "Senior Citizens"; the euphonious nomenclature that segregates and declasses us. We want to be considered persons— citizens, too, of course, but, first and last, persons, for there is a difference.

Aristotle defined man as a rational animal and also as a political animal. In other words, he pictured man in his two important aspects as an individual and as a social being.

As individuals, we, for the most part, are concerned with ourselves as individuals communicating with other individuals, but never forgetful of the self within our own skin; never losing that sense of uniqueness of self in the social complex of other individuals. It is this self to whom we of the West pay respect and about whose destiny we are concerned and whose sense of freedom we protect.

But it is not enough to see man as an individual in the same way, as is an individual man in an army or a crowd. The difference is so great that there is a special word for an individual man, a word of power and importance; the word is "person."

Originally the word was a sacred one, derived from the Greek and signifying the face mask worn by the actor. Its significance was taken over by the early Christian theologians to explain the Trinity, carrying with it the idea of rationality, that a person, being a human individual, has a reason for being and a significance of his own. As a corollary, it carries the thought that every man has individual duties to himself and to others. Also there is added, too, the idea that every man has individual rights that exceed those of the group of which he is a part. A man, because he is a person, may not be disregarded or cast out, like any other kind of individual, vegetable or mineral, in order to improve the group of which it is a part. In other words, here again we face the precept that the state exists for the man, not man for the state.

The concept of the person as a social being is that society has no existence apart from that of its individual members, and the member is in it and of it, the whole of him.

The significance of the word *"person"* in the title of our Association emphasizes for us this truth: first, that retirement is opportunity; and second, that man does not live by bread alone; that together we can work toward a many-splendored maturity; growing, not just growing old.

The individual needs of our older colleagues are the same as our own, but sometimes their needs become social problems to ourselves as persons. These social problems of theirs attain greater importance as neighborly communications and social communications diminish. Here is our personal challenge in the service of our older friends—to try to replace with vital interests the monotony and the lack of stimulation they may meet in rural areas and the anonymity and passive entertainment in urban areas. We need to help by actively being and doing something with our less fortunate colleagues; we need to incite and stimulate them to make balanced and creative use of their leisure and to accept, as actively as they will, their responsibilities as democratic citizens. Citizenship is not a passive time-consuming affair for the onlooker and critical spectator. Citizenship is participation, the sharing of responsibilities in the enterprises of government and likewise the supporter of its policies, sentiments, ideals and aspirations.

During the past few months, platform speakers and commentators have shown a distressing propensity to describe the hopelessness of our being able or even aware and eager to change the tragic situation which they depict our country as facing. The picture they paint is not a consoling one—nor is it a novel one.

The Assyrian commentator on the world's situation of his day carved into clay the tablets which we 4,500 years later can decipher. He finds his current age morally far inferior to that of earlier days. His complaints are these: "Our youth is degenerated. Children no longer respect their elders. Every man wants to write a book."

Twenty-three hundreds of years later, Socrates bears witness to a like lament. He deplores the fact that "the children now live in luxury, have bad manners, show contempt for authority, are tyrants to their elders, contradict their parents, chatter before company, gobble up the dainties at the table, cross their legs, and tyrannize over their teachers."

However, the world all these thousands of years has been facing like problems; sometimes trying to solve them by edict, sometimes by appeasement, and always, I imagine, with a sense of urgency. Today we face similar criticisms, and I hope we meet them with a stubborn faith worthy of a great nation and a great people who have the capacity and the resources to deal with them. The urgency with us is that we focus our attention and our efforts upon them.

Today we sense keenly the anxiety and concern and often even alarm for the well-being of our society. Vast sums of money expended in the interest of expansion along lines, scientific, technical and mechanical could be better spent, some believe, if a large share were allocated to the improvement of the status of man, the enhancement of his cultural opportunities, and the enlargement of his vision and potentials. Things are happening that shock and disturb us to which, regrettably, we respond with dismay and a growing callousness on one hand, and a sense of personal hopelessness and an urge to resist involvement on the other. The growing disregard for standards of what is right and what is wrong is a source of much disillusionment, despair, confusion and distrust among those of us who should be and many who are eager to help change the escapist moral climate to which we are gradually becoming accustomed. The bitterness and angry resentment at the snail's pace of social progress in the abolition of intolerance and hate and prejudice can be easily understood; but, if we are really to recover our national self-esteem, to reestablish our sense of values, to recover our moral standards, to end violence, we must bring all the pressure at our command to support our law enforcement officers, and, help restore the respect due to self-discipline and decency. But, to do so, we must realize that each of us has powers of which we are unaware, that each of us has a circle of influence, that our limitations are the product of our own thinking and self evaluation; if only we think we can!

I am mindful of a story about President Jackson. At his funeral service, a neighbor asked his body servant, "Do you think the General is going to Heaven?" and the man who knew the President best answered, "He sure is, if he wants to." We sure can. What is needed is our "want to."

John Gardner, the scholar who headed our Health, Education and Welfare Division, reminded us that "Leaders have a significant role in creating the state of mind that is society. They can express the values that hold society together. Most important, they can conceive and articulate the goals that lift people out of their petty preoccupations, carry them above the conflicts that tear a society apart, and unite them in the pursuit of objectives worthy of their best efforts."

These are the thoughts with which you can welcome those hesitant and uncertain of a goal into the warm circle of our brotherhood and the exciting challenge of leadership and service.

In doing so, you can find for yourself and your new-found friend the joy of making life worthwhile.

George Eliot assures us:

> *"Every soul that touches yours—*
> *Be it the slightest contract—*
> *Gets therefrom some good;*
> *Some little grace; one kindly thought;*
> *One aspiration as yet unfelt:*
> *One list of courage*
> *For the darkening day;*
> *One gleam of faith*
> *To brave the thickening ills of life;*
> *One glimpse of brighter skies*
> *To make this life worthwhile*
> *And heaven a surer heritage."*

"Alone, and always alone, must we meet great issues.
As an individual we entered this world and,
as an individual, we depart from it.
The individual man is still the moving force,
the dynamo, the energy which moves the mass
and drives into adventurous seeking for what lies
forever beyond the ever receding horizon."

The spirit of altruism

ver the mantel of the dining room of the home of my childhood there was engraved on a plank of manzanita these words:

Three pleasant things—
To be here
To be here together and
To think well of one another.

As I have talked and visited with you, and have listened to the marvelous tales of your achievement those words of old kept surging through my mind: how pleasant it is to be here together and think together, one with the other.

This assembling brings me great joy. Meeting, in person, this glorious sample of the dedicated men and women from the four corners of our commonwealth, is to see in microcosm a dynamic America, faith in the self, and in each other, and the work of all of us together in helping build the American ideal.

Just so, America was pioneered by people moved by faith in themselves and in a future which they could and would build together.

When we speak of the immigrant coming to our shores, do we

51

realize that every one of us is a son or a daughter of a pioneer? It is not a matter of great concern when they came. By the way, did you know that the average speed of the Mayflower during much of the voyage across the Atlantic was *two miles an hour?* It doesn't matter how patient they need to have been. It doesn't matter what brought them. Perhaps they came to enjoy freedom *from* persecution or army conscription or freedom *to* own a bit of land, before denied them or beyond their wildest dreams. It might be that they were led hither by tales of fabulous wealth. No matter what the particular lodestar that beckoned, the end of their rainbow always was to better their lives and the lives and the futures of their offspring. And—and this is the important thing—no matter what unexpected dangers they met, what cruel disappointments they encountered, no matter how many of their illusions were destroyed, still *they stayed;* for here they found the two great freedoms, the *freedom from,* and even greater, the *freedom to.*

And we, the sons and the daughters of these immigrants, glory in the courage that it took to break home ties and the fearlessness that empowered them to meet conditions which, even in the boldest of their imaginations, were uncertain and perhaps perilous. Still they came, not creatures of unrest, absorbed in short-term material quests, but always following the gleam. No matter what discouragements they found, they made and brought with themselves new opportunities, new vistas, the promise of a tomorrow destined to be free and fine, built as it must be on the spirit of the past. As we thrill with pride at the realization of what vacuums they found and what vacuums they filled, still our fondest pride is in that individual pioneer, who, perhaps with wife and child, ventured alone; no matter that he might have come in association with others of like feeling and intent, alone he had to make the decision,

> *"I am a part of all that I have met yet all experience*
> *is an arch where through gleams that untraveled world*
> *whose margin fades forever, and forever, when I move."*
>
> Tennyson's *Ulysses*

Alone, and always alone, must we meet great issues. As an individual, we entered this world, and as an individual, we depart from it. The individual man is still the moving force: the dynamo: the energy which moves the mass. Each individual, unlike any of the other myriads of persons that inhabit the universe—that is part of his magnificence that he is uniquely himself—progresses through human existence with a fundamental drive: constantly pressing against boundaries; possessing an enterprising spirit that drives him into adventurous seeking for what lies forever beyond the ever receding horizon.

It is that instinctive respect that we feel for man that haunts the traffic of the busy city, and we stand still and uncovered when a funeral goes by. It is man, paying a finite and final gesture of respect to the infinite we find in us all. Is it not, perhaps, that bit of the infinite in each of us that makes us realize when we pray. "Thy will be done," that it is only through us that Thy will can be done; that we are Your agents and only through us will Your purpose be realized. Thus we know that we are a part of the infinite, if we choose so to be. If spiritually we are alive, Thy will will be done! Perhaps it is this instinctive love and respect for ourselves as individuals, who "have fought the good fight and have kept the faith," that makes so hurtful the current common concept of the aged as a group of persons who have lived beyond their usefulness, whose presence and services are no longer needed; for whom the playthings of adolescence, games, and dancing, are provided; for whom a dole is planned, with the expense of their care computed as a peculiar danger to the public purse.

It is this instinctive regard for man as man that makes us hope that the man in the street will refuse to conceive of the aging as a mass, old and ill, and indigent, needing only loving care and compassion, but will instead picture, as he thinks of aging, those millions of older folks whose dreams, and labors, and sacrifices have helped fashion the America he now lives in, as persons who have discovered that there can still be zest and enjoyment and purpose in life for them; that there are satisfactions and contributions and companionships which are to be enjoyed and savored.

We hope that the man in the street and the lad in the school may come to look upon aging as a source of inspiration and a resource to be used not only for leisured reminescence of days and deeds gone by, but also for prophetic forecasting of things to come, to dream about, to realize. We hope, that all may learn that creative energies and the knowledge that comes from fruitful living can and do materialize into constructive activities and worthwhile projects, needing doing but hitherto never done.

And the way to bring this about?

The AARP member, proud as he may be, as a representative of this great association of dynamic folk, still knows in his heart of hearts that the best contribution within his power to make is the giving and the extending of himself in wider interests, in deeper understandings and in an increasingly greater concern for the welfare and the future of his own, his community, and the nation that claims his allegiance and his love.

Life in a great city sometimes resembles a revolving door, impersonal and individual. But life can be humanistic too, sometimes. Sometimes we do good unawares.

After my father's death it was my duty to examine his papers. Among his private ones I found some letters he had saved. One was old, written on those double sheets with a little dove impressed in the left-hand corner of the upper sheet; one of thousands on sale in the inexpensive stationery shops of that time. It was a letter from a woman who signed her name, Hilda Knugine. And it read, "Dear Sir:" and it ended with the quaint old expression "Your obedient servant."

"I am the cleaning lady of the 11th floor of the Ashland Block but tonight I worked the 10th floor, too, because my friend, whose stint it was, was sick and couldn't work. This way I could cover for her and she wouldn't lose her pay.

"Just as I was about to leave, there was one office still busy and folks were talking and I was just about to knock and ask that when they left would they please remember to lock the door and turn out the lights when I heard your voice. It didn't belong there; I would know it anywhere. I had listened to it when it pleaded for my son, and I stopped and listened. You were saying, 'Let me tell you about a case I lost, a case of a fine young man, one of nature's noblemen,'

54

and you went on and told the story. And then you said, 'You see what he had done was legally wrong but, actually, morally right; a real tragedy when right cannot justify an indicated breach of the law.' And then you went on and the others talked, too, but I had stopped listening, for I knew the rest of the story only too well.

"When I came to work tonight I came as the mother of a criminal, loving him but ashamed and bitter. I left that hallway a woman refreshed, rejoicing, saying aloud to myself, 'I am the mother of one of nature's noble men.' Thank you sir, for giving me back my pride in my son."

For man is not an island. He is not made to live alone. He is made to share. His happiness is always linked with the happiness of others of those whom we know and see. Then our bonds of love are slender and weak. But, if others, unseen and unknown, can become part of his dreams of service, then the bonds become strong and binding. Indeed, so universal is the belief in the brotherhood of man that the most severe punishment that can legally be demanded of the hardened criminal, other than capital punishment, is that of solitary confinement.

I like to think that life, as we phrase it when we are discussing the potentials for happiness, might be studied from the two standpoints of (1) myself, and (2) all others. It is a meum and a tuum kind of thing. If you picture life as a long arc beginning at birth and traversing the span of life towards death, we can see on the one end of that arc the babe, any babe, your beloved grandchild it might well be. To him, the world is himself, his comforts, the attention he craves, the things he finds delight in manipulating. His anger he expresses in screams of protest. Everything must conform to his needs or he protests until again he is master of his world. And no one dare dispute his wishes. Briefly, at the other end of the arc is the Man of God, the Christ who gave his all—even his life, to the betterment of his fellows—to point the way to selfless service.

We who are older rejoice as we see burgeoning in our youth any concern for the welfare of others. Adolescence, that period of half childhood and half adulthood, shows at times in puberty a growing awareness of the alter, the other, the birth of altruism, the gradual sinking of the absorption in the personal to the more generous sharing with others that which one covets for oneself; and, as maturity advances, the sharing grows into an understanding and an appreciative caring and regard. During this transition from childhood to manhood, there is a paradoxical other trend at work: from the youthful insistency for conformity of the dictates over the fashions and the foibles of the crowd to the appreciation of one's own standards of values; the full grown recognition of one's uniqueness; and the fearlessness and creativity of adulthood.

It is along this measuring arc we find emerging our leaders, for the good of mankind is dependent upon that spirit of altruism and the work of man's hands that it inspires.

It is because of this concern for others that our founding forefathers added the Bill of Rights. It granted the individual so much *freedom from.* I have often wondered upon learning the base uses to which these safeguards to life, liberty, and the pursuit of happiness have been diverted, if it had not better to have added still another code, the Bill of Obligations. The *freedom to:* the freedom to pay allegiance and respect to others and, most of all, to our government itself.

Emerson has long ago awakened us to the truth that all things must be bought and paid for; only our love do we give freely. And if we demand love in return, that which we gave is not love, for it is only love that is given; if returned, the cup indeed runneth over. If only we, as parents, as our children grow forgetful of us, would always remember that truth, perhaps our heartaches would be fewer.

Even liberty is not free: it must be fought for and defended every day of our lives. If we merely accept and offer nothing in return, we are beggars in the sight of man and of the Lord. If we accept the privileges of the government our forefathers bequeathed to us, in return we should accept the obligations for keeping fresh and vital its fundamental fact that we are here to support that government, not here to demand support from it; it is our obligation to accept the terms of the founding, and be helpful in helping youth and the stranger within our gates to see America as beneficient, even if often failing: not impersonal and serving only the privileged. It is our obligation, in return, to help to interpret in action the compassionate and the tender hopes of every one of us.

To buy that America we must pay the bill of alert and watchful care; we must yield not to apathy and placid acceptance that permit creatures of privilege and self interest to remain unmolested in their seats of authoritarian power in the halls of our great cities.

It is our obligation to help better conditions here, now, while we still have the vigor and the vision to do so.

As we hoist the Blue Peter flag signifying that we are outward bound toward another year of helping older folk help themselves and keep their rightful place in life in this glorious government of ours as elder advisors, may I recall to you that story, beloved by all who have Scottish blood in their veins, the story of the Bruce of beloved memory.

At his death, the most precious treasure of the Scottish folk was encased in a golden casket—the heart of the Bruce. When the Crusaders went into battle, they knew that to protect this memento of their hero every man would gladly give his life. Yet, when they joined in battle with the Saracens, the chest bearer threw with all his might the heart of the Bruce into the thick of the battle. Straining to their utmost, they would recapture it, only again to throw it forward, and ever forward, while there remained a Saracen on the field.

There was a story told of a captain on one of the sailing vessels of the early days who, at moments of strain, hurriedly consulted a research document which he carefully locked away from curious, roving eyes. When the second mate became skipper at the captain's sudden death his first concern was to consult the secret orders so carefully protected by his predecessor. Unfolding the document he read to his astonishment the truth:

> *"Starboard is to the right,*
> *Port is to the left."*

Now when you, as individuals and as chapter officers or members are ready to sail on outward-bound passage and you hoist your imaginary Blue Peter Flag to signal your readiness, I know that you will have the required charts at hand and up to date and you will know how to use them.

But don't think that you must go afar to find your next adventure and challenge. You may recall the story of that vessel caught in the Atlantic, far off the coast of Brazil without drinking water, even while tossing in that surging, wild, tumultous sea. Their signal of distress, their plea for water was heard. But the answering message was not the one they sought. Again and again the call of distress was answered by the same, "Put down your buckets where you are!" In desperation they did as they were bid, and the water they pulled up, to their amazement, was sweet and sparkling. They were adrift and athirst where the mighty Amazon was emptying its vast volume of fresh water into the huge salty waste of the Atlantic.

So remember, greatness and rewards are perhaps within your grasp, if you see the needs of the people about you and apply yourself to the fulfilling of their needs. The messages in your chart locker will read, "Do what you can with what you have where you are today." If you put down your buckets where you are, you may find the goal you seek.

Life is a sea, where, we are told, the proud are humbled; the shirker is exposed; and the leader is revealed.

You sail it always. You will be carrying with you the heart-warming assurance that, in the discharge of your duty, you carry with you the esteem and the regard of all of us who cherish you for your ideals and who admire you for your courage, your perseverance and the love you show in your concern for your fellow man.

Come, my friends, 'tis not too late to seek a new world. Push off!

VALUES WE
LIVE BY

I wish you some new love of lovely things, and some new forgetfulness of the teasing things, and some higher pride in the praising things, and some sweeter peace from the hurrying things, and some closer fence from the worrying things.

John Ruskin

*"We are often dazzled like the child playing
with the kaleidoscope and watching the fragments
shift in endless array. We need instead
to put our eye to the telescope and, looking past
the fragments that confuse it, to see the true
proportion of things as they are."*

Bases for decisions

he peppery little conference leader was harranging his fellow members, "Even though we expect to reach a concensus— and hopefully we shall—still in the implementation of this decision upon going home," and after a pause, with his eyes twinkling, he added "every man must skin his own skunk."

And, he might have added, we grant that after all our deliberations in common with our fellows, the final decision must always be reached by each of us, individually and alone. Yet with our widely variable human behavior each of us, the product of many types of social adjustment and different kinds of culture, will have been heard differently and will therefore interpret differently what we think we have heard. Nevertheless, incumbent upon each of us will be the objective demand to make a decision and after it a plan for action. Often we must accept the dual roles of both judge and of administrator.

It behooves us, therefore, not only to listen attentively to everything that is said on the issue at hand, but also as attentively to all that is not said, to identify, if possible, the missing steps, to try to see the problem as a whole—as far as it is possible for us to do so—to try to establish in our thinking a sense of the relative values concerned to build a kind of perspective. Then to realize that, like the judge whose procedure we are emulating, we need to take time to reach that decision no matter what may be the immediacy and urgency of the issues involved.

We need to call upon all the insight we can muster; we need, like the artist standing back from his picture, to see the parts in relation to the whole. We need, too, to pause and recall that there is a rhythm of the spirit. We need to consider what the psychologist calls the value of spaced learning. Truly, to be just, we must retreat at times from society to solitude, from deeds to thought, from action to meditation. Then, and only then, with our mind fortified by peace and quiet and refreshed in spirit, should we decide both what we believe to be our best judgment and our best plan of converting thought into action, decision into planning.

So true is the evidence that we all hear and see differently and report differently. When the testimony in a court of law conforms identically although offered by various witnesses, the jurist naturally suspects that there has been a prior conference of the witnesses and a decision met as to the sequence of events to be reported or the emphasis to be stressed and details to be suppressed or ignored. Even our professional reporters, such as our news commentators and our drama critics, often vary widely in sharing with us their impressions and viewpoints on the identical event or portrayal.

The story is told us of a Perisan Shah among whose self-determined duties it was to sit in judgment on disputes brought before him. One day he commissioned his four sons to take over this obligation that he might judge their fitness for this role which some time might be theirs. Appalled to hear the finality and the immediacy of their decisions, he made no comment, but on the following day he called to him his oldest son and sent him on a mission to report the condition of a mango tree on the south terrace of their northern palace. And when the young princeling returned his father waived aside his report for the present and when spring came, he sent his second son on the same mission and in the summer, the third and in the autumn, the fourth.

Only then did he ask for their reaction. The lad who had seen the tree in winter stripped of its foliage reported its stark appearance, skeletonized and forbidding. The lad who had seen it in the spring thought the greenery as charming and as delicate as that of the maidenhair fern. The summer reporter stressed its opulence and the shade that it offered. The autumn visitor brought with him the luscious fruit it was bearing, both delectable and nourishing.

And the father assured them all of his pleasure in the definiteness of their report, each differing but each true. And then he stressed to them the need in reporting on the tree—in reporting on any case at issue—the need first to see the tree in all seasons and to judge every contention by studying it under all conditions possible—before considering the decision so that that decision should place first things first, be impartial and, where need rose, merciful rather than merely just.

One of the problems facing us as we ponder our position is that we, in seeing the whole picture, see what are the essentials, discover the insoluble factors beyond our control and, not magnifying them as deterrents to our own planning and possible action, not depreciate that fragment with which we still can grapple and improve. It is essential that we maintain a perspective of the whole affair, determining in our thinking the major issues involved and subordinating the lesser to the greater.

The trouble lies, not in our not knowing the basic right from the basic wrong, but in the emphasis we sometimes place upon the various factors. Our sense of proportion should dictate the relative merits of the component parts we need to hold in mind. Particularly if the problem appears to fall within the scope of one of our predetermined interests should we watch our reactions that they be equitable and not prejudiced either for or against.

We are often dazzled like the child playing with the kaleidoscope and watching the fragments shift in endless array. We need instead to put our eyes to the telescope and, looking past the fragments that confuse it, to the wider horizon that it can afford of the great wide wonderful world and then see the true proportion of things as they are.

To gain this perspective we need to retreat at times from the world, not in the thought of shirking a responsibility but that we may free ourselves for the small things that daily fret and disturb us into the quiet and the peace, not in apology for our comfort, but intermittently and occasionally to refresh and recreate our spirit, to enrich and enlarge our life.

We must regard such withdrawal, not as an escape from duty but as recognizing the tidal life of the spirit, the rhythm of life, from day to night, from wakefulness to sleep, from the grave to the gay, from the world of work to the world of recreation, We need, for our well-being, the sabbath of living—the day of rest and of meditation. We are told that the French in their zeal at the time of their Revolution, advocated the universal application of the decimal system and so changed the workaday week from six days of labor and one day for "dwelling in the house of the Lord." But the strain of unremitting and continuous toil for nine days proved so exhausting that, to restore the needed balance of life, regretfully, the seven day week became again established. We need at times to let the flood-tide of the spirit wash away the absorbing, hurrying, worrying pursuit of things yet undone and, true to the tidal force, with its ebb and flow, cleanse our minds from the demands of worry and concern. We must, when great issues are at stake, respect the tidal laws of life. So we gain in wisdom and in peace.

And then, following the natural law of variation, we are again keenly aware of the intensity and the overwhelming demands of living, and, ready and equipped with renewed growth and power to do our share, our balance is restored, and we find that the decisions we have been seeking we know how to make. We feel in ourselves a renaissance, a personal significance; our ideals are resolved and we strive again to translate our judgment with courage, persistence and hope into worthy actions and projected plans.

There are among us many whose added years have brought to them the lack of incentive and a feeling of uselessness. To them life offers no joy. They have not learned that to get one must give. How to bring meaning into their lives, new hopes for happiness and the more fruitful use of time is the problem of those more fortunate older folk who are concerned. It is part of our problem. How can we convince them that it is not too late to change; to help them learn to give of themselves, to be on the plus side of living, to look forward to some desired end, to think well of themselves, to realize that respect is more rewarding than pity.

Medical theory and psychological studies teach us that we are in a constant process of growing, growing more tolerant, growing wiser, growing in independence and in purpose, or growing more prejudiced, growing less perceptive, growing more dependent, purposeless, senile in fact.

How can we help redirect the direction or the seeming lack of it, how to awake the apathetic to the danger to himself that lies ahead? How to deliver him from the slavery to self to an interest in his fellows? How to bring him to realize that his mind too needs "three square meals a day?"

Lewis Carroll, the author of *Alice in Wonderland* and a scientist of note, tells the story in this humorous fashion:

"Breakfast, dinner, tea; in extreme cases, breakfast, luncheon, dinner, tea, supper, and a glass of something hot at bedtime. What care we take about feeding the lucky body! Which of us does as much for his mind? And what causes the difference? Is the body so much the more important of the two?

"By no means; but life depends on the body being fed, whereas we can continue to exist as animals (scarcely as men), though the mind be utterly starved and neglected. Therefore Nature provides that, in case of serious neglect of the body, such terrible consequences of discomfort and pain shall ensue as will soon bring us back to a sense of our duty; and some of the functions necessary to life she does for us altogether, leaving us no choice in the matter.

"It would fare but ill with many of us if we were left to superintend our own digestion and circulation. 'Bless me!' one would cry, 'I forgot to wind up my heart this morning! To think that it has been standing still for the last three hours!'

'I can't walk with you this afternoon,' a friend would say, 'as I

65

have no less than eleven dinners to digest. I had to let them stand over from last week, being so busy—and my doctor says he will not answer for the consequences if I wait any longer!'

"Well it is, I say, for us, that the consequences of neglecting the body can be clearly seen and felt; and it might be well for some if the mind were equally visible and tangible, if we could take it, say, to the doctor, and have its pulse felt.

" 'Why, what have you been doing with this mind lately? How have you fed it? It looks pale, and the pulse is very slow.'

" 'Well, doctor, it has not had much regular food lately. I gave it a lot of sugar-plums yesterday.'

" 'Sugar-plums! What kind?'

" 'Well, they were—'

" 'Ah! I thought so. Now just mind this: if you go on playing tricks like that, you'll spoil all its teeth, and get laid up with mental indigestion. You must have nothing but the plainest reading for the next few days!' "

We are witnessing a great revolution in the practice of the medical profession. The change is a shift of emphasis from the repair and the rehabilitation of the stricken body to the constructive approach of a program of optimum health, of prevention rather than of cure. We are shifting the emphasis from contagion as a quality of disease to contagion of health as a potent force. Science does not hope to render extinct the germs of disease but it is turning its attention to the more promising and the possible task of fortifying life against them, of barring them out by starvation, by the immunization of the individual. So the germs become powerless, uncontagious, because they find no material upon which to feed and no soil on which to fatten. One such immunized life can become the safety of a thousand.

Just so, there is the contagion of spiritual health. A good man spreads goodness just as the sick man gives disease. The quiet, unassuming mother leading a life of kindly and helpful service leads a fortified life in a medium of social immunity. Some people serve by being just themselves. You have of late often heard that statement quoted by the niece of Masaryk. She had returned to Czechoslovakia after having been successful in traveling to the freedom of the West. When asked why, of her own volition, she had returned, she answered in some such fashion as this. "When the people of Prague see a Masaryk on the street, they know that there is still in our beloved city a Masaryk. I am a symbol of the freedom that Thomas and Jan Masaryk typified in their lives of devotion and service. I, too, can serve by just being here."

Truly, there are those among us who are unheralded and unconscious "carriers" of goodness. Some do serve by being and some by doing. Let each man carry his own burden and he, too, in that fashion is contributing to the value of the common life. Let him give of himself in service and he is doing more than helping others. He is reinforcing his own strength to bear his own burdens.

The story of many lives, alone, unnoticed, unpraised, like the lighthouse keeper on his barren and rockbound coast, nothing can be more solitary, less regarded and less extoled. Why does he stay there, alone and lonely, keeping his little flame alive and flickering? Why does he not sleep on and let his light go out? The answer is "It is not his light." That is the reason for his careful watch. That is what makes him significant, his service essential and to him important. He is performing a trust. His country has put in his keeping a sacred obligation. When the lights of his country are gone out, he stays awake and keeps his burning, and, by it, the ships are guided safely on their way, cared for by the lighthouse keeper whom every sailor has been taught to trust.

Why don't you let your light go out? Because it is not yours. You, too, are a lighthouse keeper. Do you realize you, too, have a sacred trust? You, too, have a place in the great army of service which makes the world secure, and you know that many a life that passes you by unseen and unknown may be looking eagerly from night to night to you for guidance and for help. You must not fail them. They depend upon you!

*"We feel that we are zestful, energetic,
well-integrated folk; we know we have
a positive attitude toward living and we pray
and strive for a maturing wisdom."*

Learning to live under water

eo Rosten, the beloved author of Hyman Kaplan stories, special editorial advisor to Look, was recently granted an award at the University of Chicago. In his gracious acceptance, Alumnus Rosten quoted from the close of one of his recent books, *Captain Newman, M.D.*:

"—Then Newman said, 'My father once told me a story I always think of, when the going gets rough and things look hopeless. It's about Destiny . . . Destiny came down to an island, centuries ago, and summoned three of the inhabitants before him. 'What would you do,' asked Destiny, 'If I told you that tomorrow the island will be completely inundated by an immense tidal wave?' The first man, who was a cynic, said, 'Why I would eat, drink, and carouse, and make love all night long!' The second man, who was a mystic said, 'I would go to the sacred grove with my loved ones and make sacrifices to the gods and pray without ceasing.' And the third man, who loved reason, thought for a while, confused and troubled and said, 'Why, I would assemble our wisest men and begin at once to study how to live under water.'

"I, too, never forgot that story. When our cause seems doomed and the future lost, when despair becomes unbearable and the heart is on

68

the edge of breaking, let men summon hope and honor and high resolve in yet one more stubborn affirmation: 'Come, let us assemble our wisest men and begin at once to think, to study, to try to learn—even to learn, if we must, how to live under water.' "

Together NRTA and AARP have demonstrated in their various activities their capacity to confront with equanimity and faith the problems that growing older naturally brings with it. They have proved to their satisfaction the truth of the adage, "The bee fertilizes the flower it robs." For aging has engendered many blessings. Every year the oldster realizes is a victory won. The future is ours to go on helping build and helping protect the things we hold dear in our America. In so doing we have discovered that the ultimate good for us—and for all others lies not in self-seeking but in selfless service to humankind.

Together, at least for ourselves and those whom we contact, the whole concept of age has changed. We read that Washington, Byron and Churchill, each at one time in his 30's had announced themselves as in the sere and yellow leaf. But today's journal reports the wedding of two of our members, both past their three score years and ten. They, like all happy folks, believe they can find happiness in service and effort.

We have learned to take hardships in our stride. We are braced to regard difficulties as challenges but not as fatal deterrents. We know the stop in music is part of the melody.

We oldsters know that we are living in a world of breath-taking changes. We realize that the cold war will be with us for generations to come. We have no illusions of a swift and yielding peace, but we do have *faith*.

Nor are we older folk afraid for ourselves of the word *old*. We are amused and a bit dismayed at this caption of Senior Citizens planned for us by the Junior Citizens of our Nation. We do not like being fenced off in a minority. We feel that we are zestful, energetic, well-integrated folk; we know we have a positive attitude toward living and we pray and strive for a maturing wisdom.

Together we have demonstrated that age is not a defeat but a vic-

LEARNING TO LIVE UNDER WATER

tory, not a punishment but a privilege. We have encouraged the
American tradition of self-help and human service. We have striven
for excellence. We know ourselves to be social innovators.

Maurice Maeterlinck, the famous Belgian poet at 84, made use of
Cervantes' words to express his own philosophy which we think is
ours too. He wrote of Cervantes' speaking of age as a journey between
pleasant inns.

"The real goodness of living comes with the journey itself, with
the striving and desire to keep moving. Now I find that I can look
back on my 84 years with pleasure and, what is even more important
to me, I can still look to the future with hope and desire.

"I have learned to take each inn along the way with a traveler's
stride—not as a stopping point but as a starting point for new and
better endeavor . . ."

We have started early in the direction we wanted to go—there has
been no slackening down—we have been on our journey, been living,
growing and contributing to something. There is naturally no single
pattern in our combined achievements, but we do know that in the
accumulating of our associational accomplishments by individuals
there are thousands of experiments and solutions at work.

We like to say our thanks, too, to our founding association and
our younger and bigger organization. The pride we feel in the outgrowth of this Renaissance of the Older Folk is largely due to their
union. A fine tribute in this regard was given your president recently.
One of the most powerful legislators "on the Hill" said to me just
before the Congressional adjournment, "The reason we seek the reaction of you people is only in part the vast number you represent; it is
that you represent a group that features many segments of society—
teachers, lawyers, doctors, business folk, industrial workers, farmers,
housewives. We get in your combined groups a wide cross-section of
America that we know are not being pressured; we are being informed.
We highly respect both your associations, their independence, their
integrity—but even more highly their inclusiveness—not all of just
one kind. That's their real strength. That's how you have achieved
status." And that strength comes from both our associations—the

70

NRTA for its fostering sponsorship of AARP — and AARP for its recognition that in diversity as well as in numbers lies strength.

A half century before Christ, Cicero said: "Gratitude is not only the greatest of virtues, but the parent of all others." Our associations give of themselves in gifts of mind—ideas, dreams, purposes, ideals, principles, plans, projects, poetry. They give to each other in gifts of the spirit; vision, faith, aspirations. They give to each other the gift of the challenge of a constructive and a creative life. They give of themselves in their humane activities, their modernity and their comradeship.

Why do they do this? There are many reasons: perhaps an inquiring mind; perhaps interest in each other, and perhaps in appreciation of the gift of life to us, sharing the joy of that gift to others—gifts of kindness, of understanding, sympathy, forgiveness, tolerances, by word and deed with those who mourn because they have not that which we take for granted.

But the end is not yet; together we face the problem of how best to meet certain flattering challenges that have come to us. One challenge to our two associations comes through individual, local or state groups urging our interest and commitment in trying to help the newly discharged juvenile offender find his way back to his valuing the American traditional virtues of industry, integrity, and responsibility.

The Peace Corps offers another opportunity. Early in the history of the Peace Corps, those who were entrusted with its growth and development came, on our invitation, to our headquarters and we later filed with them applications of 300. The agency expressed itself as amazed both at the promptness of the applications and the willingness of our membership to go anywhere where needed. Miss Noneka Douglass, a 71 year old former school-teacher, a Negro, reports that she has been accepted to teach in the Philippine Islands. Formerly Miss Douglass was a teacher in the St. Louis public schools. President Kennedy met and praised a group of 12 Peace Corps volunteers between the ages of 60 and 76 as reminders that people growing old still can live useful lives in countries as peace-time ambassadors.

71

Mr. Kennedy called them "an extraordinary group of men and women" and said they disprove the impression that only young people join the Peace Corps. He singled out for special notice the oldest of the group, Ralph Cole, 76, of Dallas, Texas, a civil engineer who is going to West Pakistan. Asked why he had joined the Corps, Cole said: "Who knows?"

And there is the ever-recurring call of service to the Veterans Hospitals and domiciliaries where the friendly visitor who has warmth and interest can give the patient, starved, hungry for human friendship, both lifegiving hope and faith.

It seems so natural to turn to aid the young and so unusual to relieve the consuming hunger for love and care of the aged, perhaps because they are no longer charming in their manners or delightful in their looks. Particularly though is the oldster in the great city needful of human contact because there the social controls that govern human behavior are weakened, cooperative action is less active, fewer people know each other, the individual is often lost and alienated. The factor of bigness and the enormous concentrations of power often dwarf the individual even in his own esteem, both the potential helper and the possible friend-to-be.

Voluntary service is not new to America although it is unique to it. It began when the 41 founders of the Mayflower Pact came ashore and pledged to work for a "just and equal way of life."

And today we are saying to our thousands of volunteers words of appreciation for their enthusiasm, admiration for their fire, interest and energy, pride in their magnanimity that keeps alive the American spirit of neighbor helping neighbor and together helping their community become a neighborhood.

> *"With never a blare of trumpets*
> *With never a surge of cheers,*
> *They march to the unseen hazard*
> *Patient volunteers."**

They are America in action.

* *Mark Antony de Wolfe Howe*

72

"We earnestly seek not eternal youth but
a constantly increasing maturity, the wisdom that
will not need or seek praise, striving to realize
each day a little more of our goals—goals of helpful,
happy and enjoyable living and of growth."

Let our symbol be
the golden key of faith

n Colonial Days, when advertisements were limited to an appropriate symbol hung outside the proprietor's store, the Golden Key identified the Wet and Dry Goods Store, but also to all the passersby it represented a pledge of integrity, quality of friendly service and a promise of personal, neighborly solicitude: Shorebound sailors from the King's Navy—country squires and colonial dames all knew the sign of the Golden Key—the place to buy with surety and peace of mind.

The Golden Key can, too, be our symbol—the golden key of old age—a guarantee that we care for our fellows and that faith will unlock for us and them the door to a pleasant and buoyant life— faith in ourselves first of all, faith in our fellows, faith in our country, and faith in the future. Faith is the golden key of age—perhaps, too, of youth, but youth finds few locked doors that need a ready key of gold that will not tarnish or decay.

I am not ignoring the fact that we are all individually different, that some of us are impatiently liberal, some congenitally skeptical, but I am talking about you and me, the ordinary run-of-the-mill folk who cherish a lively sense of traditions, and enjoy a keen awareness

73

that our new leisure empowers us to become more directly responsible for what concepts the world will hold of us elderly, responsible too for what testimony of unselfish action we advance, and of the validity of our belief that we should and do participate in the business of government, not only in the limited sense of electing officials and reacting to measures submitted for referendum but also in finding the goals for the common good and in living a serviceable life.

When the Alumni Association of the University of Chicago desires to honor a member who has measured up to his standards in "pursuing the good life" it confers upon him the title of "Useful Citizen."

That title, "Useful Citizen," should be ours through just desert. It is the verdict, the award we seek on our being and our actions, for it bears witness to the faith we have in ourselves and in our sense of mission in living. It tells the world that we sense life as an evolving, an adventure, that we fear death-of-the-spirit more than we dread death in person, that we experience a sense of belonging to that beyond ourselves and the here and the now. It is our faith made real in our actions and our reactions. It is the belief made manifest that we are alive—growing up mentally and spiritually, that we are a part of that great movement of which Arnold Toynbee speaks—making to the limits of our ability, the sharing of the benefits of civilization among all men:

"Three hundred years from now," so said Arnold Toynbee in 1951, "Twentieth Century will not be remembered for the splitting of the atom, nor for the diminution of distance and disease, nor even for its shattering wars, but for having been the first age since the dawn of civilization that dared to think it (possible) to make the benefits of civilization possible to all mankind."

In our own efforts, each in his own fashion, to touch other lives, of course, we do not expect to be considered Allahs. Look at the world about us that you and I helped to make. But we can look back at the great changes—innovations at one time—through which we have lived and we can hopefully look forward to a spiritual renaissance that we can help generate. It's fun to recall that once upon a time even the word *automation* was itself a novelty; it's greater fun to

74

forecast in imagination what tomorrow can bring. It is electric in its intensity to realize that as we move into the future it becomes the now, the appointed time, that it is being tolerant *now,* being forgiving *now,* being happy *now,* instead of postponing purposeful and positive living to some indefinite future—that is to be great, great in that you have recognized that courage, hope and love are always right at hand, that you open your life so that they may be part of your every day being. And our lives will be supporting evidence that we now recognize the four instinctive drives and needs of our being: work, play, love and faith.

Not to all of us will go that great satisfaction that work entails, but to most; they can echo the poet's acclaim.

> *"Work!*
> *Thank God for the might of it.*
> *The ardor, the urge, the delight of it.*
> *Work!"*

Given for pay, or given freely, it can be creative, can enrich life and lengthen it, make you, the worker, count for something, and that something will be good!

Do you recall the epitaph on the favorite pupil by the Village Schoolmistress in Master's "Spoon River Anthology"?

> *"My boy, wherever you are,*
> *Work for your soul's sake*
> *That all the clay of you, all the dross of you*
> *May yield to the fire of you*
> *Till the fire is nothing but light*
> *Nothing but light!"*

We earnestly seek not eternal youth but a constantly increasing maturity, the wisdom that will not need or seek praise, striving to realize each day a little more of our goals—goals of helpful, happy and enjoyable living—and of growth.

In this open-end, ever expanding tomorrow, if it is granted to us, we want to know—we want to want to know. The wanting to know is half the battle, that longing, that hunger, that developing appetite are the forerunners of the victory—the cause for celebration—the pledge that America and her ideals are safe.

The pioneers of America were a great people. They were sturdy of body, broad in outlook, they dreamed a vision of a glorious future. They laid the foundation of a good and a great government. We are their proud and grateful inheritors—we are also their responsible trustees. Ours is the obligation to pass on the traditions that have made our country great—to inspire in the youth of our land the basic concepts of freedom underguiding our country's government.

In answer to the question, "What Can I Do?" Bonard Overstreet answers, "You say that the little efforts I make will do no good; they never will prevail to tip the hovering scale where justice hangs in balance. I don't think I ever thought they might, but I am prejudiced beyond debate in favor of my right to choose which side shall feel the stubborn ounces of my weight."

Of some things we are sure. When we were young, we were brought up in a stern financial creed. It could be summed up in two words, *work* and *save.*

To learn the first, one was sent to school and to encourage one in the second was given a moneybox. Into this metallic object one placed any small coins that came one's way. The lessons so laboriously drummed into us—sometimes with the assistance of a paternal hand or a maternal hairbrush—make me still mindful that the end product was real delight in sustained effort and a bit of pride in financial self-sufficiency. What our elders failed to teach us—the thing that they did not themselves know—is that legislators perhaps then aborning ordained that the more a man made by his labor the larger the proportion would be taken away from him often to subsidize the less industrious, and though some social good and some social harm have come out of it, the harder it seems a man works, the less proportionate remuneration he receives.

It is of interest, too, in this same connection to note how the youth of today reacts:

Opinion Research, one of the most dependable research institutions in the United States, in a recent survey of high school seniors, revealed some facts that are enlightening; for example, 61% of the students think "that the profit motive is not necessary for the survival of our system of free enterprise"; 76% think "most of the gains from new machinery go to the owner"; 82% believe that "there is practically no competition in business today".

What youth thinks today becomes the philosophy of tomorrow. This becomes all the more significant when we consider that the young men and women who will be graduating from our high schools and colleges, today, will be the future leaders of our nation.

If we are not content with things as they are, we must concern ourselves with things as they might become. We know that again the prescription is simple but it is not easy to compound. We are told that Galileo said you could not teach another anything but only hope to help him find that thing burgeoning within himself.

In the doing of it you can enjoy the thrill of the explorer, the adventures of changing conditions, of helping the world about you grow in sweetness and in light, while you, yourself grow tall in stature, your horizon broadens and you follow where the gleam might lead—fully alive—sharing, knowing, that the future is made up of the total of today's experiences.

Bernard Shaw says it for us, better than we can say:

"This is the pure joy in life, the being used for a purpose, recognized by yourself as a mighty one, the being thoroughly worn out before being thrown into the scrap heap; the being a part of nature instead of being a feverish, helpless little clod of ailments and grievances, complaining that the world will not devote itself to making you happy."

May you keep by you the Golden Key of faith. Remember that we appreciate what we share, not what we receive. The real bonds that tie us to others are the insights we share, the appreciation we hold in common and the moments of inner experience in which we meet. There is no one who does not carry a treasure in his soul, a memory he loves, a dream of excellence to which he aspires. Let's hope that sometime we can share with others those dreams and those visions.

"Our community is the place where we,
as older individuals, can be most effective.
In no other place can we gain so much cooperation
and win so many champions and supporters."

We who are
practical idealists

We are faced with a strange paradox. The newscasters of today tell us that the financial recession once predicted for this year has not materialized, that the economy of our republic is riding at even keel, that never had the people more comforts, more luxuries; indeed that the luxuries of yesterday have grown to be the necessities of today. A witty lecturer commented in this regard that America is the only land where the poor now have a parking problem.

On the other hand, these same newscasters report that mental illnesses are increasing, that millions of our countrymen are confined to mental hospitals and other millions outside are suffering from mental disturbances. One commentator has named this period of our living as the Phenobarbital Age; another, the Age of Anxiety. And this in a time of plenty—this at the same time that our South Asian friends are considering starvation much as we do cancer, as highly regrettable but unavoidable, and so accept it as part of life.

Living in a time of national strain and uncertainty, we seemingly have lost the thrill of derring-do, of adventuring; we seem mainly to want security; we want to escape and particularly we want to escape responsibility. We have become apathetic. Yet what is happening now

78

was foretold over a century ago. Writing in 1840, Alexis de Tocqueville predicted that the United States would enter a period when—for the first time in all history—people would have so much social, political and economic freedom that they could choose what they wanted in practically every aspect of life. But that, he said, would not be an unmixed blessing. With so much freedom and so much abundance, we are confronted with a surfeit and hold of little value the liberties so won. Yet we know that, whether we like it or not, we are engaged in a bloodless struggle to preserve our American way of life! We feel ourselves righteously outraged at the fear and the suspicion even of our kindly offers of aid aroused among the other nations of the world, and we justifiably feel so, if we ignore the fact that we have become the unwilling heirs of the cruelty, the oppression and the humiliation of other peoples of other days.

We are great salesmen, but we have tried to sell the wrong commodities. Instead of sharing with other nations the American dream of individual responsibility, of creative measures to relieve suffering, we have stressed the efficiency of our technology, the products of our inventiveness and effort. Before the world we are regarded as the exponents of the TV, the washing machine, and the deep freeze. We have not realized that things do not stir one's imagination. It is the poetry of life, the philosophy, the creed that excites and stimulates. We, who are practical idealists, have forgotten that it is our idealism, never yet realized, but progressively being pursued, that should be our greatest article of export.

We face both Russia and China with their philosophy, their program, their passion for their realization. We are told that Peking, in spite of its tragic situation of hunger and privation, is eager, excited and militantly prepared to die for her cause, and we are apathetic even though deeply concerned. We seem to be expecting a catastrophe, waiting—for what? Can it be that, instead of the financial regression which we feared, we are suffering regression of the spirit so that we have adopted an interim morality? Our college lads say there's no need to decide yet upon a life career, that they expect to be drafted and after that there'll be time enough; our growing sex irregularities are explained away—why wait for respectable marriage when the opportunity for emotional stimulation and satisfaction are offered?

We have had a dangerously trivial contact with psychiatry. Glibly we report that the consciousness of guilt is debilitating; that scientifically if we can locate the cause, the deviation in ones behavior is explained away. To know all is not to judge. Even in murder trials, we find this same sentimental attitude at work. Is the accused a product of a divided home, an unwanted child, a product of financially distressed people, a naturally rebellious victim against a parent, dominant and puritanical, a brother forceful and brilliant, a sister captivating and charming?

The lad caught cheating explains away his acts by the necessity of so meeting too high a standard of achievement. Explanation is sufficient; confession wipes the slate. Outside circumstances have determined the act. Why he "was forced" is not relevant; neither is his lack of capacity or failure to spend the needed time considered. He has successfully avoided the moral issue: "Should he have done it?" And even more tragic than his complacency with closing the issue with a frank confession is the acceptance on the part of his fellow students of both the act and the doer.

Just what is needed to counteract this lethargy, this escape from reality, this frantic search for pleasure, for excitement for the shocking to be tolerated, and the ever-broadening and lowering of our moral and aesthetic standards?

We remember in wartime how united in purpose we all were, how we produced beyond the wildest of speculations, how significant each of us felt in his or her share of that mutual, horrible conflict. Does it need such a dreadful catastrophe again to awake us, to unite us, to make us realize the great heritage left us not only to protect but to advance?

Are we, as a people, willing to accept the Russian viewpoint that the moral imperatives are outmoded and no longer pertinent? Are we willing to surrender our age-old convictions that the nation is the product of the individual, his servant; that the individual has the

80

obligation to make a choice, and only on choosing the right, the good, the beautiful, does he become moral? Are we willing to scrap the necessity of complying with the laws of God and of nature, represented as they are in our western world by the Golden Rule and the Decalogue and throughout the world by similar expressions of the universal and the unseen? You and I believe that we are not.

Here we are, then, each one of us, with manifold claims upon us, the claims of parenthood, of citizenship, of neighborliness, of friendship, of associational obligations in human concern. We cannot ignore them; we can do nothing but honorably meet them. In this regard, we are reminded of the story of Crito and Socrates. Crito pleaded with Socrates that he leave Athens, which no longer treasured him, that he need not drink the hemlock, and that he could save his life by flight. But Socrates answered, "I have enjoyed the privilege of Athenian citizenship; I owe it therefore my allegiance. Why should I break down the power of the state by disobedience? As I have accepted, so am I obligated. No, Crito, one does not deny or defy the claims upon us that once befriended us, even though they may now desire to eliminate us."

Can we not see that actually the conflict between America and Peking and Moscow is not really one of economics or even of politics? The Russian economy, we are led to believe, is in a process of change, gradually assuming some of the features the Russians have so glibly stigmatized as capitalistic. Are not their politics planned to suit their advantage, their reactions changeable at will? Does not the real difference between us lie in the place of the individual in society? Are we forgetful of the great achievements we have won in the freedoms we enjoy—the right of assembly, the freedom to worship as we will, the freedom of speech and of the press, and our suffrage? The universal or basic fundamental truths of our heritage from Judaism and Christianity are still our guiding lines and our dynamic goals which we admit we have never realized, but toward which we hopefully are advancing.

If once we could only realize that we as Americans should be militant defenders of these freedoms we could then multiply many millionfold our surety of national defenses.

The story is told of a river in the Holy Land that flows southward from its source and empties into two seas. Along the shores of one placid and smiling sea and on the rich and fertile banks of this little river are pleasant villages and sparkling foliage. On the shore of the second sea all is sear, drear and barren of foliage and the water itself dark and bitter. And the reason is the Jordan, as it flows through the sea of blessed memory which we call Galilee, accepts the stream and graciously passes it on. The sea of dread accepts the same sweet water of the Jordan but there the water is bitter and brackish. And the secret—the Sea of Galilee receives and passes on its blessing. The sea which we call the Dead accepts and holds and never gives—never shares itself, contained, accursed and alone.

In our lifetime, we have seen Hitler galvanize into action the German nation; we have seen Mussolini awake a flame of enthusiasm in Italy. They evoked a loyalty that while the goal was ignoble and the means often infamous—still they gave their people a philosophy and a program which they pursued with passion. Can we not in like manner awake our people to a loyalty to loyalty itself, to the realization of an ideal that will be helpful to all mankind, to further God's will of peace throughout the world and hasten the ultimate goal of brotherhood of man?

I once heard the great scientist, Arthur Compton, the first man ever successfully to split the atom, tell us this story. I remember his saying to a little group of Christians and Jews to whom he was talking that there was enough potential power locked up in just such a small conference to change the history of the whole world if each of us would only realize his full potential and unselfishly put it to work for the good of mankind.

Our own community is the place where each of us can come to grips with this challenge. Our community is the place where we, as older individuals, can be most effective. In no other place can we gain so much cooperation and win so many champions and supporters.

Only there shall we come to practice our belief that we are conscious of our own measure of responsibility for the planning of our government, local, state and national; only there can we realize the need not to delegate to our lawmakers the welfare of the state but actively to share with them our thinking, our honest reactions, and our hopes. There in the microcosm of the greater world we can become increasingly alert to the need of creative service to the suffering and the distressed; there, to express a renewed dedication to the ideals of individual growth, independence and service, with the hope that through our efforts each of us can do his share in helping America and her traditions and her way of life radiate with ever-increasing lustre and prestige.

"If we see the wide perspective of life and
appreciate the fact that we live in an orderly
world and feel that we are a part of that process
of infinite wisdom, if we are mutually helpful
in accepting love and giving it,
if we strive to be versatile, knowledgeable
and serviceable—then we have found the way."

Searching for some
sustaining, stabilizing concepts

B ut," I would persist, "Dad, how can you be sure?" And, towering above, he would pat my shoulder and with that quizzical smile, "Because," he would answer, "because, my dear, you'll just *know!* And that is the only assurance I can give you. You'll just know!"

I cannot remember just when I first realized that tomorrow always followed today, but very early the promise comforted me that, if I would go to bed *at once,* there would be mañana coming in which I again could explore, adventure and play to my heart's desire. And then when mañana came, there was always tomorrow waiting!

It was a long time after when I first grew conscious of the shift of the seasons, the waxing and waning of the moon, and the rising and the setting of the sun. But gradually the certainty and the continuity of the seasons dawned upon me—the surety and the security of knowing that there were order and planning.

And then came wonder and awe. My sister and I watched at San

84

Juan Capistrano for the swallows predicted to return on St. Joseph's Day. We thrilled at their characteristic patterns in orderly formation and their graceful swooping. We marvelled at the intricate pattern of the cobweb, so rarely seen nowadays in this cleanly antiseptic world but not so rare in the olden days. And we marvelled at the precise, jeweled crystals of Jack Frost on the window panes—the geometric artistry of the snowflake on the sill—at the uniform symmetry of the leaves, at the orderly placement of them on the branches. All of the natural order became a part of our everyday lives and yet beyond our bidding, giving us shivers of sheer delight and awe—at the wonder of it all.

And when spring came, we saw the rippling waves of the sand, windblown-patterns of curving beauty, regular in their finery of parallels, yet each a bit different and distinct from its adjoining neighbors.

Gradually we became aware of the orderly process of the world in which we had our being, and gradually, too, that we also were a part of this same world of continuity and meaningful patterns, each of us different in many ways but all of us alike in the great ways that mattered—all a part of the natural process of infinite supernatural wisdom, transient for us but continuous and perpetual and uncompromising.

And then as the years passed, came school where we learned how man had contrived to adjust nature to his needs; how when he disobeyed natural laws, there came disaster—floods after the hills were stupidly and ruthlessly robbed of their protective trees, desert when the fertility of the earth was exhausted and not replenished, illness, when nature's rules were abused or defied.

And there were even more marvels when we learned how precise are the mathematical bases of beauty—always specific, law-obedient yet still amazingly versatile, complex and individualistic. And we discovered that the science we began to explore was also built upon the natural laws of this same predictable behavior throughout the universe. Increasingly we became aware that these patterns disclosed a meaningful mind: an ineffable "Something." And then, to our amazement, we learned that even the "everlasting hills," too, are answerable to these same laws of continuity, growth, and pattern of changes of movements which respond to the surge and urge of life.

Our awe grew with the cumulative revelations of these meaningful patterns in nature. We came, increasingly, to the realization of the triumph of human understanding with Galileo's statement: "With regard to objective certainty—the few verities known by the human mind are known as perfectly by man as they are by God."

And so at long last we began to see the larger perspective of life —the world about us and ourselves, too, as inseparable parts of that orderly process.

At times we felt as one with it, somehow so inextricably woven into its very fibre that, in empathy, we experienced the thrill of identical movement as we watched the circling and wheeling of the birds in flight, in the gushing swirl and sweep of water in cascades of dashing, foaming falls, the rhythm of horses in gallop with mane and tail flowing. We had projected ourselves in them. We were taken out of ourselves and felt at one with the objects that entranced us.

So we began to expand our horizons: we began to realize how immeasurably great to the world was the Jewish contribution of sensitivity, in a time of terror and confusion, grasping this universality and proclaiming the oneness of a single Deity Who was at once both the embodiment of this law and yet One who respected and obeyed it.

We *knew,* as my father had assured me long ago, and we knew *we knew.* We realized that the principles we had learned are not subject to compromise; yet definitely are open to our choosing, our obedience, our conformity to shifting situations; or to our violation, disregard or ignorant defiance.

We came to believe that in the microcosm of the world about us we could imagine the wide world in all its majesty and awe-inspiring complexity. Now the central mystery was still insolvent. Yet now we had a framework against which we could wonder why we are here and where we are going.

We knew that we had consciousness. We had, we believed, a freedom of choice. Convinced and bulwarked by a passionate intuition and our own life-experiences, we built our enduring hope—our faith that with hope for the future and love and service for our fellows, we would find a rewarding serenity of spirit. We had faith that there are enduring values in life that bring inspiration and comfort, that these universal human experiences have a profound emotional and social impact upon any and all of us—that makes us not shrink from danger, from hardship or from bitter toil. We learned how truly Seneca spoke 2,000 years ago when he said that wisdom allows nothing to be good that will not last forever. No man, to be happy, needs other happiness than that which he has within himself; no man to be great or powerful needs other power than mastery of himself.

We saw changes—inevitable changes—and we saw adjustments to the imperatives of stability, of balance, of motion with its corollaries of growth and, when abused, of decadence. From them we deduced certain conceptions, such as the essential equilibrium between the liberty of choice so essential to moral responsibility and license which abuses it, between one's rights and one's responsibilities, between one's obligation and the joys of doing one's duty.

We grew astonished at the various interpretations of the concept of leisure, ranging all the way from the dictionaries' definitions of "idleness," and "freedom from work and duties" to the power one has to spend one's time according to one's choice and one's potential powers and one's philosophy of growth and service.

So we have grown to recognize meaningful patterns in life, to enlarge our perspectives, to appreciate eternal values, to enjoy everyday events that offer permanent values, to hold every moment as precious, to develop a concern for human society in this troubled, confused, technological world in which we live.

We saw changes—inevitable changes—and we saw adjustments to them. When adjustments were not made—well, we saw tragedy follow. We watched those who were adaptable—and those who resist in stubbornness, apathy, indifference and must therefore pay the consequences of senility. We saw the great mysteries of life flash before our eyes, giving us glimpses of greater insight—flashes of aspiration and hope, or again we saw about us folks who had learned to live well. They may not have been famous or wealthy or even schooled, but they were alive—active, alert, aware and dedicated to the advancement of some idea, or some person, or some group, or some movement. They were putting the most into it; they were finding life interesting—they, too, were interesting—and valued and treasured. Yes, we warmed toward them with a sunny smile, a delightful apropos quip; we found them "good medicine."

We see, too, daily, transcendent beauty in the early sunrise—and in the glowing sunset, and for a moment we are exalted. But some do not look, and, if looking, see only the utilitarian prediction weather-wise they think they discover in it.

I remember, as a child, beguiled often in being terror-stricken at nine o'clock for fear that my feet would not be "toeing the mark" on the chalked line of our planked schoolyard. Intrigued in watching the farrier, I would tarry watching him shoe a horse. It was a thrilling sight; he was so absorbed, so at one with the animal whose shoe he was fitting, so dextrous with his bellows and his fire, sometimes smoldering and smoky and sometimes shooting up in brilliant flames. With glowing iron in hand, his shop so redolent always of that pungent acrid smell of burned hoof, he would say at just the right last moment, "Scurry along, Sissie, or you'll be late!" Scurrying away, I would feel the call of service, of joy in work, of being meaningful.

Even today as I write I am thinking as I did then that one of nature's masterpieces is a man absorbed in his work and loving it. He was one of the first of those great successes I have known through life. He had the art of sharing, the graciousness to accept love, and the depth of heart to return it! Many years later, again I saw the farrier, much older but still happily at work, still comforting his charges, still building in them confidence in himself, proudly stilling their uneasy fear, still self-renewing in his service and friendliness.

On my desk I have a letter that tells of the sudden death of a life-long friend of mine—a Japanese man who long before World War II had his neck broken in an auto accident. All these many years he has lain prone, supporting himself on his elbows, ever black from the strain. For years to me he has been a beacon, a pillar of light by day, a pillar of fire at night, a man who never mentioned his plight. Always thoughtful of his unseen friends, he was quietly reassuring to his vast

88

host of telephone shut-ins to whom he was a cheering friend, a wise counselor, a man who "just somehow" happened to find the leisure time always to be available, always to be helpful. People who knew him did not feel sorry for Peter Kondo; they felt proud that they had known him, that he had trusted them with the secret of his disability, trusted them and loved them. And I, and all those who must today be grieving for his passing, loved and trusted him.

And so I came to the faith that each of us, as individuals, can help toward the realization of the American ideal. If we see the wide perspective of life and appreciate the fact that we live in an orderly world, and feel that we are a part of that process of infinite wisdom, if we realize that the natural law is the compass that helps guide us in our world of continuity and recurring patterns, if we are mutually helpful in accepting love and giving it, if we strive to be versatile, knowledgeable and serviceable—then we have found the way. Then we *know* that the goal is always in the process, not in the arriving, in the doing, never in the ending. Then we are actively at rest, for we have acquired a "dynamic maturity."

*"The tradition of faith and courage is
still the yeast ever at work among us—
faith in ourselves, faith in our fellows and
faith in God—and courage to go forward."*

Man's destiny

We realize that man's destiny is a great one perhaps in part
because the essence of it is tragic. All that man builds
crumbles; all that he embodies turns to dust; all that he
loves most he must one day leave behind him. He comes at
long last to realize that that which alone endures on earth is the spirit
in which he understands and meets his fate. This he passes on to his
children and his comrades: that spirit is only a breath of life, but it
still embodies the essence of his being. It is that intangible thing,
though yet the most durable—his faith and his courage.

The tradition of faith and courage is still the yeast ever at work
among us—faith in ourselves, faith in our fellows and faith in God
—and courage to go forward. These attributes are the sources of our
strength and our inspiration. You see them reflected in the sturdy
growth of unity among our older people everywhere. They are in turn
made visible to the society about us by the loyalty and the industry
of many thousands of our leaders who, without reservation, contribute their time and effort to serve far beyond the call of duty.

We need not be versatile men, such as was Thomas Jefferson, about
whom it was told that he could calculate an eclipse, survey an
estate, argue a cause, break a horse, dance a minuet and play the
violin. Nor do we need the over-concentration of Lord John Russell,
about whom Queen Victoria remarked, "He would be a better man

90

if he knew a third subject"—but he was interested in nothing but the Constitution of 1688 and himself.

The opportunity to live a dignified, productive and satisfying life is within the reach of all of us, if we but will to do so. Like everything else in life that is worth having, it comes to us only if we pursue a dynamic purpose with zeal, endeavoring to reach an ever evolving, ever expanding goal.

We must frankly recognize the changes not only in ourselves but in the social role we can play. We must redefine for ourselves the activities that we realize are within the limits of our capacity and our social possibilities. We must relinquish or at least minimize old activities that we can no longer successfully pursue and adopt new ones that we can. We must graciously and progressively accept changes in the standards we place for our self-assessment and the retention not only of respect which we hold for ourselves but that which we desire from society. We must face fearlessly the great problem of life —one always with us from youth to age—what are the goals that bring value and purpose to our lives?

And then we must convert these goals into action. When we are invited to accept a volunteer assignment—such as this one here being offered—do we automatically decline, giving all the reasons why we believe in its value but at the same time explaining that we just cannot do it? Or are we willing to assume service beyond that of self and see in such volunteer contributions of time and energy a way of increasing the enjoyment of our own life? That is one test of how graciously we are aging.

Are we narrowing our fields of personal interest? We are assured by both the medical profession and the psychologists that the tendency to withdrawal is fatal to forward growth. Pray God that we never reach the point where we cannot cheerfully strive to grow.

Do we instinctively avoid something new and strange? Do we resist learning new things and the "how" and "why" of old things? Learning is a form of living; let us keep alive our sense of curiosity, of wonder and of concern.

Are we overly concerned that our looks are not as pleasing as they were when we were younger? Do you really believe that beauty is reserved only for the youth? Don't we ourselves know among our acquaintances those who in their older years are more attractive, more vibrant, more interesting than they were when younger, whose courage, confidence and enthusiasm bespeaks a real beauty in living, a higher morale? Surely we have often seen their living and the purpose of their lives reflected in their faces.

Do we not know persons who progress through life solving their own problems, living purposely, lending a helping hand to others where needed and keeping love in their hearts for their fellow man? These persons have developed an inner beauty that does much to soften wrinkles and sagging chins, to lessen irregularities of features and even to challenge chronological age itself.

It is this inner light that we must keep alive; for the strength of folks like you and me, and of our Association, like the strength of a nation, while it rests largely in our thinking does even more so in our feeling. The heart of our Associations is just as good, just as fine, just as warm, just as genuine as the heart of the people who compose them, and outside that heart there is no life. Out of the heart springs the sources of life and action, so we must see to it that we do not hold aloof, that we throw our lives with all our energy and our spirit into the welfare of the lives of others. We must see to it that these others feel themselves necessary to our well-being.

Such is the object of all noble institutions. Strength and happiness depend upon all of us getting together and pulling together as a single team.

Can you imagine an association more ideally suited to help advance the right of mankind of every sort everywhere? This plea is not a sermon to the despondent or the lonely; but just a sincere welcome to join a great fellowship and to ask you to go along with all the rest of us in triumphantly illustrating the spirit of America, concerned and helpful in the service of mankind.

GROWTH AND SELF-FULFILLMENT

Take time to think
  It is the source of power
Take time to play
  It is the secret of perpetual youth
Take time to read
  It is the fountain of wisdom
Take time to pray
  It is the greatest power on earth
Take time to love and be loved
  It is a God-given privilege
Take time to be friendly
  It is the road to happiness
Take time to laugh
  It is the music of the soul
Take time to give
  It is too short a day to be selfish
Take time to work
  It is the price of success

Courtesy of Squibb Nurses Notes Magazine

Direction—
secret of the good life

Many of you have seen the old McGuffey's Readers, books which were used by the children of one hundred years ago. In a Fifth Reader in the McGuffey series there is this story. An old clock which had stood for fifty years in a farmer's home without giving cause for complaint, suddenly stopped. The pendulum did not try to blame anyone else for this stoppage, but said, "I am responsible and I shall tell you why. The truth is that I am tired of ticking. I have just figured out that in the next 24 hours I shall have to tick 86,400 times. This thought was disconcerting enough, but when I began to multiply that number by months and years, it is no wonder I got discouraged. And so, think I to myself, I'll stop." The dial, seeing the trouble, asked the pendulum if he would give just a half dozen strokes. The pendulum did, admitting that it did not tire him at all but that he was not complaining of 6 strokes, nor of 60, but of millions—the 31,536,000 seconds which he would have to tick in the year. "Very good," said the dial, "but recollect that although you may think of a million strokes in an instant, all you have to do is one, and that however often you have to swing, a moment will always be given you to swing in." With this the pendulum took heart and began to run the clock again.

In those old days of the McGuffey Readers, such a tale was usually ended with a postscript marked *Moral*. So that you will feel this same sense of completeness, let me tell you another tale. The discontented pendulum seemed never to have heard the story of the man who traveled all the way to India to seek out a mystic and ask him how one could live a full and satisfying life that would banish thoughts of boredom and of death. And the mystic said, "For your soul's sake, there is but one word for you to know." "And what is it?" queried the traveler. "Others," answered the mystic. "It is both the alpha and the omega of the true life."

The discontented pendulum, on making his decision, did not consider the dismay and consternation the cessation of his swaying might cause the world which he served, aside from the unpleasant consequences to himself in the possible form of discord and abandonment. Also he missed the true joy of life—of his life's being used for a purpose recognized by him as a worthy one—of dividing time into measurable lengths, with its possible use by all within the range of its motions. Missing the vibration of the sweep of the moving disc, the man rising early for a try at the brook stops uncertain. The tantalizing odor of the coffee and the sizzling of the bacon in the skillet lack a bit of their usual hearty relish by the disturbed householder. The lad dawdling over the treasures he must leave for the present, wonders if the school bell might ring and make him tardy. The world about, while it does not cease its necessary and insistent duties, suffers a disturbing sense of a comrade lost, a friend who has failed; it clouds a bit the glory of the morning. The ship of the household somehow seemed to have lost its compass and its rudder.

And when again the pendulum begins its rhythmic swing, changing on its downward curve the future into the present and on its upward swing the present into the past, the world about, a bit puzzled but at once relieved, marches on its way to the future, never arriving but always in the process of becoming.

The pendulum, however, obsessed with pity for himself and the formidable future went back to the drab routine of his days, feeling that if he refuses to take the long view of his participation in the affairs of his world, he can better accept the daily treadmill of the

96

immediate present. Surely this is a most unexciting role, plain duty, robbed of imagination and of the thrill of companionship, the joy of meaning and the sense of adventure that might have ennobled his service and added to his sense of being an efficient and a necessary member of the team, with a purpose of good will and a direct bearing on the course of events that might alter history.

And so it is with many of us older folk. A dull despair, and, in this mood, failure is certain. We know that "life is not lost only by dying; life can be lost, minute by minute, day by dragging day in all the thousand, small uncaring ways." Only a consistent picture of life as it ought to be, as it can be, can catch our imagination and make us face life with zest. If we fail to clarify this picture for ourselves, the zest is not ours.

People who visit Peking report that there is to be found there a mood of inexhaustible expectancy with a lift of enthusiasm that has come to that poverty-stricken city because of a fanatical devotion to an ideal—false and cruel and unworthy as that ideal may be.

But here in America in a time where material well-being is at its height, we find depression. Increasingly we are numbering those mentally ill among us. Books telling how to gain peace and poise are among the best sellers. Is it not sad that a sense of boredom comes as the reward of relief from routine and responsibility? Often it is reported that we do not know what to do with our released time and, like the discontented Pendulum, we just give up.

We blame the mechanization about us that has brought us more data to worry about than any generation before us. We blame the times with their unrest and their tensions. And yet we know that peace is a dream still to be realized, still to be earned, and that we must wisely and well go on living in this period of stress. We must realize, as did the man in prison, that we can determine the direction of our thoughts. We can see only mud as we peer through the restraining bars, or we can see the stars! Should we not cultivate the attitude of looking for the stars? Like Socrates drinking his poison, we must keep our mind untroubled because we know that we are sure of ourselves and of our purpose; so we gain a sense of inner well-being.

If, however, we do not have this source of inner happiness, we are truly at a loss. We see round about us the frequent sadness of the very rich and the very beautiful as often in the case of Hollywood, but we do not see the lives of these people as noticeably enviable because of that wealth or that beauty. It would be silly to say that money is unimportant; we know that it is so because of its often being the means of untold good, and it is equally silly to insist that the mere possession of money or of beauty can guarantee one a good life.

We know often these same people in times of war were happy. In the anguish we all suffered, and the sense of dedication it demanded from us all, we were forced to live on a higher plane in which we gained a sense of significance from our lives. We can bear great sorrow; we can carry great responsibility but we must have a sense of meaning in our lives; we must feel that our lives count; we must not see ourselves or our activities as trite or trivial. We need the conviction that we are contributing something and that that something has in it an enduring quality.

If as the day dawns, a man sees in it just another day—with no call for him, he is truly a part of the unburied dead. As William James tells us:

"Whenever a process of life communicates an eagerness to him who lives it, there the life becomes truly significant. Wherever it is found, there is the zest, the tingle, the excitement of reality and there is the important in the only real and positive sense in which importance anywhere can be."

And how do we gain that importance? We know that we ourselves are not important, even if we desired to be so. But this we do know, that we gain importance by sharing ourselves with some ideal, some ideal preferably to be found in a concrete cause, be it either a person, a cause or an institution.

And here we come to a seeming contradiction. We say happiness comes from within but we know equally well that unhappiness comes also from within; it comes because we dwell too long and too intently upon ourselves. We learn the inner secret of happiness when we learn to direct our inner drives—our interest and our attention on some-

98

thing outside ourselves.

The famous Harvard professor, Joseph Royce, summarized this thesis in these words; "There is only one way to be an ethical individual and that is to choose your cause and to serve it." And again— "We are not speaking of a good that comes to a few men only . . . to heroes or saints of an especially exalted mental type. The mightiest and the humblest of any social order can be morally equal in the exemplification of loyalty."

Man needs to *belong*. "Member" is one of the most splendid words in our vocabulary. Man needs to be a *member*. He reaches his fullness of self when he finds something to live *for*. Whenever we espouse a cause and give ourselves to it, our lives gain a greater value, a finer sense of purpose, a real significance.

And that cause is best for us which harms no other but serves to unite all of us and all our powers, and dedicates us and them to something outside ourselves. "And so," concludes Royce, "A cause is good, not only for me but for mankind in so far as it is essentially a loyalty to loyalty. That is an aid and a furtherance of loyalty in my fellows."

The Association that we serve is a cause which is universal in its sympathies, even though it works through small units. Few joys are greater than the joy of participation with a dedicated group and that is a boon we offer to all men. We are all recruits in the total human enterprise that is hoping to contribute to the ultimate good. So we enter into a community of service and of hope. By so doing we transcend our allotted span of life; we deny mortality. We live for that which passes far beyond the *here* and the *now*.

Happiness, we know, comes from within, but it is equally true that our greatest unhappiness comes also from within. When our inner happiness is self-centered, we lose it. When our inner-self seeks an "other's" goal, we gain it. If the aim is centripetal, it defeats itself; when it is directional, it brings with it well-being.

Truly as George Ade, that gentle humorist of yesterday once said— "Them as gives gets."

Shouldn't this have been the *moral* that McGuffey failed to add?

"To take another perspective on our lives in the swift pace of contemporary living is to think how much we need to grow if we would play our part in this age of modern complexity."

For what shall we strive?

The New Year brings with it obligations of inventory and assessment. The accomplishments and the shortages of the past are reviewed and weighed, their record and their memory filed away. A new year stretches before us, and with it the vast opportunities of choice. For what shall we strive? Just what is our goal?

We see ourselves in a world of increasing mechanization and automation. To both we are grateful for the relief they afford us and for the leisure they accord us, but we want, too, to remain human, alive, functioning, and helpful. As we survey the things in the past that we have done and the things we have left undone—our sins of commissions and of omissions—we discover that perhaps that which brings into our heart its greatest sense of security, of fullness and of warmth is the love and the friendship of the people who have blessed us with their regard. Yet, the disturbing question vexes us: have we failed in our busy lives to keep these friends heart-close? Many of our beloved ones are already gone away and their love remains in our memory— a cherishing thought and a soothing solace. Many are still here, but in the rush and the negligence of daily duties and routines we have unconsciously slighted and sometimes ignored those who are near and still daily contributing to the richness of our being. We are failing to acknowledge now and often the priceless gift they are giving us,

100

the contribution they are making to our lives and our happiness. This then is one thing we hope to do now—to nourish our friendships —taking time and giving care to keep in flourishing condition the finest gifts of life, the protecting insurance of love and friendship.

There are so many ways that we can take the pains to have our love speak for us: we know them, and let us use them!

Another phase of this same need is the continuous adding of new friends—younger folk—to our treasury of friends. In doing so, we learn that the art of friendmaking pays great dividends, for friends share our problems and double our comforts.

Because we are older, have learned courage and have outwitted handicaps, we can help youth do a better job. They have the advantage of youth and an idealistic realism. We have the advantage of having made most of the mistakes that mankind can make, and having learned from them we now want, in the fullness of hope and love, to share old dreams with them. We perhaps can arouse the apathetic to new endeavors. We can help awaken dormant ability and direct it. Maybe we can make others aware of their strengths, their potential skills, their inherent abilities. So we can find joy in learning their unawareness and watching them grow in courage and in strength.

Making friends is an art that anyone can master; all we need is to try. Difference in age is no deterrent. And experience can help enlarge their horizon. So we can enrich, with our friendship, the lives of others, and we, in doing so, may enrich our own.

To take another perspective on our lives in the swift pace of contemporary living is to think how much we need to grow if we would play our part in this age of modern complexity. We need, as never before, to be versatile, to be knowledgeable, to be perceptive. We owe it to ourselves and our fellowmen to develop a rounded personality. Henry Brandon in the *Saturday Review* reminds us:

"It is not enough today to have a knowledge of one's own country, its history, its politics. One's range must encompass a far wider world than was ever required in the past.

"It is not enough to limit oneself to becoming familiar with one's own surroundings; one needs to be acquainted with other civilizations.

101

"It is not enough to have an idea about the American Constitution. It is vital to pay attention to other important political systems—particularly those with a world-wide impact.

"An isolated life in one's own back yard, however much one may yearn for it, is out of date."

And then we want to make our contribution to society. The Royal Bank of Canada recently published an article on the *Volunteer in Our Society*. In it was this statement:

"One does not need to have a romantically heightened view of giving yourself away, but only to remember that the contribution made by individuals and groups voluntarily is the real foundation of democratic society, and that it is one of the ways in which, in spite of mechanization and automation, we remain human."

Dr. Paul Moody is quoted as saying, "The measure of a man is not the number of his servants but the number of people he serves." The oldster who shares himself with his neighbor has found the solution, practical and constructive, to the answer of "Why am I here?" He is here because he is concerned about people and cares what happens to them. He wants to help.

There are so many ways he can help. One of the most compelling ones is to introduce retirement to those in or out of our profession to whom it is still only a word—one fraught with dread or one wrapped with illusions of leisure. To have the opportunity to help folks cross the border line and find in this new release of time and control of one's activities not boredom but, if they have the grit and courage, to find a more active, a more dedicated and a more articulate way of life.

Most folks on approaching older age really cannot imagine its potentials. As teachers—if we are discussing them—there often comes a vital change in living. Perhaps there is the loss of a sense of mission, a lessening in prestige and social placement that may follow, the lack of contact with fellow-workers in a crusade and with the association and guidance of youth that have been the main purpose of our being, or a lesser financial income. Perhaps these shortages, as they suddenly come, are the great dividers between the association of active teachers

102

and that of the retired. The active is immersed in the assured present, in the education scene *per se;* the retired face not only an entirely new present but the unknown future; his problem becomes a highly individualized one and a social one. He desires to keep in the full stream of life and he can do so only if he *strives,* only if he keeps on earning the prestige and dignity which before came naturally to him because of his function. He may resent not being considered a person, a personality, a doer; he may even resent the euphonious nonmenclature of "Senior Citizen"—what indeed are the Juniors? Why should he be segregated and declassed? He can find the answer only in himself and in the love and the service of his fellow-man, in not growing old but in growing, not in being a problem to society, but in helping society solve its problems.

The world is full of things to do. Here are suggestions we have gathered as real projects that gave pleasure and profit both.

Collecting is one of them; Coins, spoons, wild-flowers, stamps, cartoons for one's self and the enjoyment of friends; magazines for hospitals, clothing for the needy, funds for one's pet charity, etc.

Making things is another; Scrapbooks for filling, scrapbooks for the well ones, and the ill ones in hospitals; candles, paper-folding; dressing a doll for an unknown child, making its clothing historically or occupationally correct; doing typing or stenciling for your club or association; knitting squares for afghans; rolling bandages for Red Cross; building a miniature garden on a pie plate, building an orange crate dollhouse, party favors, etc.

Doing something you have never done before; like taking a walk on a Sunday morning at 5:00 a.m.; joining a drama group; following your bus routes to their termination; talking to some folks you have never seen before; experimenting with a new hairdo at a beauty training school, letting the novice experiment on styles best fitted for you; trying some foods at a gourmet shop that are strange to you; using a new recipe for a family surprise; buying an utterly frivolous bit of finery, a pair of shoes or a funny hat; learning a new card game; taking a walk turning left at the first corner, right at the next and alternating at each corner; reading a book picked up at random; attending

a foreign movie, churches of other faiths, luxury stores; visiting the city
council meetings; growing plants from orange pips, avocado seeds,
carrot tops, sweet potato; joining study groups of folks of similar
interests; planning a dream journey and getting illustrative materials;
starting a neighborhood magazine.

Tracking down the initials of organizations and learning their
function, e.g., SEATO, SAC, FAD, NATO; the history of your
family, your town, your association; derivations of words used on
this page; finding a civic need and developing a project to help answer
it.

Studying the history and the people of a certain country; a specific
subject like quills, shells, heraldry, the various breeds of dogs, cats,
horses; flower arranging; learning a foreign language; myths of ancient
days; the geography of the '60s; the life of people in the 17th, 18th,
19th centuries; the international problems today; wood carving, pup-
petry; reviving an early interest in the arts; becoming an authority on
jewels, roses, fuchsias, geraniums; studying a city of your dreams,
e.g.: London, Florence, Paris, Rome, Hong Kong and from its maps
gain an armchair acquaintance with it.

With big enthusiasms, the conviction of need, and the resolution
of effort, we, as individuals in the context of like-minded persons can
obtain a measure of ourselves and the satisfaction of personal acceptance by others, so becoming more adequate and gaining a sense of
importance beyond our own individual orbit.

In summary, each of us can fulfill his dream of self. Still curious,
we can follow national affairs, the politics that engage us, the geography in the making, the history of countries formerly only words in a
social studies class, the social trends, the tensions and the uncertain
future. We can strive for at least a minimum knowledge of the
advances of science, of biological, atomic and space science, of psychology and the fundamental laws of trade, and the economic processes of the various nations. We can realize the urgent need of
friends, perhaps gain a new concept of our human and familial and
neighborhood relationships. We can feel the need to participate both
modestly and with humility in the hoped-for advancements and the

more speedy solution of cruel and needless inequities. We can accept as part of our active citizenship a social role, joining with our fellows in finding the sought-for answers to our social problems. So at long last, with courage we face our needs to eradicate prejudices and commonplace judgments. In so doing we earn for ourselves self-esteem and status with experience that absorbs and satisfies.

"What makes life worthwhile?" questions R. M. MacIver in *The Challenge of the Passing Years,* and he answers:

"The answers offered have been themselves various and conflicting. But whatever they are, whether they find salvation through a way of believing, a way of doing or a way of feeling, they have all had at their base a common element. The way they prescribe must enlist the personality in wholehearted unison with some reality that absorbs and fulfills the being. The fulfillment of personality is thus a form of communion, whether it be with the God a man worships; or with nature under some aspect; or through intimate communication with ideal things, the inexhaustible quality of beauty or truth that pervades the universe; or with some cause that calls into action all one's power; or even with things of lesser significance so long as they suffice to satisfy the human craving for union."

For such we strive.

*"Shall we ostrich-like bury our heads in the sand,
be part of the great unthinking mass? Or shall we
stretch our faith, our hope, our love to try as onlookers
to understand and marvel at the new world emerging?"*

The art of
knowing yourself

I f we look upon our retirement from paid employment as also being our commencement, our graduation into a new unexplored world, our 65th year is no longer tragic, but, instead, is a time when we can plan our own individual time schedules and our own program of activities and can either develop or ignore our own potentials for growth and for service.

To prepare for that earlier period from which we have just been graduated, a score or more of our years were spent and much familial and professional efforts were expended involving a considerable financial outlay and much thoughtful planning.

To prepare for the two score or more years ahead of us, little attention probably has been paid either by ourselves or by others and yet we know that the preparation for those earlier periods of our life is no longer adequate for equipping us today to meet the problems and the frustrations which are foreseeable. Nor are we the same persons we were in those earlier days, nor are our values, our interests and our life goals identical with those we held as guidelines and ends toward which we then were working.

Were we now about to retire from some certain lines of endeavors, we would find being offered to us a pre-retirement counseling service

106

in which the major emphasis might be psychologically structured to help us in our need to develop a systematic approach to self-study, and so to save time, anxiety and to improve our approach to adult life, life planning and improved social intercourse.

Barring that, we can ourselves arrange a self-improved study of ourselves and our environment which can anticipate later adjustment and, perhaps, help prepare us for years of active productivity despite the society-imposed retirement fictions of institutionalized living, incapacity, family rejection, and/or indigence.

There is no easy way open if we would make the most of our lives. Even those who have pleasure as their goal have to exert themselves to make that possible. It means we must work, study, analyze and understand what we can learn about ourselves, why we behave as we do, what equipment we have with which to behave and our social concern in the world and people about us.

We must try to look at ourselves as objectively as we can, as truthfully as we can, our own personality, our health, our interests, our friends and those things or persons or movements that give us satisfaction and reward.

Psychology tells us that we all share certain basic drives with all human beings. These are not equally dominant in all the lives of all nor are they always dominant in any one person's life. How we react to them, what wide variables they offer us, what conflicts they engender in us are some of the characteristics that help differentiate us one from the other.

To help us understand ourselves we must decide the comparative importance of each of the basic drives in our own lives: which are the dominant ones, which are the ones that seem likely to trigger action or to sway our sentiments and build or destroy our sense of values.

1. To live long—not to get old but to grow old.

Probably the basic one is the desire to live—live long—but not to grow old. We must decide first, how important to each of us is our own life? How much joy and beauty does life bring to us? All stories of derring-do, of pioneering, of physical heroism are stories of folks eager to live—live in spite of danger and in face of it—to increase the vigor, efficiency and happiness of living.

2. *To be loved and to love.*

And the second drive—like the first—is basic—the drive to love and to be loved. Babies respond to it, and when deprived of it, fail to develop normally. We older folk may deny the need of it, but the confidence man knows that pretense is futile. One tragedy we know is that older folk are often deeply loved, but grieve because they are denied the privilege of showing their love for their beloved by little acts and deeds—concrete and measurable. How dominant is this need in our lives, the need to give service? Could you sacrifice love to gain wealth? Do you actively feel that basic need to be needed? That is one of its manifestations. Philanthropy stems from the desire to give love.

3. *To belong.*

And then there is the need to belong. Just how important to you is that memorable word "Member"? How great is your need of others? How tragic in your life is loneliness? How strong is your sense of loyalty to family, to clan, to school, to AARP, to your friends and your fellow countrymen? If we retire from life, life retires from us.

4. *To feel secure physically and spiritually.*

How great is your sense of security: physical security, economic security, and that intangible one of spiritual security? Does it make us cowards, fearful of taking risks? Does it force us to conform, to accept the undesired present, rather than risk the possibility of failure in an ardently desired future occupation, residence or condition? Where physically would we seek security: in town, in country, at sea, in the mountains?

5. *To think highly of one's self.*

How dominant is the need for us to think well of ourselves, to

108

have our self-respect, to maintain our spirit of self-reliance? Do we need to make a fortune to think well of ourselves? Or do we need to give that fortune to others to maintain our integrity? How do we feel about honor? How good is our spoken word?

6. *To have others think highly of us.*

How much does the regard of others mean to us? What do we do to gain approval of others? Do we deny ourselves financial security to buy luxuries we cannot honestly afford because we need to have our confidence bolstered by the approbation of others? How dominant in our thinking is the status symbol?

7. *To have something to look forward to.*

And last but far from least is the need to have something to look forward to: How easily does boredom come to us? How dreary and routine is the tempo of our living? Where do we find—or do we find—romance and adventure in our life planning? We are told that among the four great healers, light, love, sleep and change—change has a dominant place. Travel, adventure, new experiences—all so easy to contrive for the creative and the imaginative! Are zest and enthusiasm ours? Or are we natively slow in thought and sluggish in action? Have we kept alive and awake? Do we look forward to tomorrow with anticipation because we know we have lived fully today?

These seven basic drives are not all of equal value in our lives. If we have followed them, we have identified the urge that makes us different from our friends, our relatives, anyone we know.

We, then, should likewise assess our skills, our talents. We should realize that that which we have done is a measure of our capacity then. But remember Henry Ford's dictum, "Anyone can walk right through the boundaries we ordinarily believe are our limitations." Our past performance is in our grasp; we still can reach and extend ourselves.

Having given ourselves as searching and as objective an analysis as we are capable, we have inventoried our equipment, then we look about us in this world of massive change in which we live our uncertain lives with a hope that somewhere we shall find a challenge that we dare accept as ours. And what do we find?

We find the great leaders who have helped us in days past have either gone or are silent. Churchill, despite his faults (and like our own, they were many) still gave us courage and confidence and faith. Gandhi is no longer with us, but his spirit lives on. Schweitzer is gone. DeGaulle, valiant and self-reliant, still is only a French leader, not a global one. Yet we know that the world's destiny and future depends upon the sufficient numbers of them with imagination and compassion and understanding as wide as the world is wide.

For the world is a larger place than when we were young, a larger place and yet a smaller one too, made so by invention, speed, ease of transportation, communication techniques formerly undreamed of, and beyond the dreams of even a Jules Verne. It is a world of bewildering, of massive change, more populous every minute. We are told that while it took 1500 years to double the number of people on this earth, yet the statisticians tell us that this same doubling is expected in the next 50 years! Added to that amazing and arresting situation comes the equally startling statement of that wizard of figures, Luther Hodges, that automation is releasing 40,000 jobs in the United States, in industry. The world picture of peoples, too, is changing. In the last ten years 800,000,000 persons have moved from the oppression and repression of colonial domination and primitive conditions to political independence and modern development in technology, science and art.

At home we find bewildering, intangible changes; upsetting and disturbing.

The family is different. Father is no longer the unquestioned head, priest, and lawgiver. Today, if he still is a member of the family, he settles for a "palship." Mother has become perhaps a part of the work force, maybe a nucleus of an entirely different family group. Traditions disappear. They have faded in their grip on our imaginations and our ideals seem to have evaporated. They are dwarfed; religion has a lesser hold on our lives and upon our actions. Indeed there seems to have been a shocking decline in moral standards. Law enforcement seems to have suffered a deterioration. The smattering of psychiatry we have picked up has convinced us that a sense of guilt is weakening. Uncovering causes and frankly stating them seems to eliminate the necessity of either feeling guilty, or facing the moral imperative of repentance and rededication.

This is our world, a world of insecurity and of anxiety, of fear and distrust; a world where many find their response in some form of escape; escape from the necessity of sharing responsibility, escape into a feverish pursuit of so-called pleasure—the theatre and the motion picture with its delineation of a decline of moral standards of integrity and decency where topics are discussed that are destructive to our fundamental values, or into the oblivion secured by barbituates and sedatives: sleeping pills and apathy!

Nicholas Murray Butler, the noted leader of Columbia University at the turn of the century, once said something like this: The world can be divided into three groups; a small one that gets things done; a larger one that observes things that are being done; and the larger one that doesn't even know that anything is being done and probably cares less.

The question that we must ask ourselves is to which class shall we belong? Can we stretch our humanity to become eligible to that first class, or the second?

How wide is our imagination? How great is our understanding? Are we limited to live at ease only in the land we used to know? Can we in our thinking, in our sympathy, really be concerned with the welfare of all mankind? Can we feel kinship with those of a different color, of a different race, those who embrace a different faith, whose standards vary from those we know, whose values are strange to us?

How deep is our faith and how high are our aspirations? How wide is our willingness to understand, how broad is our vision? How vast is our compassion?

This is a world with which we must move, in which we must proportionately grow big, in which we are becoming increasingly near

111

neighbors, to those of whom we knew nothing—neither their names, their place of habitation, their hopes and fears nor their sense of insecurity. And still placing even greater demands upon us—they have learned often to fear and to hate us, to doubt the sincerity of our purpose and the reason for our offer of helpful service.

Truly whether we like it or not, we have no choice, except as to our attitude to this world of incessant change and complexity. We can ostrich-like bury our heads in the sand—to be part of the great unthinking mass, or we can stretch our faith, our hope, and our love to try as onlookers to understand and marvel at the new world emerging—or we can escape, if we will, and be fearful, suspicious, and insecure. Can we try to grow in conformity with its new dimensions? The decision is ours.

"If there is one important resolve that is both urgent and self-protective for us it is to break with the past—for the past cannot be changed or cured. A man cannot go forward and stand still looking backward at the same time."

Life just gives us time and space— it's up to us to fill it

n Grecian mythology, Uranus, the personification of Heaven, is wedded to Gaea, the Earth. Their son is Cronus, Time, and he in turn fathered Zeus, the god of the thunderbolt and the rainbow.

Such is the story of Time, Time born of Heaven and Earth, and antedating the gods themselves. Always has it intrigued mankind and later philosophers, and scientists have discussed it today—still to us a mystery.

Not only is Time intangible, seemingly unreal; it holds for many a fear and for more a comfort. To the young it is a laggard that moves tardily and should accelerate its pace; to the middle-aged it is at times insufficient, at times nonregarded, but always demanding. To the aged it seems for some the archenemy, offering only an empty void of boredom; it engenders a sense of guilt to others of this time of life, but for still others it opens endless opportunities for a rewarding fulfillment.

It is the only aspect of existence over which man has no control. We have learned to conquer space; we are enthralled with its immensity for us to explore, its potentialities for our use. But Time—

LIFE JUST GIVES US TIME AND SPACE

Time is always so elusive; ethereal, tenuous and spiritlike that we feel baffled and inept in facing it. In relief we turn to things of space finding comfort in things that we can hold and touch and count and secrete. All we often find to do with Time is either to fill it with things, or kill it, or while it away.

In imagery Time seems an endlessly moving belt upon which at birth we step and hold our place, at first unaware of its movement but, as we age, sometimes we grow apprehensive and fearful at its speed and the uncertain shortness of our stay, that we waste it, trading existence for living. Yet for the first instance in our crowded lives we have the full twenty-four hours of each day to do with as we will. While we know that the things of space may divide us, we know too that Time should unite us in its universal identical gift to all with, it would seem, a certain bonus to the aged. However, of only one thing are we certain; living imaginatively in both the past and the future, we know that we live significantly only when we live intensely.

Recently a member sent me this quatrain. It teaches a truism, very obvious but nevertheless it is good medicine:

> *"Life itself can't give us joy*
> *Unless we really will it.*
> *Life just gives us time and space—*
> *It's up to us to fill it."*

It is a good recipe for the performance of any heroic enterprise, ambition, or martyrdom. It holds just as true for the business of daily living by just you and me.

In filling life with both time and space, our existence, we all realize, is a compromise—three instincts pull us three diverse ways: the instinct to relive the past, to hope really to live one day at some future time, and the instinct to live here and now—and we meet all three instincts every day, and we must make a choice among them.

Naturally we deplore the tendency of many of us as we grow older to live in the past, carefully chaining ourselves to some immovable rock at the bottom of a steep cliff and at the same time hopelessly striving to climb the heights.

If there is one important resolve that is both urgent and self-protec-

114

tive for us it is to break with the past—for the past cannot be changed or cured; to dedicate our existence to its reliving, for us, is a sad waste of life, marring the present, and achieves no earthly or heavenly good. Grief and remorse are for the past; and should be of the past. They with self-pity are indulgences we must quickly and definitely eschew; a man cannot go forward and stand still looking backward at the same time.

Then too there is the drive to defer life to tomorrow. "Tomorrow I will live; today's too late."

We deplore the tendency we see about us—you see we ignore ourselves in these comments—the tendency to put off living a full life to some future day. Sometimes the reason is the denying of a treat from a Puritanical sense of guilt. Also we see our neighbors denying themselves some small luxury that they would enjoy, so that some day the money that it would require might be left to someone—a young relative perchance—about whose very existence there is no certainty.

Our "active" years were absorbed in the preliminaries of the business of living. Now, freed at last, we face the challenge of making a life rich in expression without friction and without futile desires. This existence today is life itself. It is much more life than we will be living a score of years from now. Consider that. This is our day, the only time of which we are certain. This is our good hour, *bonheur,* the French word for happiness.

Tranquility and serenity—and happiness too—we know are chiefly matters of temperament. We know, too, that it is highly improbable that we will develop them in the future if we have not even glimpsed them in the past. To savor the present, to squeeze out every bit of its flavor, its scent, its quality, to enjoy it is to live it to the full. It's folly to believe that tomorrow will be uniquely different from today. Today is ours! It will be significant as it is purposeful.

I read somewhere this challenge: if we were today to come into the world about us for the first time and knew that there would be only one similar tomorrow, think of what an experiment, a novelty, an adventure each thing, each person would be to us, and imagine the glorious excitement at the things we now take for granted and the ecstatic thrill of how differently we would face tomorrow. Today is ours; let's live it to the full. It's the only time we have, for tomorrow, when it comes, will be today.

With Time, if we wish, we can discover beauty in the intimate and the immediate, and the usually-not-observed. It makes possible to us to think out the meaning of things; it shows us the unity of all beings; it develops in us compassion and purpose; it helps age become completion.

The Indian proverb says: "I met a hundred men on the road to Benares, and they were all my brothers," all on the way to bathe in the Ganges and so to be sanctified.

A British soldier at Dunkirk answered to the query, "What were you thinking of as you waited there on the beach, with the sea in front of you, the German army at your back and the German bombers over your head?" "I was thinking," he answered, "every man here is my brother."

Satisfying stories, for both men were surcharged with a sense of the unity of life, both were experiencing the breath-taking concept of consecration and deliverance.

Wouldn't it be fine if it were possible for us to feel that same sense of brotherhood without the need of any impelling circumstance other than that of our own sense of commitment?

Such it seems to me is the opportunity we face as we grow older. Age can become life's Sabbath, the day of tranquility and peace, of serenity and repose, when freed from the tyranny of things of space we seek to become attuned to the holiness of Time. Then in our thoughts we turn from the marvel of created things to the mystery of creation, from the world of creation to the creation of the world.

Age needs time:

> *"Time for vision*
> *Time to dream*
> *Time to be kind*
> *Time to be useful and purposeful*
> *Time to be at home in God's universe."*

116

"The human contribution is the essential ingredient. It is only in the giving of oneself to others that we truly live."

According to one's power

e stand, in awe at the disclosures and the conquests of today's research—the victories won in nature and the visible world. The gigantic discoveries and achievements of technology, science and the arts move us to marvel at the power of man, and we realize that the end is not yet. The year 2000 will offer homes run by finger-touch, planes winging 5,000 miles an hour overhead, food enough for all harvested from sea and interspace; the weather under control, and the great deserts in full bloom; hurricanes turned around and headed back to sea. Such is the prophecy of General David Sarnoff:

"Every discovery reveals more clearly the divine design in nature, remarkable harmony in all things, from the infinitesimal to the infinite. Physical processes and laws are logical, all-embracing, wholly dependable. They imply a supreme architect."

And they all are in accordance with Natural Laws which man can neither veto or alter. Cause and consequence is a concept that is basic to all relationships.

Just as significant—so it seems to me—as even the genius and the achievements of these great ones, past and future—is the patent of nobility each one of us holds—the right of choice—the capacity to decide for one's self, again limited only by the moral natural law which is a force in the universe, moral as well as physical. No man can alter, can, of course, ignore, can also disobey, but he cannot

117

change. Some call it God; some, the supernatural. We see it manifest in the ethical precepts found in every religious faith, under whatever names, these concepts help people to realize and practice the moral truths of human contact. We call them in our tongue and faith the Golden Rule and the Decalogue. Other faiths have their near equivalents. Conscience, we hold, is our greatest prize and treasure. And so again we marvel at the potential power of man, at the fact that the seeds of moral advancement are planted in the heart of man, but they have not flourished as dramatically in the social or the spiritual world, either with self or with others, as have the seeds of the intellect in the areas of science and technology. The future holds great possibilities!

We, as older folk, do not want to be thought of only as critics of the order of today. We want to see our America without prejudice, without bewailing the passing of the old days gone forever. We realize her many culture traits, her love of physical comfort, her cult of bodily cleanliness, her finance capitalism, her holding certain values from our British heritage—fair play and tolerance—her material generosity, her outgoing, genuine benevolence, her missionary spirit, her love of laughter, her high regard for women, her belief that "work counts."

Yet we note, at times, in America a growing placidity, an apathy, an indifference; this is a reaction and an emphasis new to America, a seeking for security rather than adventure, a disposition to delegate authority rather than the old individualism which insisted on drawing the designs for this nation's political and economic life.

President Eisenhower in one of his messages to the American people, reminded us that, "It is a good thing for us all to talk about America, about the great heritage of the past that must be preserved, of the great enterprise of the present that must be advanced, about the great vision of the future that must be nourished. We must realize that the mission of America has been—and is—the expansion of individual liberty, self-reliance and personal responsibility, within a system where a Government—of conscience and heart—is the servant of every individual, doing for him what he cannot do for himself. Rather, we are a Republic of free individuals, each working out his

118

own destiny, each making his own contribution in his own way to the common good. At the same time, in the deepest sense, we are a united people, spiritually joined in a tight loyalty to great ideals."

Today we find in the world about us great issues at stake. The problems are so vast and intense that we stop to wonder: Are we nearing the close of an era or hearing the prologue of another. Civilizations that have developed different traditions and different viewpoints and standards are suddenly brought close to one another, with their atomic weapons near at hand while their minds are still a world apart. We are all aware how dangerous the situation is for all mankind; we, as older folk, should want to do anything we can to relieve the tension. For any age, never has there been a greater opportunity, a greater responsibility—a more awesome obligation.

Each of us is involved, whether or not we choose so to be. We must study the issues involved—if local and national—with the goal that we have a fair, just and ethical government and a growing realization of the democratic objectives; if national and international that we recognize the value of differences among people, their customs, their religion, their traditions, the things they treasure—this calls for imagination in recognizing just interests of all nations and in watching the patient and wise negotiation that must ensue in the support of the rights of others without sacrificing those essential ones of our own. The method is not easy and the solution is not imminent.

Let us not forget that many people in many lands perhaps will have in their hands the very existence of the world as we know it. We have developed great power with terrifying potentials—weapons with no soul—no wisdom—no conscience, but equipped with the power of destruction. Can we ignore the great responsibility that is ours? To make such a vision of peace real calls for the vitalizing energy of all of us. The venture demands a course analogous to religious faith —a courage that realizes that it can be made real only if powered by the fervor of passion and faith and zeal.

The University of Chicago reports the same disturbing story, of man's indifference to the stirring events and dangers that confront the Nation. A survey of adult education reports that of eight courses offered the American citizen—or at least the 25,000,000 of them so enrolled—education for citizenship ranked next to the bottom. More adults were enrolled in dancing lessons than in the combined fields of public affairs and general political education combined. The Gallup poll also revealed that 20% of those interviewed could not identify the Bill of Rights, that part of our Constitution that houses our basic freedoms, and that only 60% exercise their franchise on election day.

And yet before we—you and I—are anything else—workers or idlers, retired or active, homemakers or industrialists, parents or single folk, we are citizens—and we should be citizens who understand and uphold the nature of this, our American way of life which we call democracy, not through the fear of communism, but for the far greater purpose of being worthy of the awesome responsibility of this precious stewardship which we all of us share alike.

Do you not realize that the measure of a man is told by the type of topic—cause, injustice, weakness or strength—that calls forth his energy and his enthusiasm?

But often we ignore these great issues. We see only the immediate as pressing; often question the value of any other kind of effort. I am reminded of the story that when Farraday was explaining to Parliament the great mystery of electricity, Gladstone, the statesman, critical and unconvinced, asked, "But what is it good for?" and Farraday, inwardly amused, answered, "Sir, so that some day you may be able to put a tax on it."

The American gift of oneself in service for the good of all is not new; it is older than this nation. The 41 settlers of Plymouth, while still aboard the Mayflower, signed a pact, each to work for a "just and equal way of life." Today 50 million Americans are giving of their time and their talents and their energy to further that "just and equal way of life."

Down through the years of our country's life, the volunteer has been one of America's vital strengths. In early days volunteer fire departments sprang up. "Barn raisings" recall the neighborly help that was always ready for a call. "Good works" became even a status symbol of social standing. The "Lady Bountiful" was to be depended

120

upon for comfort in the aid of the sick and the distressed.

We are told that such volunteering service is a good barometer—not only of free enterprise but of our American way of life; it certainly is prime evidence in our associations that the member is alert to the duty that is his—the rendering of service.

Will Rogers is reported to have found that the only way to true happiness and contentment was to take up each day's tasks with confidence and cheerfulness and lay them down at night with no lingering worry. One day, a friend asked Will Rogers if he only had 48 hours to live, how he would spend them. The cowboy philosopher laughed and replied; "One at a time."

The "why" of working as a volunteer is not important. It may be a recognition on the part of individuals of the need of united action to meet an emergency; it may be in the cause of self-interest to help improve his own welfare in some fashion; it may be the memory that he too had had such a problem; it may be the possession of a talent, the expression of which is also a satisfaction; it may be his desire to be associated with others of like background in a communal exercise; it really doesn't matter *why*. Indeed, the Talmud tells us that it is a wise thing to do, even with an ulterior motive, for the doing of it will teach the doer the joy of doing the right thing simply because it is right; it will give him a glow of satisfaction and an impulse to continue.

With dismay we often hear of refusals of our members to assume great responsibilities other than that of paying dues and attending meetings. When I hear such comments from our volunteer leaders, I often wonder what it is, in refusing, that the reluctant members are defending—time for trivial things—perhaps essential things. But do they ever realize what it is that they are denying themselves? Do they not realize that all movements, like our association's—and any other project of like kind must begin under mechanical and material laws and then at a certain point they become personal, human and spiritual? Then every moment needs for the next step the help of man. Do they not realize that not even God himself can develop the possibilities of any plan of His without the help of human beings. Do you not see

121

that His ends are met not by laws but by the sons and daughters of men. It is only in the giving of ourselves to others that we truly live—only with the meeting of our minds—thine and mine—do we become conscious of the divine spark each of us shares—only in sharing in our daily contacts, one with another, in our mutual hopes and fears do we find real peace. The human contribution is the essential ingredient. Without it all is sterile, an unrealized dream.

Here, for instance, is a vessel at the port, eager to be on her way, the wind fresh and fair, the tide favorable. Yet the vessel does not move until man contributes his part. The captain spreads her sails, and the craft, lifeless and useless, becomes a thing of life and motion. So it is with the help of these officers of whom I spoke. They may create the best of circumstances, yet until man helps, all the work of dedicated and patient expectation waits its realization and may never be realized.

This is to me the answer to life's problem—until we grasp the truth that God's purpose must always wait on man, we really do not interpret the significance of man's life here on earth. When we look at our lives and see how infinitely unimportant they are, how aimless and ineffective is our striving, we wonder at times why should we struggle as we do against the temptation to attend only the trivia of life? That is the defense of many in explaining a wasted idle life. For one person who foolishly thinks too highly of himself—there are nine who fail in their thinking well enough of themselves. They have lost the self-respect of knowing their place in the purposes of God. How does anyone of us know whether our insignificant life may not become one of infinite importance to someone. May not be the bit of the jigsaw puzzle that is needed to complete the whole? Where men fail, God fails—how dare we refuse to do a worthy thing proferred us that is within our power, if we really realize that we may be hindering a purpose of infinite good?

Dag Hammarskjold in his autobiography, *Markings,* gives us this legacy—when we fail to do the thing we ought, we fail God. His exact words are: "If you fail it is God, thanks to having betrayed Him, who will fail mankind." That is a thought of indescribable solemnity. It is as if a great factory with its leaping millions of shuttles weaving yards of clothing might stop because one little thread had snapped that might mar the whole fabric.

It is not that we are great or notable in ourselves or for ourselves, but that each of us completes his insignificant and slight, yet essential share, in the big plan underway.

You may some day have seen a lighthouse on the bay and have been greeted by its rugged old caretaker on his rocky wave-tossed coast. What life could be more desolate or more lonely? But he spends his weary nights tending the light. It is not his light. Inconspicuous, solitary and unobserved, he keeps guard. He is not its owner, only its keeper. Why does he stay there through the weary night, tending its flame? Why does he not sleep—unobserved and let his light go out? That is what gives him significance. He is not the owner, he is the keeper. That is his name. He is a lightkeeper. The government has given him a sacred trust and night after night, year after year the lights burn brightly and ships are guided to safety by that unknown lightkeeper whom the nation and every sailor trusts and man rarely sees.

That is the story of many of our lives. Alone, inconspicuous, unobserved, unpraised, you live. But you do not let your light go out and sit in the dark. Unconscious of your vision and your service you are each a lightkeeper to help make the world safe. Many a life, that passes by, all unseen in the dark, may be looking from night to night for that beacon light of safety and go on its way, trusting and hopeful. Who knows where your influence is being felt. How far and how bright your little candle may shed its beam.

"For what shall we strive?" My answer is that we give of ourselves to others, each one, as Socrates has bid us "according to his powers." In the world about us we find a world crisis of conflicting ideologies and interests. Concerning them we dare not be apathetic; we must help in our simple fashion to avert a world catastrophe; we must help advance life plans that will bear fruit in a life more abundant for all.

*"The opportunity is ever ours, beckoning us to share
in generous endeavor; to feel in a finer, truer sensitivity
man's eternal struggle to make life meaningful; to live in
dignity and independence; to make someone happier for
our being here—these are today's heroics."*

Something to grow upon,
Something to grow with,
And something to grow for.

here but in America would a man who was to become the mayor of its greatest city make his entry into that metropolis as the hind leg of an elephant in a traveling show, and in that capacity first pass the city hall of which in a decade or two he would be chief?

It's certainly an unusual albeit an undignified way to glimpse one's future. In doing it, Fernando Wood out-Whittingtonned Whittington; the years, too, are not fictional but in the 1860s and the city is not London but New York.

I imagine many are the tales that each of us might relate of like quaint and whimsical happenings from our own families' lore; legends of our people in their pioneering search for the America of their dreams. Many might be tales of heavy hardship and of harsh cruelty, reports of shrewd and selfish cunning, and galling grind and some, even, laments of apathetic lethargy. But more often they will be the thrilling saga of derring-do, retailing sobering experiences, recalling

124

the threat of implacable challenges overcome, and the sustaining eulogy of faith and hope and communal enterprise and effort.

These are the tales we must share with our young people, for they are the stuff of which history is made, where heroes of our blood are reborn to live again letting us pace with them the intensity and the rate of their absorbing feats, bringing to us, old and young alike, a special sense of expectation, gratitude and pride.

The Spartans extolled the fame of one Tyraeus as one of the most valiant defenders of their country, but Tyraeus was a crippled school teacher who never ventured from his native village; but he was the writer of their songs, and the spirit that they evoked was faith in self, conquest of fear, surety of victory.

We, too, can contend with ideas, inspiration, insights.

This same spirit of adventure we, too, can experience today without stirring from our place in home and community. We, too, can be spacious-minded Americans right at home in the great world; outside we can be and are a part of the vast chain of life.

The opportunity is ever ours, beckoning us to share in generous endeavor; to feel in a finer, truer sensitivity man's eternal struggle to make life meaningful; to live in dignity and independence, yet with one another; to kindle our enthusiasms to appeal to the act of making someone happier because of our being here and now, and being capable.

These are today's heroics for us; these are the ways we can seek in helping build a greater America, the America of our dreams; for it is the quality of our seeking that shall determine the nature of the America in which we are to dwell. This is the America *we* can build, not an America for which *they* must be held responsible. This is our job —the job of us older folk.

Booker T. Washington in his legacy of wisdom left a message that a minority has the opportunity to generate respect for its worth by its activity motivated by faith in itself, by facing forthrightly the task at hand, however simple and humble it might be, and doing that task to the best of one's ability, ennobling the task by the manner of its performance.

Charles Ferguson tells us—"This is eternity now; you are sunk as deep in it, wrapped as close in it, as you ever will be. The future is an illusion; it never arrives; it flies before you as you advance. Always it is today—and after death and a thousand years it is today. You have great deeds to perform and you must do them now."

We who are the older ones in America have been segregated in the thinking of some as a minority group, chronologically determined. About the term "senior citizen," which they have adopted, fencing us apart, they have made a stereotype that is both regrettable and misleading and cruel, a pitiful image and caricature which can become in time a boomerang to its makers, who some day too will be old. We who have been so pictured and maligned think it highly important that we meet this challenge. Whatever our individual roles may be, as a group we need to have our communities know us older folks as we really are. We realize that as individuals we shall often fall short of the projected ideals we would like to have people hold of us; but we need at least to build an image that is fairly recognizable as that of a segment of our country that is both self-respecting, individualistic and positive. We need to be recognized as constructive citizens in community life; honorable and dependable members in family relationships; stable and cooperating volunteers in matter of religion, welfare and service; and substantial folk of dependability and integrity in business life, loyal to all those virtues and values that America holds dear. We are people of pride with heads high and a forward look—not suppliants for pity and palliatives.

This image of stable and responsible persons cannot be effective unless we ourselves think that it is true. It cannot be effective if it ends with only one group's accepting it. We must watch lest there be a critical gap between this image we hold of ourselves and what others think of us. They will judge us rightly by our observed purposes, our actions, and our sincerity. This image of the aging is something that will be tested every day by everyone we meet on the merits of its believability as we, each one of us, furnish the tested proof.

Little things, we are told, count; we will be judged not only by little things but also judged in times of strain and tension. We will be assessed every day for what we are, by what we do, anywhere, everywhere—in our homes, on the street, in the office, the elevator, the store, the theater, the church, the concert hall, the parlor and the kitchen—because there, our actions speak louder than our words; they unguardedly come from our heart and are revealing. It is what we are and do with vigor, imagination and enthusiasm that will shape for aging the image of older age. This is the great contribution our membership can make for their fellows in this period of life.

Each day come many letters from our members. I wish I might share with you the delight they give me, the challenge they offer, the tragedies they often tell. Often there are stories that pulsate with the vigor of achievement, are dynamic with growth; sometimes they tell of happy incidents, of having something to do, something to love and something to hope for, proving the truth that happiness is largely the outcome of what one does and, best of all, what one does for others.

Some recount community ventures and the spirit of the people, of being dissatisfied with anything but the best. They relate, too, the stories of gratifying work; they stress the basic values and virtues, emphasizing the need to answer time and time again the three questions of life: is it right or wrong? is it true or false? it it beautiful or ugly?

These letters make us proud to know them, these persons of maturing wisdom and unselfish service, with something to grow upon, something to grow with and something to grow for. They paint the picture of doing more than they had dreamed possible.

Another pleasure I wish I might share is visiting with just such folk. Often they drop in at the office just to say "Howdy!" They attend the Congressional hearings when they know we will be represented. They invite us to their gatherings, and we love meeting and knowing them personally. In turn we are saying to you that sometime this year for a couple of days we shall be somewhere near to where you live. We of the staff are planning to attend each one of our Area Conferences and we wish, with all our hearts, that you would plan to come at least to one of them and that then we could meet personally and together could exchange ideas and study solutions. We need your help. We are looking forward to tapping the creative resources of all our members realizing that their advice is a bonus value that we shall treasure and can be, in the words engraved upon the building of the Detroit News:

> *"Reflector of every human interest.*
> *Friend of every righteous cause.*
> *Encourager of every generous act.*
> *Mirror of the public mind.*
> *Troubler of the public conscience.*
> *Interpreter of the public intent.*
> *Nourisher of the community spirit."*

DYNAMIC
MATURITY

Staying Young

To be young, is not a matter of years. Youth lives forever in a love for the beauty that is in the world, in the mountains, the sea, and sky, and in lovely faces through which shines the kindliness of the inner mind.

It is the tuning into the orchestra of living sound, the soughing of the wind in the trees, the whisper and flow of the tide on wide beaches, the pounding of surf on the rocks, the chattering of brooks over the stones, the pattering of rain on leaves, the song of birds, and of peepers in the spring marshes, and the joyous lilt of sweet laughter.

Youth lives without counting the years in a fluid mind which is open to new theories, Fresh opinions, changing impressions, and in the willingness to make new beginnings.

What is it to stay young? It is the ability to hold fast to old friends, and to make new ones, to keep forever our beloved in dear remembrance, and to open our hearts quickly to a light knock on the door,

Youth is to remain faithful to our beliefs, to preserve our enthusiams, to trust in ourselves, to believe in our own courage, and to follow where courage bids us go.

And, at the last, youth means that, like an unquestioning child, we place our hand without fear in the hand of the Gentle Guide, who will lead us through the little gate at the end of the Winding Road.

Cornelia Rogers

"It has been wisely said that whatever many may say about the future, it is ours, not only that it may happen to us, but it is in part made by us."

The past is prologue; what's to come is your and my discharge

ging, we all grant, is universal. There is about it, in the minds of the young and middle aged, a fear of dependence and decay. The challenge that we elderly folk must accept, if we will, is to destroy that myth—this fear of dependence and decay. We must present the truth by the testifying assurance that growing old has many facets—many benefits and many delights.

We know of course that we can find in all its range of aging in old folk as well as in youth, smugness, lethargy, inequality, discrimination and even violence, and of course conformity, but we know, too, that there is a world also of truth, tolerance, generosity that makes possible, for all, access to opportunity.

To take from their younger folk fear and the distrust of aging, the foremost challenge is to have them see that, in us older ones, there are still active virtues. That is the challenge, to live up to our better selves, to believe well of our fellow men, and perhaps by so doing, to help create the good we believe in, to experiment, to explore, to change and to grow. With self-reliance, we older folk do build foundations for living our lives better, using our energies constructively and making our work productive and creative.

131

The retirement situation

Just as in the days of our active work, we studied the situation and the people round about us, identifying the life-shortages we could perhaps do something about it.

We knew from life itself that the tragedy of *loneliness* is one of those shortages—that we could help dispel by being cheerful in greeting, warm and gracious in our manner, in our interest and our solicitude. We knew that we could smile—that it takes 72 muscles to frown and only 14 to smile. We could be alert to help, help "save face" and be ready and willing to do for others things they *couldn't do for themselves.*

We saw apathy: we learned, to our dismay, how quiescent and receptive—rather than outgoing and constructive—many people were —passively accepting the boredom of life, engaging only in that *busyness* that would kill time but still not fill the aching inner void of lack of purpose or of interest. These people are not living life—tasting it only on the surface, getting life to pass in trivial and uncreative ways, as onlookers. They give nothing of themselves, but instead they waste the greatest and most precious thing they have—time—for that is the stuff life is made of.

Dr. Eric Fromm, in discussing this supreme consumer-danger, facing older people, of passively squandering time, believes that the desirable opposite is to be interested—to be so submerged into something that is not *mine,* as to forget all personal and possessive things; instead to reach out and *be in,* heart and soul—*in something*—maybe a plant, a book, a person, a cause, an ideal, an association. "Interest," he says, "is to be active, not in the sense of modern busy-*ness* where one must be doing something all the time, but active in the inner rather than in the outer sense." He reminds us of the derivation of the word, "inter - est"—to *be in.*

How can we help these free-loaders at life's feast? How can we arouse them to a feeling of self assurance and so avoid being just a consuming parasite, "passing the time decently while they wait for death?"

132

Think of what we, as AARP and NRTA members, can do to help those who have no program—who in retirement have lost their road map—how they keep developing new vistas along the highway of living. Severed from their sustaining life force—their work, can we not pledge ourselves to give them an hour or so a week—perhaps a listening ear? For we can be a confessional for their shedding a sense of failure or of guilt. We first can become a comforting friend—then at last a challenger to action. We, who are living life to the hilt, can perform a miracle through our investment of self—perhaps bringing back to these forlorn souls the releasing comfort of something beyond their mirrored walls in which they can lose and find themselves. We know from experience that these mental changes are responsive to treatment. We can hopefully stay their drift into day dreaming and decay. Let's help them keep alive their sense of timing and coordination. For instance get them interested in even the simple games of skill and accuracy as a start. A dollar's investment of a bowl and gold fish, an African violet plant—have often done wonders.

The future is ours

It has been wisely said that whatever many may say about the future, it is ours, not only that it may happen to us, but it is in part made by us. To enjoy the present, to extract from it every jot of its flavor, its scent and its quality, to have faith in man and in country, that's the way to build the future. It's folly to think tomorrow will be uniquely different; even though we know it's bringing changes to us with the speed of light. Today is ours—it will be significant to us as we make it purposeful. The essential values will never change, only our adaptation of them and to them. Each generation either brings new values by bringing vitality to our ideals or allows them, through indifferences, to decay. "The nurturing of values maintains society's moral tone."

These values of ours are intangible. Granted that we may not always live up to them, still do we not at heart hold them dear? Do we not really believe that America is a land of ideals, not a materialistic country only, as is charged? True, we like comforts and even luxuries and gadgets, of course, that save toil and routine; granted, too, that we have the techniques and skills to obtain them. Still we know in our heart of hearts, there is in us a groping desire to do something fine and serviceable for our country, and that, called upon in an emergency, we will not be found wanting. Granted, too, that while we do not always work toward our goals, still do we not believe in those things, at present unattainable, with time Americans will achieve? We can no longer condone the hypocrisy of talking about human equality and then denying it.

We live in a new world

Too, we are often conscious of our leaders saying that we live in a new world—nothing can be truer. America, from the day of its discovery, presented to the old world, a wonder, a new promise and an opportunity for generating new ideas, more magnificent, wondrous, fantastic and unique.

Cortez, when he led his 400 men to the heights overlooking the city of Mexico, voiced his wonder. Could this golden glow be real? One of his soldiers, Bernal Diaz, tells the story of their awe and incredulous amazement. Looking to find a City of Gold—was their goal—it led them ever on—Cortez to the plains of Kansas—Raleigh to the Court of Elizabeth and finally to the Tower of London and the executioner's block.

Always, in this new America there has been a wonder and the pursuit of a dynamic goal—a conviction that America was different and that here miracles could happen. And America has not failed to realize these dreams.

In New England, the dream was to form a state with religious rigidity and intolerance. John Calvin's preachment was the determiner, but, thank God, there was also a Roger Williams there too, the dissenter, who believed and put that belief in practice and welcomed others to his exile and free brotherhood. And Virginia, although its founders in their beginnings were disappointed, for they dreamed of a land of gold and princely leisure, produced a Jefferson, who in defiance to a king seeking to impose the restrictions of the old world with its fantasy of the divine right of Kings, proudly proclaimed a new doctrine, "We hold these truths to be self-evident."

Throughout the world—and often in the colonies themselves, the question was—what truths? This idea of rights not emanating from an overlord but from God was a novel one—would it hold? Did all men really have equal rights to the good things on earth? A revolutionary idea indeed And "self-evident?" Yes, to the man thinking, to the man feeling, but how about the masters of men? "Self-evident" was a radical and subversive statement! Yet those words and the concepts they embody are the greatest of our treasured American heritage. They are the keystone of our democracy. And yet so few realize either their novelty, their startling significance or their as yet unfulfilled promise. They are however America's basic creed. It is faith in those words that makes the American unique; it is a faith that is deeply religious, yet often accepted as so natural and right that the wonder of it we often miss. For there is wonder in such a theory— a theory that waited 1776 years for its utterance.

Where do we go from here?

Knowing these commitments, where do we go from here? The answer is, we start here and now, we, every one of us. There is no time for breezy optimism—nationally we are on the brink of a precipice. Folly of hatred or power-pride may plunge us in the abyss of nothingness. The defense to this threat of our possible annihilation that our Nation offers, is massive retaliation. Every day we hear of inventions of still more awesome engines of destruction; and yet, we know that the finest, most dependable reliance for our country's life is the faith of the people themselves in her and her ideals; our greatest weapons are the people's courage to believe and intelligence to understand. We are the prime and the ultimate weapon of America's defense. We are potentially stronger than anything which the Pentagon can contrive or any drawing board design.

In the fourth century the ruler of Greece was approached by a visitor and asked why of all the cities and states of Greece, only Sparta lacked walls. He turned to a group of young men nearby and said

"Sir, there are the walls of Sparta—and every man a brick."

Every man of us—and every woman too, is a potential atomic bomb of faith and trust. Every one of us born in America, or accepted into our citizenship on their plea; should realize the trust that is ours and theirs—the inner obligation we and they owe for the rights enjoyed —and that that inner obligation demands the conscious recognition of these privileges, of our citizen's commitment to the doctrines of opportunity, of access, of respect for the individual and the God-given rights he should be permitted to enjoy in peace and dignity.

We need to contact youth

The need, too, to help the youth with whom we are in contact, realize that life, liberty and the pursuit of happiness demand discipline and effort and perseverance; and discipline and the others mean self-knowledge, self-dedication and self-control, not force from without or power they might resent and ignore. We need to help our youth respect the universal laws that control the universe and are basic to all the epoch-making achievements of today. Theirs is the task to build, upon these verities, their new world, a world we may never know, on their adaptations and expansions of the values that we know today—and we marvel at the essential intelligence, the precision, the accuracy, the cooperativeness that this work will need for the future, and we stand humbly at salute.

The mission of the retired

But, while we are still able to function, let us not forget our own mission, as divinely entrusted to us as that of any desert-traveling son of Israel believing in his faith, that we owe our country the best we can give her, that we owe God to whom we make our supplications the realization that we are His instrument on earth, and, as Dag Hammarskjold has told us, we must not betray our fellows by failing them, and by failing them, fail God Himself.

Faith is inherent in all living beings

Albert Schweitzer tells us that faith is not a product of religion, but

136

is inherent in all that lives:

"Imaginative power, determined by ideals, is at work in all that is. The impulse toward perfection is innate in us—beings, as we are, endowed with freedom and capable of reflective, purposeful action —in such a way that we naturally aspire to raise ourselves and every portion of existence affected by our influence to the highest material and spiritual degree of value.

"We do not know how this aspiration came to be in us and how it has developed itself in us. It is an intrinsic part of our being. We must follow it if we will not be untrue to the secret will-to-live which is rooted in us."

Our life assignment

An old legend tells us there was an old man up in the mountain who had a reputation for being very wise. And there were two young doubters in the village who said, "Let's make a fool of that old man." One boy asked how. The other said, "I'll tell you how. We'll catch a small bird, and I'll hold it in my hand, and we'll go up to the old man, and say, 'What have I in my hand?' Being a wise man, he'll say, 'You have a bird.' Then I'll say, 'Is it alive or is it dead?' And if he says 'It is alive,' then I'll crush it and show him a dead bird. But if he says that it is dead, I will open my hand and let it fly."

And so they went up to the mountain to the old man, and sure enough, when the boys asked the question, the man replied, "You have a bird." And then one said, "Old man, is the bird *alive* or is it *dead?*" He replied, looking the lad sternly in the eye, "Young man, it is *as you will it.*"

Life is as we will it

That is life, after all, isn't it—"as we *will* it?" Let us keep our zest for living, for the joy we can find, and the warm human friendships we can make, and, mindful of our life as a trust, do what we can to make it useful.

"The past", Shakespeare tells us in *The Tempest,* "is prologue. What's to come is your and my discharge."

*"We are in great measure the architects of our added
years. It may not be in our power to arrange for ourselves
good living quarters, a decent wage; but it is within
our power to enrich our later years by maintaining
wholesome personal contacts with our fellows and by using
our leisure time in some useful activity."*

The aged and the retired

ld Age, like every other ordinance of nature, ought not to be
looked upon as evil. If people fancy that it will never come
upon them and consequently complain of being taken by
surprise, they have only themselves to thank for the delu-
sion."—Cicero, De Senectute

"Grow old along with me! . . .
Our times are in His hand
Who saith, 'A whole, I planned.
Youth shows but half; trust God: see all,
nor be afraid!' "—Robert Browning.

When we think about aging, the questions at once arise, "When
is a person aged?" "How old is old?" But individuals, on the evidence
of different cases, give different answers to these questions, so that we
are forced further to ask, "Is aging then?" or should we accept the
arbitrarily fixed age of enforced retirement, 65 years, as the begining
of aging? Then, another question looms, "Is aging desirable?"

Aging has always been with us, but today aging is in the process
of revolution. Science has lengthened our lives but science, through
industry, has taken from us, in part, the means to enjoy that life in
action. The stereotype of old age as a disease, increasingly costly

138

and troublesome, however, is contradicted by the host of happy and productive oldsters participating and serving beyond the call of duty.

While aging is universal, it is really still intensely personal. Although the aged group is interesting statistically—often dramatically—it is not a homogenous entity. In it we find great extremes: economically from vast wealth to utter penury, physically and mentally from the sprightly well adjusted octogenarian to the senile chronic invalid with varying degrees of normalcy. Aged people are more than statistical material.

There are those who even in youth and adulthood have always felt abused and unprized. There are those who are chronically aggressive and pugnacious toward life and living. These, we can predict, will not enjoy a happily adjusted old-age. But to those others—the mature, the naturally passive, and the independent—older life can be pleasant and rewarding. And among them all is the common denominator of mutual needs and positive requirements.

Perhaps the most compelling drive is the wish to live. Progress in medicine has extended the span of man's lifetime by postponing death. And yet there is a hidden danger here. Dr. Davidson of New Jersey tells of a venerable and celebrated physician's saying, upon accepting an accolade from the younger members of his profession, "When one has escaped the lesser hazards of life—which is dying too young— he faces the greater hazard of living too long." A Chinese doctor asked what the speaker meant. How could living too long be a hazard? In his country the old man and the old woman are respected and given an important place in the community. Dr. Davidson did not know the answer, but reported that on the staff of the Essex County Hospital in New Jersey there are doctors from the four corners of the world and they testify that in their respective countries old people represent only 10 to 15 per cent of the mental hospital population and not 55 per cent as in the United States. Yet we comfort ourselves with Browning's plea, "Grow old along with me!"

Second only to the desire to live is the natural yearning to be wanted and needed, to feel that one's contribution to life is essential. But this yearning challenges the oldster and impels him to give generously of himself to circulate among his fellows, to participate actively in the little world about him, and to share whatever he may have of talents, strength, means, wisdom, or skill. This is the basis of his self-respect; in this way he earns his sense of dignity and worth.

Aging need not be synonymous with loneliness. No oldster need be without friends, if he himself seeks to be one; no one will be unsought if he is known to be kindly and ready to serve. There is no exercise better than reaching down and lifting another up, and no surer cure of loneliness.

Wilfred Funk, it is reported, in naming words that are vitally significant, listed these: the most bitter—*alone;* the saddest—*forgotten;* and the most tragic—*forsaken.*

Florence Nightingale at 31 felt that death alone could solve her distress, and Abraham Lincoln we know, was a man of sorrow. But they both found their peace in caring for their fellow men. Only so do the elderly find solace in themselves, feeling grace working, faith replacing doubt, health overcroming sickness, and darkness giving way to light. This pronouncement may sound sentimental but the medical profession assures us that it combines the finest of therapy with the soundness of common sense.

Longevity and health are not inherent rights; these privileges carry an obligation to earn them. The oldster must stop thinking of the treatment of his ills as merely applying a temporary patch to a worn fabric. He must think positively how to keep that fabric in shape for long and comfortable use. He need not put up with handicaps and infirmities that can be corrected. It must be admitted, however, that all of us have two-way feelings. We want to be independent, yet we want to be taken care of. We seek the reassurance of our earlier satisfying experiences when some one did take care of us. So often the aged, seeking affection and the assurance of being cared for and being important to someone, enjoy and prolong their disabilities. But their real need is to accept the disabilities of age and to live with them, adapting themselves to their physical limitations.

The elderly are often worried about money. Economic independence, in part, colors all the rest. The retired person is probably faced

140

with having less income. Does this lesser income necessitate a change of residence? A lower standard of living? Retirement may cause no disturbance in the case of those who can earn a supplemental salary, but to the great majority the problem needs an honest facing. If income is smaller, is need of material things correspondingly less compelling? Smaller quarters and simplified housekeeping are found to be sensible *musts* with many oldsters. Health and accident insurance pay rich dividends in peace of mind. If social role and status are still a matter of pride and one's own personal concept of self remains undisturbed, changes in economic status and mode of living are accepted as matters-of-course by friends for whom, later perhaps, the same fate will be in store. For the truth is that wealth and freedom from financial worry do not of themselves spell peace of mind. And if economies and retrenchment are necessary, let them be taken in good heart. Let one learn courageously to eliminate all but the essential, to remember Thoreau's conviction, that "a man is rich in proportion to the number of things he can afford to leave alone."

It is scientifically as well as imaginatively true, as the Psalmist said: "The heavens declare the glory of God and the firmament showeth his handiwork." And in the wonder and the majesty of the universe the older person finds relief and comfort and faith.

The wonder and the glory of the world create an urgency to know, and that urgency—that output of curiosity—is a craving to know. There is in older folk—as in those who are not older—a wide diversity of curiosity both in kind and in vigor.

It would seem that we are in great measure, after all, the architects of our added years. It may, of course, not be in our power to arrange for ourselves good living quarters, a decent living wage; but according to our vision and our health, it is within our power to enrich our later years by maintaining wholesome personal contacts with our fellows and by using our leisure time in some useful activity, no matter how humble, with meaning to ourselves and to others.

There is one thing no retiree can afford to do without—and that is companionship. For that, man has a craving that is never sated. And here with one's advancing years and loss of friends, and with one's retiring from active work and loss of daily contact with former colleagues, the elderly person is vulnerable. Up to the day of retirement he had enjoyed friendly intercourse with fellow-workers. Now many of these folk whom he still holds dear continue with their absorbing duties. If they come to seek him out, it will be for the reason that the retiree has some powerful attraction—a vital common interest, a merry soul, a congenial master of a mutual hobby, a good host, or a sympathetic friend. If the elderly retiree is not so sought, it behooves him to make himself desirable and interesting to his fellows. Even sheer contentment has the compelling charm of relief. Social concern for the welfare of friends can be a powerful attraction. The oldster must keep alive not only his old friendships, but he must form a circle of new friends with freer hours for intercourse, and consciously he must learn to love and help some younger people so that he can keep in touch with other phases of life's parade than his own. Youth can and should be courted.

The craving for new experience differs with each individual. Some persons tragically cease to be curious at twenty; others regretfully at forty, many—and these are the fortunate ones—never cease to be till death. Yet there are others who cease to look for new experiences. When this happens, senility approaches and the oldster tends to live in his memories to exalt the past. The doctors call it *misoneism,* a dislike of and a distaste for something new. This is the cardinal symptom of senility. After it appears and is recognized, it may be already too late to do anything about it. The Chinese proverb tells us, "Learning is like rowing up stream; not to advance is to drop behind."

Dr. Edward L. Bortz, chief of the Medical Services at Lankenau Hospital and past president of the American Medical Association, emphasizes the importance of the aged utilizing the known facts about nutrition, the importance of their avoiding prolonged fatigue, the importance of recreation and sanitation.

Independence—economic and familial—is greatly to be desired, to be planned for, and hopefully to be realized. The man-made tragedy of compulsory retirement has not only deprived many of their work

142

but also of all of its concomitants—the feeling of contributing to the common wealth, the satisfaction that comes of "pulling one's own weight," the comforting conviction that one's work was better done because he did it, the solace of the companionship of fellow-workers —a boon he perhaps never rightfully valued until he lost it—the routine and responsibility of a duty, the pride of family recognition as its financial support, the awareness of social acceptance as a producer, and last, but far from least, the joy that comes from work well done.

Happy is the man or woman who, on growing old, can quickly adjust to necessary changes and find satisfying substitutes; who looks upon retirement from a job, however devoutly served and treasured, as a challenging opportunity for a second career. Happier still will that fortunate person be if this second career expands his circle of friends, raises his sights to service for his fellows, challenges his powers, absorbs his interest, and makes the activities of each day a necessary part of the future he is helping to build for others as well as himself.

Rare indeed is the job that will satisfy all the oldster's needs. Creative activity, however, can supply this sense of achievement. Developing a hobby will challenge one's spare time, conquer (or can happily promote) frustrations, and certainly destroy all sense of loneliness and boredom.

Special centers and Golden Age Clubs can open doors to warm friendships, avenues of reminiscence and pleasurable activites, summer camping, and excursions by bus. Best of all, the public library and the adult school are spurs to action and the building and enjoyment of ever-widening interests. Play, laugh and relax, and enjoy oneself is good medical advice that pays off when followed. We are told that even exercise is not so essential to a happy life as a merry heart, a laugh shared, and "work to do and no work to be done."

Mens sana in corpore sano: This is our answer to those of our thoughtful members who remind us "of the extraordinary power for good which is inherent in the retired group," and that our program is "wonderfully conceived to carry out the ideals and functions of maturity of thought, maturity of experience and maturity of judgment." We feel humble before the spiritual reserves within the retired group which make for a deep yearning for a betterment in government and world understanding.

We all know that we shall grow old, yet we do not plan for the meaningful continuation of the interests essential to our happiness; we vaguely imagine retirement will offer opportunities for catching up with the unrealized dreams of yesteryear, yet we are likely to fear and postpone building the foundations for their positive realizations.

Surely, in spite of all other conditions and factors, success in retirement is largely what the individual makes it. Negative feelings can be converted into positive experiences for graceful aging, but it largely depends upon how well the oldster can adjust to change and philosophically accept his waning powers. How he will do this depends in turn upon his capacity to see humor and express it, to enjoy a chuckle at his own follies and forgive his own shortcomings and those of his intimates.

Dr. Paul D. Moody is quoted as saying, "The measure of a man is not in the number of his servants but in the number of people he serves." The oldster who loves his family, who shares with his neighbors, of his time and of himself, who helps his community become a happier, healthier place because he is in it, is truly successful. For him, aging ceases to be a problem—he has become the answer to it.

"After all, what can a man give except himself?
And what can a man really give except himself?"

We who are mature
know a nobler way to live

oday we—who are in a certain sense the elder statesmen of our time, who love the old traditions and glory in those days of creative initiative—of pioneer deprivation and sacrificial achievement, need to see that the youth we hold dear knows these stories, balances them with modern standards, and hopefully values them as we do. This we know—that our freedom needs constant replenishing, and we know that we can have a part in keeping alive the dash, the venturesome outlook, the thrill each day of rediscovering America. And we will do this best in giving ourselves—after all what can a man give except himself? And what can a man *really* give except himself?

We do not need to dedicate ourselves from this moment onward to be a Nathan Hale volunteering as a spy and being hanged for our patriotism, without even a trial. We can do it so simply. I don't mean that it can be done easily—just simply—for we must do it from within, joining this assumed duty to our normal living—the kind of normal living you and I want for ourselves—and can have if we want to pay the price.

Robert Louis Stevenson defined for us this same prescription. It is now engraved on his memorial in San Francisco's Portsmouth Square. "To be honest; to be kind; to earn a little; to spend a little less; to make upon the whole a family happier for his presence; to renounce when that shall be necessary and not be embittered; to keep a few friends but these without capitulation; above all on the same grim condition to keep friends with himself—here is a task for all that a man has of fortitude and delicacy."

You see Stevenson's good life begins—as does ours too—at home, with folks we not only love but much more important we like as well. And if we keep before us those "home" values we find all the homely virtues that make life liveable and people lovable—honesty, courage, forbearance and sympathy.

If you and the family are lucky, you and they will enjoy maturation also; for maturity is not easily come by—it is not a gift, neither is it always a concomitant with aging. Maturity is the cultivated, continuous growth of the mind; it is relative, never fully acquired, never symetrically attained. It is that part of our intelligence that is interested in the *why* and the *how* and the *what,* without prejudice, or rancor or pre-judgment.

When we really can feel we have, along with our years, gained maturity, we know that we must have called upon all our resources of honesty, intelligence and courage, to have seen ourselves objectively and comprehended realistically our potentials and our shortages, pleasant or unpleasant, and to have accepted them emotionally with as considerable objectivity and equanimity as we could muster. We must have learned not to expect too much from ourselves or from others, either too much, too soon, or from too little effort.

We must have realized, too, the fine balance that always exists between privileges and responsibilities, and when we are really ma-

146

ture we shall have realized that that balance is ever an inseparable one.

Then, too, we shall perhaps have learned the lesson so hard for youth—the ability to reserve judgment and, when made, to act upon it for long term gain rather than for the satisfaction of immediate desires.

All these—like all the phenomena of life—are not only correlated and integrated but are also variable. This is the picture no matter what is our environment, no matter what is the social, cultural, economic or political frame in which we live.

When our house is thus happily set in order we have found the serenity which sets a man free to enter into the joy of service.

Of folks like these comes the "aristocracy of virtue and talent" that the great democrat, Thomas Jefferson, prophesied as needed for the perpetuation of a democracy. You see them all about you; they cross your path daily. They are creative in their every-day lives; they bring up their children decently; they help their neighbors; they are fond of people. You can trust them; for reliability is not a matter of contract; it is a matter of the heart which signs no formal agreement. They are sensitive, considerate, plucky folk; they are our aristocracy, victors over cruelty and chaos. We see them behaving as if they were immortal and if society were eternal. Both assumptions —we know are false but with them we accept them as true; that is their strength.

Is it not a tragedy that no device has yet been found to transfer such private decencies to public affairs? The newsboy can leave unguarded his pile of papers and know that the appropriate coin will be placed in his money box, but grave public-affairs somehow breed no such honesty or trust. Here in the ascending ranges of power, the higher the public life—the more you find of a spiral of suspicion, falsehood, even treachery and finally armaments, and yet we are confronted with the paradox of a world we are told is pretty generally growing better as to the sentiment of mercy and the sense of justice.

And it is still of *home* of which I speak—my home, your home, our homes; be they permanent or transient, they are the place where the homely virtues we prize have, with our *Lares* and *Penates,* their abode. And wherever they are, geographically speaking, we face two weaknesses that we deplore. We might perhaps give aid in a reorientation or adding a bit of starch, or tested steel or firm backbone—whichever is indicated.

We find sometimes among our youth, a softening of fibre—seemingly they have adopted as wholesome the doctrine of unrestrained self-expression—do what you want to do when you want to do it—inhibitions?—acknowledge none!

And we who are old and were once young know that there is a nobler way to live, that discipline is good and self-discipline is best. We know in such a situation that no counselor—no legislator—no anguished parent can do more than give advice. The youngsters give the conduct, and only they can change—can make of themselves the man, or the woman, they once hoped to be, and only then because they themselves want to. We realize that they will live in a world as different from today's as the one we grew up in, but the eternal verities will be the same. They need a sense of ethics. How to help? It is not easy; it is not simple, but the call is there, right at home.

And also in our own home we find another case of indulged weakness—this time we face the erroneous assumption that aging is all decline—the exaggerated apprehension by social workers of aging folks "insecurity", as if security ever will exist except to give us a hope or a wish. Like the advice to youth of the dangers of inhibiting impulse, these well wishers turn to the aged, with the characteristic idolatry of youth, equating aging with depreciation. The transferring of the Office of Aging by the Department of Health, Education, and Welfare to the supervision of the Commissioner of Welfare clearly indicates this same premise that as age increases, competence declines, so correspondingly the value of the individual decreases.

The false assumption that aging is all decrement, added to the fact of no recognition of the continued maturation and development of skills and understanding, is destructive to the drive of older persons to maintain their usefulness and health.

"This defeatist attitude," I quote Stieglitz, "has led to the generous but stupid philosophy that all relatively handicapped people (whether by age or otherwise) *must* be given assistance. Our present society does much to make disability of any sort profitable, parasitic, and pernicious."

This philosophy—this absurd stereotyped thinking—touches our home—our people—ourselves; we hold it to be a real disservice. We do deplore such erosion of the will—we need the strengthening of the will to battle the concept of discord and waste, of "no mission." We refuse to be displaced persons; we refuse to be forgotten men.

Our home—our homeland—needs us; so, too, do our youth and our aged friends. In the words of Ulysses we say:

> *"I will drink*
> *Life to the Lees. All times I have enjoy'd*
> *Greatly, have suffer'd greatly, both with those*
> *That loved me, and alone . . .*
> *Yet all experience is an arch wherethro'*
> *Gleams that untravell'd world whose margin fades*
> *Forever and forever when I move.*
> *How dull it is to pause, to make an end,*
> *To rest unburnish'd, not to shine in use!*
> *As tho' to breathe were life! Life piled on life*
> *Were all too little, and of one to me*
> *Little remains; but every hour is saved*
> *From that eternal silence, something more . . .*
> *. . . but something ere the end,*
> *Some work of noble note, may yet be done . . .*
> *Tho' much is taken, much abides, and tho'*
> *We are not now that strength which in old days*
> *Moved earth and heaven, that which we, we are,*
> *One equal temper of heroic hearts*
> *Made weak by time and fate, but strong in will*
> *To strive, to seek, to find and not to yield."*

"If," said Abraham Lincoln, "my father's child can get to be president, your father's child can make his heart's desire."

To find again
a role in life

During the 40 years following 1900, technology shortened the working week from 60 hours to 40 hours, at the same time more than tripling the per capita income and raising ever higher the standard of living. The most significant product perhaps that technology has yielded, as it affects a maturing society, is the gift of time—time, oceans of it—free time, idle time—leisure time. Call it as you will, this leisure time upon retirement, once a boon to be shared only by the privileged few, has become to some upon an enforced chronological retirement only an unwelcome and a conditioned joy. Sometimes it has ceased to be an elusive vision, enjoyable and to be enjoyed to one's betterment and fulfillment; it remains instead a drab, omnipresent threat.

Our lives in our prime have been built about a core of work. In it we have found the satisfaction that comes as the end of persistent and earnest effort. The life of man, like that of other animals, is adapted to undergo a certain amount of struggle. Most of us, fortunately, have either not been born so wealthy or been so indulged and weakened that we have been denied that need to struggle, which calls for the zest of effort. Now, shorn of that life-work of ours, we face a life one-third as long as that of all our productive years—15 calendar years at least without the stability of that core about which the satisfaction of our life had been built. We miss much more than the wages we earned before we retired; we have lost the sense of significance in the performance of that job of ours, the comradeship of others likewise engaged, the prestige in the community as a worthy and respected producer, even something of the esteem and appreciation of friends and relatives as the head of a family and its provider. But, the loss is not felt at once.

With retirement there comes a pause, a resting period when the harness we have worn so long is being gladly surrendered; perhaps we even rejoice at being freed from routine and responsibility. After a bit, however, we find that we realize that with that freedom has come another freedom—not only freedom *from* something, but freedom *for* and freedom *to*. *Freedom for what* is the answer we must meet; *freedom to do what* naturally follows.

This is the crux. What do we want of life? What do we want to do in life? What shall we do with our new freedom?

Generally, *the freedom for* is—is it not?—for growth, for further service, for living significantly. Do we not say with Ulysses?

> *"How dull it is to pause, to make an end,*
> *To rest unburnished, not to shine in use!*
> *As tho' to breathe were life! Life piled on life*
> *Were all too little . . .*
> *. . . but something ere the end,*
> *Some work of noble note may yet be done.*
> *Though much is taken, much abides, and tho'*
> *We are not now that strength which in old days*
> *Moved earth and heaven, that which we, we are,*
> *. . . strong in will*
> *To strive, to seek, to find, and not to yield."*

Freedom to live up to one's highest potentials is fine, but actually so to do means that we must be convinced in mind and spirit that, no matter how humbly we appraise our own worth, there is in each of us something of the infinite. We, every one of us, can fit ourselves for great opportunities, if only we realize it—but to do so we must strive, we must study, we must think, we must observe—and then again we must go to work.

151

We are talking about going to work; yet we retired folks are living in a nonwork block of time that enshrouds us. We long to continue "to strive, to seek, to find, and not to yield," and that betokens effort—work as we see it and name it.

But with retirement there comes a shift, both in goals and in purpose. In our so-called productive years, we were concerned largely with things. Production of things yielded us an income, gave us our means of livelihood. Now the great change, as radical as the gift of time, is that we turn away from things to folks—to people, our friends, our neighbors, those we see and know.

And now we have freedom—freedom for that which has always haunted us with a vague, enchanting promise that, were we free to do what we wanted to do, this would be one of the delightful pursuits we would follow, and perhaps find in it rewarding satisfaction. This may be your answer.

Perhaps this allurement has not been yours through the years; yet you still have before you the need to find in those fifteen or more years a purpose in living—a purpose that will make those years amount to something, to make life about you somewhat more worthy because you have lived, and have, with your resources, done the best you knew how with both mind and heart.

That is the great shift in our thinking and in our viewpoint that our leisure and its enforced retirement from production presents to us. People now might well become our goal; it can become our challenge to provide services for them, intangible perhaps, but endless in variety. Of these services there can be no limitations except those of our own making in failing to identify either the need or just how one can go about supplying that need.

The goal today is to help older folk about us find again "a role in life," an active role that will restore those who are tending to withdraw into their memories and a self-enforced solitary retirement. The need is to challenge such people to participate mentally and physically in the mainstream of the life about them.

This new freedom given us demands from us the realization of *how* to proceed without offense or officiousness. That is now our obligation. We must explore within ourselves the means of helping our fellows who find their free time a burden and a threat to discover that the future can still hold for them a promise of fulfillment. The job is to re-establish their faith in themselves, that they are important in the eyes of their fellows, that their help is needed and valued by the community in which they dwell.

In *The Way of All Flesh,* one of the great novels of England, Samuel Butler tells the story of a weak idealist in a household that valued him not at all. While his friend is trying to help him in later years to adjust to the life which he had turned against, he confers with a learned doctor. "Cross him," said the doctor, "at once. Crossing is the great medical discovery of the age. Shake him out of himself by shaking something else into him."

And now in paraphrase: Take him to the zoo, and stay with the larger mammals until they begin to bore him. Then spend a part of the morning at a church service of his childhood faith—then a day of sightseeing. By all means let him go often to the theatre!

"Had the doctor been less eminent in his profession," the friend tells us, "I should have doubted whether he was in earnest," but he knew him to be "a man of business who neither wastes his own time or that of his patient," and added, "I mention this here in the hope that some one or other of my readers may find this hint a useful one; I did in the care of Ernest."

Whether or not that will be your approach, the need is there —to break through the loneliness, the withdrawal, the willingness to remain a discard from society—a nobody. You must keep your withdrawing friend occupied. "Shake something into him" so that he may begin, perhaps unknowingly, to blend into the energetic life about him. Inspire him with the sight of activities of others which he also can duplicate or better. Spark his interest with the interest of others. Soon you will find him joining in the common goals and interacting searchingly and constructively, responsive to the pulsing, eager, changing world about him. And you will have saved a life!

Or perhaps you can reawaken the love of reading—

Robert Louis Stevenson, himself a master of storytelling, says:

"The desire for knowledge, I have almost added the desire for meat, is not more deeply seated than this demand for fit and striking incident . . . A friend of mine, a Welsh blacksmith, was twenty-five years old and could neither read nor write, when he heard a chapter of Robinson Crusoe read aloud in a farm kitchen. Up to that moment he had sat content, huddled in his ignorance, but he left that farm another man. There were day-dreams, it appeared, divine day-dreams, written and printed and bound, and to be bought for money and enjoyed at pleasure. Down he sat that day, painfully learned to read Welsh, and returned to borrow the book. It had been lost, nor could he find another copy but one that was in English. Now he sat once more, learned English, and at length, and with entire delight, read Robinson. It is like the story of a love-chase."

Lincoln is quoted as saying in one of our currently famous novels, "If my father's son can get to be president, your father's son can get his heart's desire." That is the gift of the leisure time which is now ours. So we triumph intellectually and spiritually over the physiological process of aging. So we upgrade the current concepts as to the potential of later maturity. Our attitude toward leisure becomes bright with eagerness; we are not just finding commitments to fill our time; we are earning the deep rewards of being heartily in earnest, in believing in what we are doing. We persevere in spite of discouragements and impossibilities, we keep our minds alert and up-to-date. With humility and friendliness we do our best to leave the world a little better for our stay in it. If you wish, your father's son, too, can have his heart's desire.

*"To make retirement successful you need only to remember
the two precepts of the law and the gospel:
Feel reverence in the glory of the universe and love
thy neighbor as thyself. Retire not from but to service."*

It may be later
than you think

he medical profession tells us that aging begins at birth, or even before; aging is progressive living. Such a concept of a lifelong process indicates inferentially a corresponding life-long growth and development.

We who have been teachers accept the charge, in the service of our pupils, to meet life realistically and to help bravely and persistently to condition it for full wholesome living. The instinct of curiosity we seek to satisfy and to stimulate. We plan to supply the craving for companionship. We provide for joys of shared experiences. We promote conditions that will yield at once gratifying social approval, the joys of purposeful activity, and the self-assurance of individual worth. Security, too, we plan—securities of all sorts and conditions—and prime among them that of economic independence.

Considering aging as a life-long process, we face the corollaries of corresponding growth, development and service. Let us condition ourselves as guides and counselors of ourselves in the later phase of our own living, which we call retirement. Growing old we all agree is normal. It of course comes to all of us; with equanimity we see it in our friends. Yet somehow or other the fact that it can actually happen to us has perhaps never really penetrated into the realization of us as individuals. Yet one day a 65th birthday does happen, and the realization of that age and all its complications perhaps gouges into quivering tissue that never quite recovers its resiliency and health. If you have not seriously faced retirement in your thinking, if you have not realized how it will vitally affect you, then it is later than you think.

How do we feel about growing old?

The prime job for you is at once to face life and age with an individual rejoinder that you, as an individual, will be responsible for as fine an accounting for your age as you have been, for your life work.

Perhaps, to do this job objectively, you should consider yourself as counselor, guide and friend of this other self, a person you know intimately and wish well, an individual with probably 10-20 years of life ahead. You know your own needs. You can estimate your own resources. You can help yourself fairly gauge both, and gear one to the other, so that that later life of yours may run smoothly. Knowing that you are interested and qualified, you first face the problem, "What is retirement to me?"

As a welfare worker, I have heard that question answered a score of different ways. Some of the grisly answers are: Humiliation, frustration, an end without a beginning, loneliness, discard. Others, who had thoughtfully prepared and were happily adjusted, measured retirement in terms of enrichment, realization of dreams, adventure and even romance.

Many, however, even those already retired, might profit by constructive retirement planning; such planning might yield a livelier view of these precious richly-earned years. So let us first objectively examine our attitude toward our advancing age.

No matter how much illness or sadness may have seasoned our lives, every year that we have lived we prize; none we would wish unlived, even when we might long to have them lived otherwise. And so our age becomes a treasure-house of memories of the persons and happenings that have contributed to make us ourselves. The fact that along with advancing age comes the graying of the hair, the wrinkling of the skin, the waning of physical powers, we must as sportsmen-in-living accept as matter-of-fact, not worthy of serious concern, surely not of apprehension and dismay. With frank acceptance, then, of physical changes such as a smaller needed intake of food, a lesser use of large muscles, a longer time for rest and perhaps for sleep, let's consider some of the many delightful "plus" signs of retirement. First and foremost is the elimination of enforced routine, regulation of attendance, insistence of bells and schedules. Next in measure of relief is the shift in the source of decisions and policy-making from a directing administrator or a board of trustees to one's own self. Third is the delightful similarity of all days of the week, Saturday no longer being the prized free day for chore-doing. Then there is the matter of dress. With friends being seen more irregularly, there are fewer calls upon one's wardrobe for diversity of clothing—one of the savings retirement brings with it. Retirement has surely other than negative aspects.

Are we still curious?

As counselor, there comes the first item of our enforced checkup. We call it the craving for new experiences—the output of curiosity— the sparkplug of intelligent action. In it, as in all other urgencies, there is a wide diversity in kind and in vigor. But we must keep that curiosity satisfied, stimulated, and even more alert. Plan that every day will bring you a new thoughtful awareness of the interlocking complexities of this wide, wondrous, whirling world, and the harmonious unity that motivates and governs it. Dr. Edward J. Stieglitz, Chief of Staff at Suburban Hospital Bethesda, Maryland, was wont to say, "It is an axiom of clinical medicine that forcing the one-track-mind executive to retire is tantamount to signing his death certificate within the year'!'

The craving for new experience persists from infancy to a certain time in life which differs with the individual. Some persons, tragically, cease to be curious at 20; others, regrettably, at 40; many—those are the fortunate ones—never cease until death. There are others who, like the one-track-mind executive, cease to look for new experiences. Then senility approaches, and they tend to live in memories and exalt the past.

We need friends

Now let's consider the second need—the craving for companionship. Up to the day of retirement you have enjoyed regular friendly intercourse with others of like dedication, experience, training and purpose. Now many of these folk whom you hold dear will continue with their absorbing duties, and then how about you? If they come to you, you want them because they want you. So you must make yourself so cheerful, so understanding, so serviceable, and so vitally interested in an expanding world that your friends will seek you out, not from duty or pity. The relief of sheer contentment has charm. Friendliness, social concern for our friends, have powerful attractions. You must keep alive your old friendships, but you must also become one of another circle of folks with the freer intercourse hours of retirement, and consciously you must learn to love and help some younger people so that you keep yourself in touch with other phases of life's parade than your own. Youth you will miss; it has kept you young. You must replace the loss; in this substitution you must give yourself; you will find both enriched.

We need a job

Third, fourth, and fifth drives—the needs for participation, for social role and status, and for constructive activity—all add up to the importance to you of one thing, a job, a congenial job of your choosing, to replace the one you have left. That job should preferably be one at once of sharing, of serving, of recognition in that service, and of such challenge that it will require from you earnest endeavor to the extent of your best powers. "Oh," you say, "such jobs are scarce." I'll tell you, no! You can yourself name a hundred right now that call aloud for doers of deeds and dreamers of dreams. Salary may come only in awareness of service graciously given, but the rewards still are princely. You realize that many community activities depend upon competent and reliable volunteer workers. There is a need for leadership and service in Scouting, club work, church visiting, teaching DP's, PTA service, and that thrilling field of juvenile and aged welfare work. For those of you with a literary or artistic drive, still other fields are open. To others there are such delights as making a cherished avocation yield financial or pleasurable dividends, the systematic playing of hobbies, recreational pursuits that have no connection with either idleness or loneliness. To make retirement successful you need only to remember the two precepts of the law and the gospel: Feel reverence in the glory of the universe, and love thy neighbor as thyself. Retire not from but to service; give yourself to something—something unselfish, something constructive. Go about it with a "calm and tranquil spirit."

We need a sense of our own worth

The sixth drive—that of earned self-esteem—is another of life's compelling needs; yet often it is hard to come by. Florence Nightingale at 31 felt that death alone could solve her distress, and Abraham Lincoln we know as a man of sorrows. But they both found their peace in caring for their fellow man. Truly they followed the formula: "Look out, not in; up, not down; forward, not backward; and lend a hand." Only so do we too find solace in ourselves, feel grace working, faith replacing doubt, health overcoming sickness, and darkness giving way to light. This pronouncement may sound sentimental, but the medical profession assures us that it combines the finest of therpy with the soundness of common sense.

Are we worried about money?

The seventh need, economic independence, in part, as we view it, colors all the other six. Probably you are faced with a lesser income. Does this lesser income necessitate a change of residence for you? A lower standard of living? Retirement may cause no disturbance in the case of those who can earn a supplemental salary, but to the great majority of us the problem needs an honest facing. If your income is small, is your need of material things correspondingly less compelling? Smaller quarters and simplified housekeeping are found to be sensible must's with many oldsters. Health and accident insurance pay rich dividends in peace of mind. If your social role and status are still prideful and your own personal concept of self remains undisturbed, changes in economic status and mode of living are accepted as matters-of-course by your fellows for whom later perhaps the same fate is in store.

It's a life-long job!

And even with all this preachment, you must remember that the end is not yet. This counselor of yours has a life-long guidance program for you. If you plan first, you fare best. But don't be too shocked to find yourself at times a back-slider. Enjoy a bit of fault-finding, of self-pity, if you will—both sure signs of aging—but remember too that fault-finding and self-pity are nothing to build upon; they're only good for wallowing in. So, just take a good grip upon your sense of proportion—and of humor. Then get back on the beam. Make of your retirement a real fulfillment. Prove to the world that you have proudly retired to a fuller life, richly lived.

160

*"Reverence for life . . . does not allow the scholar
to live for his science alone, even if he is very
useful . . . the artist to exist only for his art, even
if he gives inspiration to many . . . It refuses to let the
business man imagine that he fulfills all legitimate
demands in the course of his business activities. It
demands from all that they should sacrifice a portion
of their own lives for others."*

We live in deeds, not years

s we retire, the most impelling problem facing us is "What of the future?" This we know: that the past is forever gone and the future is not yet. All we—and all mankind—have is the present—already passed as we think of it. Change we face and cannot predict. But what of us? We have lived many years, some happy, some sad, some yielding delightful memories, some provocatively doing the reverse; of them we are always an over friendly witness.

But the past is past, and what of the future? What of time allotted us—as to all people? How shall we plan it? How shall we measure it?

Calendar-wise we know that we shall be growing older. But appealing from clock time, do we not have the freedom of time—to measure our growing, not only growing older, by *conscious time?* Do we not really live, not only live through, in moments, in periods, in self-giving? rather than in years? And do we not experience in just such moments and periods of wholehearted absorption in some one or something other than ourselves, a very real sense of being in harmony with life, a feeling of union with the universal spirit, of joy in really living? Are the depths of our feelings and the width of our concern perhaps really better measuring devices for our days ahead than the clock standard? The time measurement we deplored in enforced re- tirent because of age, calling it outdated and stupid. It was, and can be, in fact, a very threat and deterrent of living life at the full.

The poet Bailey in *Festus* says truly:

> *"We live in deeds not years; in thoughts, not breaths;*
> *In feelings, not in figures on a dial.*
> *We should count time by heart throbs.*
> *He most lives*
> *Who thinks most, feels the noblest,*
> *acts the best.*
> *We all know*
> *How slowly the hours pass to the unhappy,*
> *How long the night seems to one kept awake, by*
> *pain and yet*
> *How swiftly the days go by for the man who*
> *fully lives his time, not just lives through it."*

We older folk cannot be entirely unmindful of the passing of the years but we surely need not be too gravely distressed by the limita- tions and their adjustments that aging may present to us, for we can decide that even. That very sense of the meaning of the im- permanence of life can be a vital challenge to our changing the value of our days ahead by the test of *conscious time* spent—of living life to the full, of realizing our own integrity and our own potential for growth.

Waking up should be a morning challenge to a dynamic day— utilitarian, cultural, social, contemplative as you choose but let's make it conscious; don't let us become drifters, time-wasters; let's taste life to the full.

Feel to the peak the sense of the joy, of the mystery, of the wonder of being alive, of being able to be you. Your breakfast with its manifold and magical contributions from other lands and peoples can become a marvelling treat, if you so will it; your home a coveted treasure house of memories and a stimulating meeting place for friendly intercourse; your neighborhood and your morning paper a challenge to know your fellows and their way of life and to help; and your AARP and NRTA—your opportunity to sustain and renew for those who will come after you the aspirations, the traditions, the doctrines and the vital arts and the style of living that you believe in.

Group-belongingness is, we are assured, the haven of personality, giving to us a continued identity, a solidarity, a continued oneness that withstands the impact of change. In it we not only live out our own integrity but into the fullness of the more abundant life of our fellows. This sense of freedom that time affords us permits us to choose our way of life, to preserve our sense of identity, to defend against ourselves and our desire for care and comfort, our own stalwart independence; to acquire and to hold a last worthy purpose; to have as lodestar a cooperating objective in social living and social improvement.

Of one thing we are assured in this time of rapid change and that is the achievements of our culture will never be outmoded for they dwell as treasured values in the spirit of man; they make communion in their absorption with the timeless and the universal.

Euripides, long ago, in the words of his chorus, reassures us:

"Whoe'er can know as the long days go
That to live is happy hath found his heaven."

"The common problem, yours, mine, everyone's
Is — not to fancy what were fair in life
Provided it could be — but, finding first
What may be, then how to make it fair
Up to our means . . ."

— *Robert Browning*

Circumstance, challenge and choice

hen you and I begin to reminisce about our experiences, what do we generally talk about? Isn't it usually about the times when we and our associates were called upon to over-extend ourselves—to make possible the impossible; to meet competently some unexpected change; to accept some challenge that thwarted or imperiled us? Do you recall how painstakingly we would detail just what we did—the unbelievable things we accomplished? How we averted the catastrophe? And again our joy at the outcome?

Why do we so vividly recall these hardships of yesteryear and our triumphs? Why do we enjoy recalling them?—describing hardships? May it not be because in them we again find ourselves faced with circumstances that seemed to be beyond our control and our capacities and which we nevertheless overcame? The satisfaction that we felt at that accomplishment still glows within us. We are forgetful of the hard long hours of labor that were entailed, but we still relish the taste of our successful achievement. Is it really the memory of the achievement that exalts us—or is the fact that we showed to ourselves the mettle of which we are made? That we glimpse then and

164

now the potentialities of which we are capable?

If once, why not again? Why should maturity or retirement not prove that our reach still excels our grasp?

Why not redeem the self-image of our youth and strive again toward its realization in perhaps a different guise? A different setting? A different goal? The circumstance—if we don't have it, we can make it. The challenge is there, so is our responsibility to choose. Remember the words of the aging Ulysses:

> " 'Tis not too late to seek a newer world.
> Push off, and, sitting well in order, smite
> The sounding furrows; for my purpose holds
> To sail beyond the sunset, and the paths
> Of all the western stars, until I die.
> It may be that the gulfs will wash us down:
> It may be we shall touch the Happy Isles,
> And see the great Achilles, whom we knew.
> Tho' much is taken, much abides; and tho'
> We are not now that strength which in old days
> Moved earth and heaven; that which we are, we are;
> One equal temper of heroic hearts,
> Made weak by time and fate, but strong in will
> To strive, to seek, to find, and not to yield."

Retirement can be such fun, if you work at it! We enjoyed life, didn't we, when we were meeting problems? Why let the years rob us of such challenges now? You and I know that the essential ingredient of a successful retirement is exactly identical with that of our work-a-day world—some type of work or activity that results in definite accomplishments and accepting such a challenge not only solves the problem of constructively utilizing the free time that is ours but also satisfies our need of finding a meaning in life and the realization that we are approaching, however slowly, the desired goal.

The man or woman who really enjoys retirement living wakes up in the morning with eagerness to go about the unfinished work of yesterday so as to start the intriguing possibilities of today. These folk know that they are being productive—doing something worth while, justifying their existence and making the world happier for their being in it.

Some fulfill this desire if they have special talent, finding release and satisfaction in one of the various fields of creative art. Those, like myself, who are not so gifted, perhaps find it in a continuation of an occupation of work similar to that of our "active life," without compensation but with the freedom to choose both the type of work to be followed and the amount of time to be devoted to it.

It has been wisely said that all you have is life, and you only have it if you live it. To others of us—and to all of us part of the time— there is the call for volunteers and happy are we who answer, "Here am I!" When we recall that there are 8,746 hours in the year, certainly we can find a few hours each week to give to service—"worker in the vineyard." We cannot ignore the need; we hear the challenge; the choice is ours! Our future is limited only by ourselves and the answer we give and the spirit of our participation.

And then there is another call, a call we should not ignore—the call to us, as individuals, as persons, to live an abundant life—to grow in mind, in heart, in spirit—to be truly humane and compassionate. The safety slogan, "The life you save may be your own" is true in more than the sense in which it was first meant, and even in that it is worth considering, for if one's life is a trust, then it behooves us to cherish and protect and develop that trust. And in another interpretation, we know for the portion of the life you give, you receive returns a thousand fold greater in friendship and in grateful appreciation. In real truth, the life you save may be your own.

And then there's our need for more knowledge—and we know how natural, how intimate and how precious knowledge may become. Matters that were once bold mental adventures—for instance the use of the mark we call zero—are now as natural as our breathing. You have read of the explosion in population. Have you heard that more than 90% of the accumulated scientific knowledge has been announced since the beginning of World War II; that the total sum of knowledge has increased 100% between the years 1950 and 1960, and is predicted to do even more in the decade ending 1970? Do you realize that our young people in the lower elementary grades are being exposed to scientific subject matter unknown even to scientists 10 years ago? Do we—*can* we realize that 90% of all the scientists who lived and worked in the world as we know now are alive to-day? and working on even more wonders?

Might it not be well for us, older folk, now to develop interests and intellectual concern for the future so that we may improve our understanding of the world and prepare ourselves more fittingly to live in it? And, if our zeal and zest do not tempt us to expand in that field, don't let us stand idly by and let our abilities go to waste. We can help especially with youth. We can help them to develop self-reliance and self-confidence by ourselves responding to their need and by our evident and abiding faith in them. We can help them find *purpose.* We can help them generate *courage.* We can share with them our *faith,* faith in themselves, faith in their cause, faith in their future and faith in our mutual need of them at their best.

There's all the world about us, needing our help. Do you not feel alarmed that a significant percentage of our youth are disoriented? Are you not disturbed at the growing callousness, the shameless moral cowardice with which we observe crime and to escape involve-ment "by passing by on the other side?"

Have we forgotten our sense of values—notoriety displacing fame, violence emphasized instead of courage, sex irregularities highlighted and stressed, wealth and its possession extolled above constructive achievement?

Do you not cringe at seeing our heritage of a rich vital language debased by the inclusion—yes, even the substituion—of words from the underworld of vice and crime—and the current vocabulary of teenagers of the Beatles' type?

We live our lives in the midst of storm and stress. Perhaps we dwell too much on the things that divide men and too little on the discoveries that unite men in their control of nature. Yet we know that if we are ever to solve our present problem of poverty in the midst of plenty, it must be by the study of what unites men rather than what divides them.

To be alive is to be involved in the happenings of the world about us. No doubt, as we grow older and the world becomes increasingly complex, our future will call for even greater involvement. But we must never become so involved, never so absorbed and intrigued in our world that we forget that there is magic in the simple realities of life—the beauty of the sunrise, the glory of the sunset, the delicacy of the fluffy clouds, of the acrid, tingling odor of the geranium flower, the loneliness of the chair-bound relieved by your call or messages, the miracle of the smile and the appreciative courtesy of the remembered kindness. These are miracle workers. They refresh, they relax, they re-create. They, too, are essential. They are our Sabbath; they give us sernity and at the same time they reactivate our zeal, our sense of dedication. They give us the blessed sense of at-one-ness with the world—a sense of withdrawal in preparation for a fuller participation in the life about us.

And then because we are citizens of our great country, we must remember our duties in the American political process. No matter what may be our partisanship, we know the value to society of the clash of parties, the formulation of issues and the resolution of conflicts by compromise and court-finding. They are the dynamics of our democratic structure.

If the great issues of our times are to be resolved in sanity and with considered judgment, we must learn to hold politics in high regard and respect, for politics deals with the destiny of all of us—it is the process by which social issues are settled without violence, and survival may be safeguarded.

We, everyone of us, should devote part of our time and our thinking to this changing of world values, the emergence of new world problems—to the evolving for ourselves perhaps a new set of goals based as before on the fundamental proposition of the Declaration of Independence, Preamble to the Constitution and the Bill of Rights. This we must do, for in the words of Albert Camus, "we have nothing to lose except everything. So let us push forward. This is the challenge of our generation." We have the circumstance, the challenge and the choice! Let us accept them zestfully!

168

WORDS OF
INSPIRATION

Dig a big hole in your garden of thoughts. Into it put all your disillusions, disappointments, regrets, worries, troubles, doubts, and fears, and – forget. Cover well with the earth of fruitfulness, water it from the well of content. Sow on top again the seeds of hope, courage, strength, patience, and love. Then, when the time of gathering comes, may your harvest be a rich and plentiful one.

"Everything that we call nobility—conscience, ethics and religion—challenge us to share with all our contemporaries the chance to think along new lines, to grow into new capacities, to see the sunshine. That's the challenge —to see the sunshine of age!"

The crown that
dynamic maturity earns

hen traveling in the West, you may have seen the glory of that towering plant named by some Our Lord's Candle and by others the Spanish bayonet and by the scientist a certain kind of yucca. Its myriad of blooms startles and delights with its singular beauty and magnificence.

That same yucca, for an indefinite number of years has continued the slow routine of ordinary life, close to the ground. Then, suddenly when it has stored vital force sufficient, it shoots a plume ten feet into the air and flowers into stately breath-taking grandeur.

Just such a change sometimes comes to people in retirement. The stored-up energies, of which perhaps they were unconscious, when freed from the every-day hampering stress and strain of making a living, often burst out into regal splendor, and their retirement years bless and amaze.

It is this kind of thing that, when it happens to us—and we pray that it may—fills our world with hope and keeps it young. It really can happen to us for all the essential ingredients are here—they are at everyone's disposal—this mysterious force we call Life. If only we will

171

glimpse its possibilities for us, then we can imbue it with spirit and power; then we can tower over our former selves, like the flowering yucca.

We grow conscious that there are capacities within us hitherto dormant and knowledge hitherto unappropriated.

We may not be so prosperous as other men; we may be much less so, but our superiority over them will be commensurate with the freshness of our feeling, the creativity in our spirit and the quality of our activities.

You have heard the story of the Persian Monarch, who in an orgy of self-pity, sought for himself the shirt of the happiest and most useful man in his empire, only to be told that, when the man was finally located, he had no shirt.

Possessions do not give us distinction. Nor can intelligence or training, for Robert Hutchins tells us that one of every four of the dreaded SS troopers of the Hitler regime were Doctors of Philosophy. If not wealth nor learning is the essential ingredient, we come to the realization that character and the love of one's fellows may be both the alpha and the omega of life's fulfillment. Only so do we see in the mechanical and material world about us the throbbing of a personal life, only as we respond with sympathy to all the myriad interests that lie close at hand, only as we relish the humorous, and enjoy the philosophic considerations of the human beings among whom we live, only as we dream vague dreams that haunt our thinking, does the flowering within unfold, do our lives grow tall and resplendent. It is not by the extent of our knowledge but its essence, not by the range of its information but by its vitality, not by the space of our activity but by the depth of feeling and compassion to which we are alert. So we are fed, sustained and grow tall in the simple, kindly, deep relationship and warm fellowship with the whole order of things of which we are a part.

This maturing is the product of years of living fully. Neither youthful zest, nor middle-aged acquisition of schooling nor the accomplishments of spectacular college life can produce the vital equipment that comes only with the ripening years. That is the crown that dynamic maturity earns. That is the glory of age.

172

Could we not, in the service of our fellows, have them see that, as we grow older, the essence of our living lies in the choices we make of the gift of hours we all enjoy? Could we not bring into sharper focus the contradictions that surround us and offer us corresponding lures and successes? Toward these contradictions we cannot remain passive or neutral. For they are interwoven with every impasse, every act of our lives.

We are offered life-constant change, a constant rebirth. But we can also, if we will, choose death-apathy, inertia, repetition. Some will choose life, and grow tall, flower and be fruitful, a delight. And regrettably some even aimlessly avoid choosing, escaping into the busyness of the trivial happenings of the day. In indolence and self-ease they shun the adventurous, they fear the untried and the unknown, they are content to vegetate—to wither and to die, unsought and unregretted.

But with those of us who courageously face life and wish to share its intensity and its depth we grow to feel a closeness with all humanity, being uniquely ourselves, but still feeling with Bunyan, on seeing a criminal pass by, "There, but for the grace of God, go I!"

He didn't picture in writing of the Pilgrim's Progress that lassitude and despair were his guides to the golden gates.

Everything that we call nobility—conscience, ethics and religion challenge us to share with all our contemporaries the chance to grow, to think along new lines and grow into new capacities, to see the sunshine. That's the challenge—to see the sunshine of age.

Then truly retirement becomes a time of promise because it may be the time for fulfillment. As Dr. Schweitzer reminds us we don't live in a world of our own; our brothers are here too!

This then is one of our challenges—to serve our brothers; a second is to bring to the attention of the world the testimony of our faith, to help the world that is still young realize that age has its grandeur, age has still its contributions to make while life endures.

173

"Just for today we will be unafraid.
Especially we will not be fearful of enjoying what is beautiful,
and we believe that, as we give to the world,
so the world will give to us."

Just for today

stroll through this little college town with its ivied buildings, broad roadways and over-arching trees can be one of sheer delight. Here, while we are still keenly aware of the mental, spiritual and political malaise of our time, we feel no desire to escape from life, but rather to delve into life, to find it increasingly rewarding, creative and purposeful—a challenge to be alive.

Where the street widens, we see the street ahead, being damaged with planned improvement. Signs for our protection and direction advise us: "Proceed with Caution," "Men at Work," and the peremptory order, "Keep to Right," "Yield," "Danger Ahead, Form Single Lane." We halt, we proceed, we're waved on our way, and then we dimly discern the purpose behind the construction—the bleachers that are being readied to serve the hundreds that will gather to welcome into the work-a-day world the young collegians full of joy at both the completion of their goals and the official attention showered upon them.

We see them, at risk of life and limb, scurrying in groups sporting in rehearsal their academic caps and gowns. We wonder if they know the significance of the bachelor's garment. To them it betokens the distinction between town and gown. We wonder if they realize that one of those lengthened sleeves of the Master's garment once carried inside his larder and "buttery" and the other the whole extent of his wardrobe? And the Doctor's regalia and his hood that served in that capacity as

174

guard and protection against the weather—humble reminders when the university was not a building but a group of scholars. Isn't that still true today that school is no greater than its teachers and that Doctor is still the teacher, the domine?

As we listen to the commencement orators we say to ourselves we, too, will accept the challenge—shall we seek opportunity—unlimited, shall we take the long view? We know it's so easy to evade, so vague to define.

With a surge of purpose, we decide on the immediate—the definite—just for today (not for tomorrow) we shall plan in the words of Ralph Cake we comfort ourselves that just for today, we will follow the gleam. *Just for today*—we will try to live through this day only, and not tackle our whole life problems at once. We can do something for 12 hours that would appall us if we felt that we had to keep it up for a lifetime.

Just for today—we will be happy. We'll prove the comment of Abraham Lincoln, "Most folks are about as happy as they make up their minds to be."

Just for today—we will try to strengthen our minds. We will learn something useful. We will read something that requires effort, thought and concentration.

Just for today—we will adjust ourselves to what is; and we will not keep trying to adjust everything else to our own desires.

Just for today—we will exercise our soul in three ways: we will do somebody a good turn, and not get found out. We will do at least two things we don't want to do—just for exercise. And today, if our feelings are hurt, we will not show it to anyone.

Just for today—we will look as well as we can, dress as becomingly as we know how, talk low, act courteously, criticize not one bit, and not try to improve or regulate anybody except ourselves.

Just for today—we will have a program. We may not follow it exactly, but we will have one. We will save ourselves from two pests: hurry and indecision. Just for today—we will have a quiet half-hour all by ourselves for meditation and relaxation. During this half-hour we will try to get a better perspective of our lives.

Just for today—we will be unafraid. Especially we will not be fearful of enjoying what is beautiful, and to believe that, as we give to the world, so the world will give to us.

We watch the graduates as they disperse, each one champing at the bit, ready to set about remaking the old world so crudely and unimaginatively mismanaged by their elders. They are planning their assault, but first the great moment is their commencement. Pray God, it will be just that, the beginning of their education, not its formal end. We wonder when they will begin to realize that their intellectual lares and penates so dearly bought and now treasured are already on their way to becoming obsolete?

As we think of them with loving indulgence and great pride, we wish that we had more deeply impressed upon them the realization that the concepts upon which our Nation is founded are more revolutionary than anything they, in their protected experience, can conceive. We wonder do they realize how completely at variance it is with that held, until that time, by every government and every people that ever lived— that the people enjoy their civil rights by the gift of God—not by favor of king, grant by chief, or right of inheritance—that the individual, that everyone of us, is equal in the sight of man and God—equality in access to opportunity is man's greatest invention and yet it is a concept, not a reality? The vastness of the thought—do they grasp it or is it to them a truism accepted as ritualistic?

But time's a-fleeting, and just for today the nation stands at salute at the anniversary of its two great leaders—the Man of Sorrows, both of kindly wit and homely parable and of unparalleled eloquence. Reverently with the child at school we repeat his prayer—"With malice toward none and charity toward all," and that other Great—The Father of Our Country, statesman, soldier, farmer, a bit austere for vast and appreciative love but in his dignity, revered, pridefully honored, and proudly treasured and respected.

And March is here—with its two patron saints. Like all the rest of us they, too, are immigrants in a land of which neither in his lifetime had ever heard—the Roman priest whom the Irish have adopted as their own and St. Joseph beloved by many lands and peoples, but often

176

now considered by the Italian a symbol of Italian youth—two days, so different, yet so throbbingly alive!

The joyous, noisy, rollicking parades on the eastern seaboard gaily honoring St. Patrick and the "Green Little Isle" are still warm memories when St. Joseph's Day brings its poignant memories. How many St. Joseph's days I have spent on the outskirts of a crowd assembled at the humble home of someone with Sicilian traditions waiting reverently and patiently for the coming of the actors in this drama of fulfillment— the votive offering of a frightened mother, perhaps once fearful and now a grateful soul, pledging to St. Joseph an altar and with it perhaps the earnings of the family for a year, restricting them to a more meager diet so that on this Day of Days, St. Joseph's altar could offer to all and sundry culinary treats of which they had heard, never dreamed of sharing and now prepared by them with loving care, at great sacrifice.

An older man portraying St. Joseph, an honored friend of the family, and Mary, carrying the Child have come and the priest has blest the occasion. Three times Joseph knocked on the door for admission. There is no answer. Then the little procession with its beggar youths—really young beloved friends of the family—wends its way to the back to enter today's "Holy of Holies" from the humble entrance in the rear. Strangely moved, I shared in the tragedy—and then with a greeting and a prayer and a coin later to be delivered, I hurry on to join another assemblage in this little neighborhood of the bigger neighborhood which is part of my self-imposed area of visitation.

The day finds me drained from emotions, and as I close my eyes, I wonder—did the swallows come today to San Juan Capistrano as they are supposed to—on St. Joseph's Day?

Spring is a burgeoning and each challenging morn, just for the day, offers us an active, vigorous constructive outlook on life. Easter is near at hand—formerly and still at times honored as a holy day on mountain tops and in glens. In other areas the Easter Parade flouts its display of the latest in fashion and in costume elegance.

Dreams of summer release, of peace of mind, a spiritual and mental balance, of vacation time ahead are pictured on the billboard as we hurriedly pass by. And in our own planning there comes the thought of those, disabled and needy who, too, need the joy of a rest and a retreat, and we wonder just for today, what can we do to help?

One of the most delightful answers we know is enacted every year in the city of Philadelphia. There on a certain day, from eleven in the morning till two in the afternoon, the staid business men of mature years don their silk toppers, their golden aprons and false mustaches, and become the proverbial barkers of yesteryear. These industrial leaders in their younger days had been Philly's newsboys and in their prosperous maturity—they have not forgotten. Members *de jure* or *de facto* of the Variety Club, every year they turn out to give a helping hand—to the handicapped. Their drive for Old Times Sake is the sale of the Happiness Edition of a four page copy of the *Philadelphia Gazette,* the oldest newspaper in America and the price—well, the price is measured only by the means and the generosity of the contributor—and the news—just the story of this yearly crusade of loving kindness. The "Weather Report" in its accustomed spot predicts "A fair and bright summer following showers of contributions after you lighten your pocket with donations for handicapped youngsters" and the price— "you name it." The Day's Events report that the women's volunteers have taken over the activity in the suburban centers and neighborhood shopping centers. To add to the festive atmosphere the noon day parade is scheduled and to top it all at twelve-thirty for three hours the jewelers of the city conduct a curbside auction of their own contributions to help swell the fund! To read of it is a pleasure—to see it an endearing delight—to be a part of it a rewarding experience. Might not it be a grand idea for a chapter seeking a project?

May on the calendar and the billboards on the roadside are reminding us that we have a mother—as if we ever could forget her! And on that one day each year (that special day of days) we do her formal recognition with a gift or a dinner or a visit—always an outlay of money that will benefit the advertiser. While we may fall victim to their snares, we know in our heart of hearts—that Mother's most dearly treasured gift will be our coming home and telling her how dearly we love her, how grateful we are to be her children and how proudly we hold our heads because she is ours! A gift? Yes, but that is only a token of our love.

This is not "just for today" but for always!

And poor Dad, he'll come along a bit later for his belated recognition! I have often wondered as I watch him on *his* day of days, if he somewhat gauges the love and esteem we give him with the respect we pay him? I've never dared ask; perhaps he would not know the answer and would not tell me if he could!

But the calendar and the roadside have told the joys to be had on Memorial Day. Do we observe it as a holy day or a day of remembrance or a jolly holiday, a time for a family gathering, special occasion or a festival? Like the Fourth of July, its original purpose, often forgotten, the dedicated anniversary of a great political achievement, it is today perhaps a day for relaxation from the humdrum and the routine—its evening a time for the enjoying of the spectacular in fireworks displayed to our amazement for their complexity and uniqueness; its significance forgotten.

But Flag Day for many of us is still a thrill. With Franklin Lane, we feel the thrill as the flag is unfurled. We hold it a symbol for our right to life, liberty and the pursuit of happiness. It is a reminder of what we always knew, that democracy, while it is the finest type of government yet evolved by man, is difficult to administer and exceedingly complex to accept and support. It grants us no security. It tolerates in us no weakness. It is for men, proud men, stalwart men, courageous men— it doesn't need a crowd or a following. It needs the individual willing to share, to participate, even to stand fearlessly alone. Only an imaginary line separates these national days in our thinking. We still feel the pulse beat of America and know that day by day—every day all goes well.

No one's taste or interest in recreation, travel, sport, is forgotten in the displays of Labor Day advertisements on the billboards. They range from pleas for the observation of safety precautions in the long weekend ahead with its continually growing number of predicted casualties, to the formal announcements of the official observances of the day and the scheduled programs, planned celebrations, contests, recreation, sports—what you will—but no matter what may be "your cup of tea," there is an invitation and a program.

Then when August is past, come again the days of active work. It is fitting that Labor Day comes early. The question of labor is and has been associated with that of work, which seems to have as its goal—activities that will pay an ample wage, that it be eased and shortened, and its nonlabor benefits to be expanded.

The amazing paradox when work is discussed is that it is both sought and that often the occasion of forced retirement, work which had been an accepted and necessary chore seems to become for many a coveted activity, an absorbing timeless application, and an emotional reward. Does the difference mean only one of motivation, of self-direction, of personal expression or are we really a work-oriented people? As one of the Greek poets has said, "Before the gates of excellence the high gods have placed sweat."

The type of work, oddly, we find is not the issue; the ditch digger may see his hand only as a claw, yet the gardener uses that same claw nobly to loosen and pulverize the soil which has become his artist's palette. Is the difference in attitude a question of spirit-values, of attitudes, of imaginative prophecy of future beauty and assurance? That work, self-motivated, may keep the hand busy with the hooks and the net, for the form of sport—and the tools, the much more primitive tools than those he is supplied in his impersonal labor-allotment. The freed laborer builds himself an arbor, a shelter, a patio—what you will. His hand delights in the feel of a hammer, axe, saw and trowel. He plans a garden. The spade, the pickaxe, the shovel, hoe, rake and clipper are the executive assistants to those hands of his which have become instruments of his mind and his chief officers.

Or perhaps his work demands pen and paper, a microscope, a telescope, or access to a library or a printing press. Mayhap, it is a chisel and mallet, a brush and a palette, a canvas or the living room wall that awaits eagerly for a mural. Or perchance the music that he marches to, unheard by all but him, calls for reed, strings, tube; if he is of a religious trend, to satisfy some inner urge he may seek to make, a Rubrick. Mayhap he is religious and manifests a prayer tool, an altar, a chalice or baptismal font.

The success is ever proportionate to either the beauty or the practical value of the products he may produce; the success is in the satisfaction

180

he feels in the effort he makes, in his self-expression, in his innate craftsmanship.

Imaginative work, creative work, serviceable work—automation can never outmode these.

Just for today—for tomorrow never comes—and if and when it does —it is today.

"There are parts of a ship which taken by themselves would sink. The engine would sink. The propeller would sink. But when the parts of a ship are built together, they float." So says Ralph Sockman. "So with the events of my life. Some have been tragic. Some have been happy. But when they are built together, they form a craft that floats and is going someplace. And I am comforted."

Just for today let us seek the road to success that Dr. William Osler prescribes for us:

"Throw away all ambitions beyond that of doing the day's work well. The travelers on the road to success live in the present, heedless of taking thought for the morrow. Live neither in the past nor in the future, but for each day's work, absorb your entire energies and satisfy your wildest ambition."

December 25th, Christmas Day, as Charles Dickens
has written; "a good time, a kind of forgiving,
charitable, pleasant time; the only time I know of
in the long calendar of the year when men and women
seem by one consent to open their shut-up hearts freely."

A Christmas greeting

And so—as the carols ring out, as the Yule log burns merrily —we share with our beloved ones the warmth and intimacies of family life; we seek, too, to make the Day memorable by bringing cheer to those whom we have the good fortune to know and cherish. We pray, in the words of Tiny Tim, "God bless us, every one."

The message of peace on earth and good will to men still echoing in our hearts, the New Year comes with its challenge.

The gift of time coexists for all of us. How we will employ these coming 365 days is the choice each of us must make. We hope that you will fill them with wholesome, happy, purposeful living, each minute an unrepeatable miracle! Let's map a life journey of the coming 365 days.

Think of what we can do to help those of our acquaintance who have no program—who in retirement have lost their road-map—develop new vistas along the highway of living. Do you know any who feel lost in their retirement, who, severed from their sustaining life force—their work—feel robbed of their pride and individualism? They are not finding peace on earth. But we can help them find that peace if we care to fulfill the message of "good will to men." How about a Christmas gift to at least one of them—a Christmas gift of yourself—a New Year's pledge of an hour each week of your free time, with addi-

182

tions of kindly purpose and interested companionship? You can give a listening ear—you can be a confessional for shedding a sense of failure or of guilt—you can become a comforting, challenging friend. You who are living to the hilt can do a creative job if you will; you can perform a miracle through your investment of self and time and interest—a miracle of restoration. You will then realize the Christmas preachment of *good will* to men.

Wouldn't it be for you a year of great achievement if you could help him recognize old age as the high point of life—help him find contentment through exploring new fields and in turn creating new happiness?

Dr. Schweitzer tells us—"You do not live your life alone. There are your brothers." These brothers of ours who have not aged well are of course all individually different and no one approach could meet all their needs. Interest in their well-being alone is the key that will unlock the barriers isolation and desperation have built. Patience and tolerance will oil those locks, will open again for them the gates to treasures which money cannot buy for them and which they have lost the knack of making for themselves—the security of emotional well-being, a satisfying sense of their own individual worth, the solace and the pride of companionship and the releasing comfort of work.

Basically idleness is a little recognized dis-ease in the medical world. Its primary symptoms are a heart-hunger, a feeling of futility, and uselessness, the fever of boredom and self-pity, and the waste of excessive time spent in examining pains and aches. The result is apathy and the desire for others to do for them what they should do for themselves.

Leisure and work! We know that they are both blessed. Leisure gives us time for friends, to play with children, to walk the dog, to prune the roses, to follow the sports, to listen to music, to watch the sun set, to talk over world news and views, to laugh and to play and to taste life and find it good. Leisure, well-spent, is the enemy of idleness. And work . . .

> *"Thank God for the might of it,*
> *The ardor, the urge, the delight of it—Work!*
> *Thank God for the pride of it,*

For the beautiful, conquering tide of it,
Mastering stupor and dull despair
Moving the dreamer to do and dare.
What is so strong as the summons deep
Rousing the torpid soul from sleep?"

Let us not belittle the powers of friendliness. Let us truly become a great organization of friendly folk, a unity amid diversity! An association of courageous, compassionate, realistic, energetic folk, tied together by mutual esteem, mutual understanding and the bonds of mutual service!

"Giving and receiving are not just reserved for the able and the exceptional; they are just as essential as breathing and as vital as life itself."

Building a happier tomorrow

How to change the stereotype of aging to that of a dynamic maturity? How to bring beauty to being old? How to regain the authenticity of age? These are our challenges.

In their efforts to realize these goals, our associations have grown great, rightfully respected in their devotion and dedication to making retirement a richer experience and a more useful way of life. They have helped in building astounding defences against the fear and the trauma of old age. They have successfully conquered industrial limitations and legal inequities and made available new benefits. They have made tremendous strides in the winning of national repute and respect. They have raised the prestige of the teacher from conditions of being "just a teacher" to being a member of a dignified and honored profession, to which Congressmen, lawmakers, turn for the viewpoints and opinions of our members.

It is at this time when we feel that we are making progress that we come upon a challenge and a prayer, a call for personal service in a field we have not handled as yet—the field of family relationships. The problems here are many and most of them need never to have arisen and some of them are beyond any help folks can give.

And there are heartaches too in the field of family relationships. As you might imagine, they come from our members who: (1) complain of certain things affecting themselves; and (2) asking for help on problems affecting others in which they themselves are deeply interested.

The story of their own problems concerns themselves and for the most part over solicitous children. The manner in which they, as parents, showed their independence, patience and purposefulness, their consistency, understanding and a sufficient flexibility to adjust or to compromise. As regards these problems, since all people are different and react differently—even to the same situations, it is difficult to generalize.

Yet there are these specific steps they agreed upon as helpful guides to others who might meet a like situation.

1—Encouragement, approval and recognition for any activity;
2—A home atmosphere that is conducive to feeling needed and wanted and having a place in the family;
3—And an opportunity to be useful with interests of one's liking. All these, they agreed, adult children can supply their parents, regardless of their economic income.

The problem that really distresses them is not those of either their own or of their own making. It is the concern they feel on seeing their friends and even their relatives present to the world a picture of petty-narrowness, irritable demands, their thinking and their feeling seemingly limited to their disabilities and coercions. They tell us that they are sick-at-heart with the failure to engage the interest of these petulant folk, who just sit and sit, and cast the weight of their unhappiness, apathy and boredom upon those seeking to reawaken in them any interest in the life about them, any hope for a future rather than this unhappy sodden present. Distraught and frustrated they write us.

I quote one man speaking of his aged father:

"Tell us what to do. We are sick at heart, we are all so powerless. Really we are at our wits' end. What's the answer? He is so miserable and unhappy. He makes us just as miserable and as unhappy as he is. Indeed, I think we feel worse, for there he sits unmoved and we guilty in our failure to help him, suffer and feel in some way we are to blame. He wasn't always so. What can we do to bring him back? One doctor says it's due to hardening of the arteries. Another says it's purely emotional. My wife says no matter what the reason may be, the result will be the death of her and me."

186

The problem is a two-fold one—first, the withdrawal of the older person with the forecast of early senility and helplessness; and, second, the frustration and the heartache of the family, wanting to help, and being punished for not being miracle workers, for it would seem to need a miracle to provide happiness to one who is content to be goalless, loveless and self-centered.

Of course I don't know the answer, and of course we·are not miracle workers, but I do believe that this puzzling question is of vital concern to many others than the members we are quoting. There are probably hundreds of harried folk who find themselves caught in just such a tragic imprisonment, no matter how strong and vibrant may be their initiative, drive, and how thoughtful their care.

Do these malcontents show any signs of hope? Without hope, the strains and tensions of life surely would multiply until life itself would have little value. We recognize that hope is a dominant force in the life of each of us, a driving power as long as life itself. How did these unhappy folk lose hope? Or really have they? It would seem that one could not live without it, even if it were for only the smallest trifle; they expect care; they surely hope to some degree even for its arrival and presence. Can we discover what kind of force can create and maintain a greater hope? Can we help change seeming hopelessness into hope? Surely hope cannot die. Can we help by going over and over again with them that "in spite of" whatever may be their disability or their grievance, there must be many things about their every day which call for hope. There's for instance, hunger and rest, confidence in service; even there's hope for a lasting love of those who love us and whom we love. There we feel a hope that becomes a certainty; can we discover their hopes, their certainties? Remember the problem is not an economic one—it is one of attitudes and personality. They are now so morose and despondent. Their condition is clearly unhealthy and unwarranted. Can we help to reorient such folk from being depressive, sullen, unloving, joyless and unlovely? Is there anything we can do to restore them to a sense of happiness and well-being?

Probably the real truth, only we don't wish to face it, is that these folk, even in their prime, probably never did feel secure or adequate, but, through social pressure and individual needs, they had to make the necessary gestures that their occupational and social status and individual pride indicated as required and really probably never did enjoy life to the full. Now, no longer feeling the need to mask their feelings and weaknesses, being safeguarded at home and buttressed by the love and the sympathy of loved ones, they have withdrawn into a state of negation, convinced perhaps in their queer self-justification that the world, as represented by their family, owes them happiness. So firmly grooved are they in this conviction that they have persuaded their loved ones of their culpability with the development of a guilt complex on the part of the loved ones and with heartache and with failure they find themselves unable to do for these petulant folk the thing they think is owing to them. Stubbornly they continue to refuse to shake off their hopelessness and apathy.

Of course the logical solution is that prevention should have made such deterioration impossible, but the apparent fact is that the time for prevention in their case has long been past. The problem is a present one; what can we do now to help, to bring happiness to one who seeks none, in whom there is no purpose and little love?

One thing we can do. Forthrightly we can recall to their attention the truth that they already know, that one of our national beliefs and the cornerstone of our democratic philosophy is the individual's divine right to life, liberty and the pursuit of happiness. The attainment and the realization of those rights are the responsibility of the individual and the individual only and of no one else.

How can we convince these cantankerous, demanding persons of the truth that life is spread before them like a cafeteria; a person is responsible for his selection of all the various possibilities life offers; he can take happiness if he desires it. One thing is definitely certain, he has no right to make the household of which he is a part unhappy as he is.

Our job is to convince this family that his is the job to remake himself. Only he can make himself a person taking full personal responsibility for his own life. We must shock him out of the delinquency of self-pity, petulance and aggressive dependence.

In spite of rebuffs let us at least strive to help him recover a taste

188

of full vitality, the real satisfaction in living. Let him know that ours is a vital interest, not a sentimental one—not that of a "do-gooder" but of a person who knows that this is within the power of the depressed person to grant, and we will help with friendship and understanding and hope.

At least it's worth our trying, isn't it, to save one person from the self-prison of senility, or of the cultivation of the feelings of rebellion, of revenge and of even hate? For us not to try might mean someone will be passively sitting and being unhappy, childishly becoming every day a greater "problem" to his or her loved ones. Let the depressed person realize that no one owes him or her happiness. Theirs is the right to seek it for the person alone, yes, and to share it with others—rather than by negative withdrawing and moping make the loved ones feel guilty. Guilty of what? The self-absorption of the saddened one?

This treatment I advise is not harsh, though it may seem so. It is the only therapy possible to alert them to the realization of the truth, to convince them of our sincerity and be willing to help in a constructive campaign, but to be unwilling—and this refers also to the loved ones who have been made to feel a sense of guilty responsibility—that the real guilt is on the part of the aged person who refuses to choose happiness and finds his content in wrapping himself or herself in the deprivation of self-pity which is good, if ever, only in exceedingly minute doses.

After all, remember your primary objective is to help people help themselves. We can do nothing and their family can do nothing to—or for the oppressed. We have to do it with them, so they can better themselves. You will find genuine satisfaction when you constructively and in humility strive to awaken these troubled ones to a realization of a fuller life. It takes patience and faith to do it, but it will give you some joy in the now, some peace in the here, and perhaps awake some love in their "thee" and your "me."

I do believe, if with all your efforts, with all the zeal of the family, and with all the rehabilitation techniques that you and they know or can arrange for, if the depressed person will make no effort, then he or she must be told that you and the family will not continue indefinitely to carry his or her problem on your heart. All concerned must realize that, without any improvement, the situation then will call for institutionalized service. The depressed person must realize from the start the importance of the effort that is being made and accept the bitter alternative.

Giving and receiving are not just reserved for the able and the exceptional; they are as essential as breathing and as vital as life itself. Our depressed and petulant member of the family takes from it concern, care and comfort; and if he gives in return nothing, he must be taught, lovingly but firmly, that either he must open both mind and heart to the "give and take" and determine in his thinking that he will make the effort to return to a fuller life offered by the family and his loved ones or to face the alternative—isolation from the family and friends. With the least little advancement, let us continue to believe that we can all together work miracles—let us believe so and not be afraid to say so loudly and frequently in the hearing of all concerned.

Happiness is a dynamic thing, a captive that stays with you. Remember our joy as a child, in following the lamplighter on his rounds as far as you dared, and sheer delight in the rare visits to the Hurdy Gurdy Man with his monkey in his red jacket and green cap with its little white feather? Do you recall the Punch and Judy Show? Does its compulsive humor still amuse you? Can you in your mind's eye see the marionette theatre with its flashing beauty? Can you remember the thrill we felt as youngsters in the first fall of snow? In the finding of a four-leaf clover? Do you oft times recall the devotion and fellowship of Rover, your dog? Can you imaginatively smell the sweet scent of geranium, the heliotrope and jasmine? The thrill of a story of Dad's boyhood, Mother's recital of her first ball and her elaborate hairdress and train? Can you still recall the tremulous fear of the Friday afternoons when we recited our "pieces"? There are so many joys in our youth, the thrill of a campfire at twilight and that hard lump that always successfully lodged itself under your hip in camping?

How about just such reminiscing about old days on your first visit in your therapy campaign? May not our recalling and listening to old joys awake a longing for new ones? Perhaps the memories of youth may

190

bring back something of their old unusual charm and glory, and sentiment may again take root and grow in minds that have long been sterile and weed-grown.

Maybe so. At least we can launch our enterprise and with hope see it come to harbor, bringing with it pleasanter thoughts and a more pliant attitude. If only it is given us that we can share with the saddened friend a realization that man is happiest when he feels that he is recognized as a significant being, (and your being there, is proof that he is) that he is loved and needed (else why the effort you all are making?) and that life has for him meaning which he can find only in anticipation and faith, in expectation and hope. Let's build with him today a happier tomorrow.

*"Somehow, within this house's framework
there is also the divine spark that differentiates
one individual uniquely from every other in the whole
wide world. Whether we call it soul, or spirit,
it calls us to reflect upon the ever-engrossing question:
What is the mission of each one of us in this
moment of eternity?"*

To control others
these are our needs

n his eightieth birthday, John Quincy Adams responded to a query concerning his well-being by saying: "John Quincy Adams is well. But the house in which he lives at present is becoming dilapidated. It is tottering upon its foundation. Time and the seasons have nearly destroyed it. Its roof is pretty well worn out. Its walls are much shattered and it trembles with every wind. I think John Quincy Adams will have to move out of it soon. But he himself is quite well, quite well."

Science tells us that the house's framework of which John Quincy Adams speaks, like that of our own, for its component parts, is valued at slightly below $3.00 at our current rate. In its composition there is enough sugar to fill an ordinary shaker, enough fat to make seven bars of soap, enough lime to paint a chicken coop, enough phosphorus to tip 2,000 paper matches and enough iron to make an ordinary nail.

In addition there is a heart pump that measures 60 to 70 beats per minute, and over a lifetime generates enough power to lift the Battleship

192

Missouri fourteen feet out of the water.

Somehow, within this house's framework there is also the divine spark that differentiates one individual uniquely from every other in the whole wide world. Just what this is we do not know, but whether we call it soul, or spirit or use some other phraseology, we do realize that it is that which calls us to reflect upon the dynamic, ever-receding, ever-engrossing question, "What is the mission of each one of us in this moment of eternity? Has each of us a specific purpose on earth? Is there a mission for each of us planned, or does the finding and its fulfillment remain for us to mold in our life's activity and thinking? If we are to make a mission for ourselves, what is to be our guide?" These are the challenging and unanswered questions that each of us faces.

Our conscious existence we live in two worlds, between which we alternate constantly. They are commonly called realism and idealism.

In the world of realism, Democritus four hundred years before Christ tells us, "Well-being and cheerfulness are the ends to be sought above all. Their attainment is dependent, not upon circumstances, but upon the culmination of the resources of the soul, the treading of the middle path between excess and deficiency and the contemplation of noble things."

If we accept this doctrine—and I do—the strength we seek is to first of all realize our physical limitations and then to look to a source within ourselves that will help us to gain dominance not only over our own environment but to help other men and women likewise to overcome theirs.

Belief

With a vibrant and determined will, we would need, for success in contact with others, first of all, a genuine belief in the subject under discussion. Emerson tells us, in defence of such a first principle: "I had heard an experienced counselor say that he never feared the effect upon a jury of a lawyer who does not believe in his heart that his client ought to have a verdict. If he does not believe it, his own belief would appear to the jury, despite all his protestations, and would become their unbelief."

193

This is that law whereby a work of art, of whatever kind, sets us in the same state of mind wherein the artist was when he made it. That which we do not believe we cannot adequately say, though we may repeat the words ever so often. It was this convert's conviction which Swedenborg expressed, when he described a group of persons in the spiritual world endeavoring in vain to articulate a proposition which they did not really believe; but they could not, though "they twisted and folded their lips even to indignation."

Confidence

A prime second principle is personal confidence in influence. Pizzaro, a Spanish adventurer, left with one vessel and a few followers on the island of Gallo, where the greatest dangers in suffering had been endured, was offered relief by an expedition from Panama. By his sword, he traced a line with it on the sand from east to west. Then, turning toward the south "Friends and comrades" he said, "on that side there are toil, hunger, nakedness, drenching rain, desertion and death; on this side, ease and pleasure. There lies Peru with its riches; there Panama with its poverty. Choose, each man, what best becomes a brave Castillian. For my part, I go to the south." So saying, he stepped across the line and they followed him.

Enthusiasm

We might call the third enthusiasm, it certainly is a large factor in personal influence. Samuel Smiles wrote very practically: "There is a contagiousness in every example of energetic conduct; the brave man is an inspiration to the weak, and compels them, as it were, to follow him." Thus Napier relates that, when the Spanish center was broken in flight, a young officer, named Havelock, sprang forward, and, waving his hat, called upon the Spaniards to follow him. Putting spurs to his horse, he leaped the barrier which protected the French front, and rode headlong against them. The Spaniards were electrolyzed; in a moment they dashed after him and with one shout they broke through the French and sent them flying down the hill.

194

Self-Mastery

Perhaps, self-mastery is your fourth principle, the seeker of a large control of others is found in the moral master of self. It has been well-written: "Keep cool, and you command everybody." A recent author quotes a good remark of Clarendon, who said of Hampton: "He was supreme governor over his patience and he therefore had great power over other men." In an ignoble way, one can control by ministering to their weakness, but a noble use of self-mastery has the sublime privilege of exerting a good influence over weakness. In either instance, the strong man is the one whose will is steady and purposeful. Sooner or later, however, men discover their degradation in manipulated weaknesses and, resenting it, often throw off the yokes whenever the motive of fear ceases to restrain them.

Motive

Perhaps, our fifth principle should be motives. The character of man's influence over his fellows depends upon the motive that he suggests for this action. One may dominate multitudes by fear—Nero ruled Rome as a madman. Or, love may become the controlling force in personal loyalty. Schweitzer swayed thousands by his own inspiration. In one case, influence is coercion, ceasing as soon as the fear disappears, or assuming such power as to break in desperation with one's own dictates; in Schweitzer's case, the motives of sympathy are multiplied and they become stronger as love's gracious spell continues.

Insight or Empathy

The sixth principle, insight, is a control of others, a demanding ability which uncovers their motives and discovers their plans. Of some people it is said that their instinctive penetration can detect the feelings of others and so often embarrass their opponents by revealing aloud their secret motives and laying open that which they were most anxious to conceal. It would seem to me when it exists, there is no mystery, no secret that these people cannot solve. We call this one of the traits by the word empathy. It differs from sympathy, as sympathy differs from compassion. We are able to identify its possession in an individual when he realizes the answer is his aptitude for personal service, whether it is as teacher, or preacher or salesman. Just what do we agree is empathy? We could truthfully say that when it is hard, for parents, to understand their own children, whom they love and for whom they would sacrifice anything, empathy is lacking.

Yet the answer, why we cannot understand them, is that they lack this feeling of projecting oneself into another until we can understand what the other says and thinks and dreams. The interesting thing, perhaps, about empathy is that we know that it is an ability we can learn to develop in ourselves and that it can be successfully cultivated. We have to realize that it is only through cooperation that you will gain it. The pleasure that one gets is gained by the pleasure that it offers in surrendering to the sense of right, to which appeal is made for loyalty or suggestion of the highest of interests as the reason for that allegiance.

Cooperation

The best rule for the control of others probably is that of the Golden Rule. In the long run, life reciprocates with those who do unto others, as they would have others do unto them. The power of the will which can compel one to be polite or gracious or considerate or patient or helpful or cheerful is sure to cast a large and agreeable spell upon one's fellows. We know that the Golden Rule is good policy, that we are not all selfish, that there is a divine reason in humanity which makes it sympathetic to sincerity and righteousness. Not a few people in high positions have unblemished manliness; some do, and a native fear of that outright honesty creates an attraction which is hard to resist. People, for instance, had great faith in Grant. They did not love him, but he had a manifest ability because that honest and that silent man seemed to be an actual person. Stephen A. Douglas with his culture and all the time's political machinery behind him was no match for Lincoln because Lincoln burned with unquenchable fire which blazed in the heart of the North. Douglas was a "Little Giant" against "Honest Abe" and here the will that years before had shaken its clenched fist at slavery rose to its grandeur and assumed the robe of a prophet and a deliverer.

196

Will Power

The indispensable will power that makes a person a leader by nature's choice, if thrown on the side of righteousness, not infrequently outlasts this bad and even treacherous life. The will and the steady purpose of Oliver Cromwell makes him even today, "Old Ironsides." And William Orange competed with subtlety and patience and pertinacity with Philip II and his was the lasting influence which that Spanish king could not destroy by the power of wealth or position or Church control. A strong man wishing the control of others should have a right motive.

It seems true not all such control is explainable. By plain methods, just what the secret is of the power which cowes the world and the wild beasts we do not know. What is it that bows the stubborn purpose of the would-be criminal inflamed by vengeance, whetted by the resolute and fearless gains of its victim? What is that we are told was able to turn a madman, who, when he came to kill Wellington and was asked by Wellington the purpose of his mission said: "I have been sent to slay you" and Wellington, looking him in the eye, said, "Well, how very odd!"

We do not know what the will is—we do know however that there is among us, all of us, people who have the power of what we used to call "their second wind." We have the story of the tightrope walker, a man who had successfully crossed on a tightrope the Niagara Falls and then advertised the fact that he would do this same feat again, but this time controlling a wheelbarrow. Before the specified day arrived, Blondin, for that is the man's name, was stricken with an attack of lumbago that made him wince even with the thought of any movement. And so intense was his will and his purpose, that he demanded that he be carried to the place where he would start the feat to show the people how powerless he was to complete it. But, seeing the wheelbarrow there, he arose from his bed of pain and, seizing its handles, he crossed the chasm with as great adroitness as he had ever done in all his days of health. Arriving at the other side, he turned about and retraced his steps but when he came to the end, and amid the thunderous applause of the audience, he found himself again crippled and unable to move. What was it that made him able to compete? It was his will.

And so with these eight different qualities of which we have spoken, perhaps we can say with John Quincy Adams, if someone asks us about our well-being, we can say, "Quite well, quite well." I wonder, though, if over the years that same will has been so manifest, that it can be said of us the story told by the man who, at the funeral of President Jackson, turned to Andrew Jackson's body servant and said, "Will the President go to heaven?" And the servant turned with surprise and answered, "I never thought of it, sir, but if the President wants to, he certainly will."

This is our story—this is what each of us, by calling upon our reserves, can do with our life and our service. It needs our will and our will-power!

OUR COUNTRY,
OUR WORLD

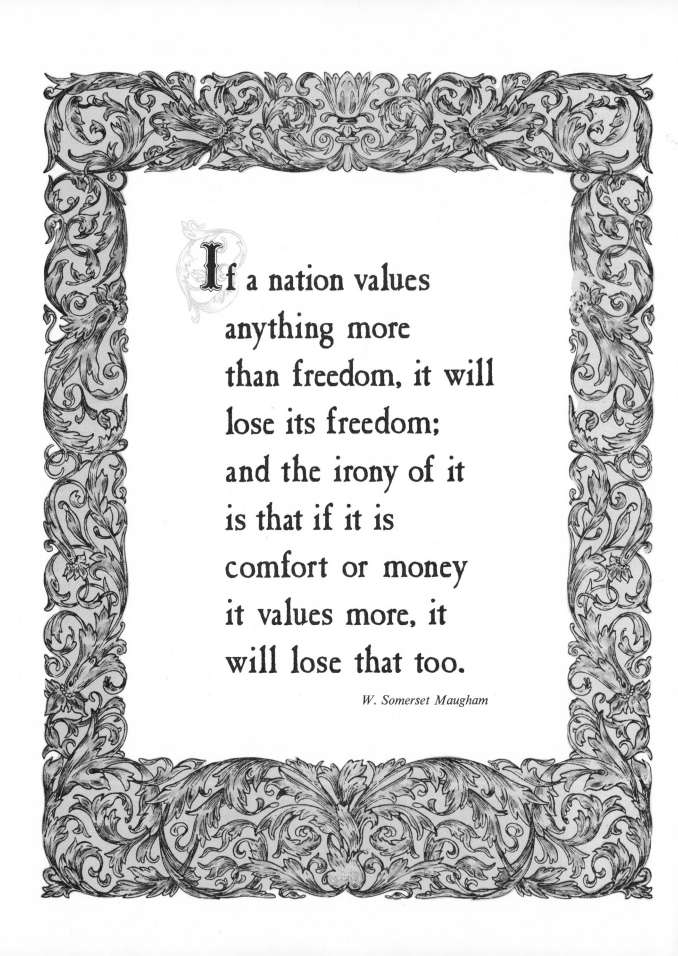

If a nation values
anything more
than freedom, it will
lose its freedom;
and the irony of it
is that if it is
comfort or money
it values more, it
will lose that too.

W. Somerset Maugham

"True it is that the forests have been felled and the raw plains are now thickly settled, but there are other frontiers that are just as demanding of our attention—these are the unexplored areas of sociology, medicine, law, psychology, government, science and personal identity."

Our pledge to America

America is unity in diversity—the heir of all the ages, of all lands, and of all peoples. Yet somehow it is itself unique, perhaps partly so because of its vast size, but even more so because of its heterogeneity, and its great religious diversity. When we speak of America, we do not think mainly of her farms, her factories, her laboratories, her schools, her homes and her workshops. We are thinking of her people, once like our ancestors, immigrants from many lands, now of one—Americans—people of hidden but deep loyalties, of groping and often unspoken love, a people that hold high many ideals but does not always fulfill them or even, it would seem at times, try to realize them, but a people who nevertheless know the right but, human-fashion, somehow ignorantly, sometimes wantonly or deliberately or through apathy and indifference, it betrays both its self and its faith; it does not fulfill its promises.

America is still a land of frontiers. True it is that the forests have been felled and the raw plains are now thickly settled and progressively alive and productive. But there are other frontiers that are just as demanding of our attention, and hopefully will be mastered just as vigorously and devotedly with the same zest and dedication as that shown by our pioneers of former days. These are the unexplored areas of sociology, medicine, law, psychology, government, science and personal identity. The axe and the rifle of the pioneer will yield to the test-tube and the computer and cyclotron of the student; the locale will shift to the classrooms and the laboratory of the workshops, and for us, who no longer work in either the classroom, or in the laboratory or the shop and office there is the challenge of the field of human interrelationships with the challenge to each of us, collectively and individually, to do something constructive about it, in it and in ourselves.

The great diversity of thought within our membership will of course generate many differences in matters of opinion and yet hopefully, may we maintain respect for one another; if only agreeing to disagree, still we can enjoy the conflict of opposing viewpoints. That should refresh and rejuvenate us. So here I speak only for myself.

If you recall, after the close of World Wars I and II, the great wave of enthusiasm voiced by all the great nations of the world, proclaimed that peace is now transcendent, now and forever more. You know how soon that dream faded. Why? Was not the outlawing of war forgotten because the people of the world, both as nations and as majorities in those nations were really not yet pledged to maintain such an ideal state of affairs? Do you not recall that very soon after these pronouncements, we began to hear such symptoms of neighborhood fear and such explosion of waves of nationalistic pride in some places that made even the advocacy of the universal brotherhood tantamount to treason to one's own land? Truly public policy seems to reflect private opinion.

No matter how altruistic may be the law, it will fail if it presumes a higher quality of character than actually exists in the persons who are expected to honor and obey it. Personal character is formed, not by man's mass hysteria but by the everyday living of the individual in the mass. Do we not agree that our personal character determines the quality not only of our personal but our common life, and that personal character in turn determines public policy?

Development of social usefulness is not a miracle, it is public policy and personal character interacting upon each other. Do we see any other source?

If we do so agree and we would have social advancement, the

202

building of a stronger individual character seems to be the answer. History tells that it is the character of the people rather than the size of the population that determines the existence of a nation and its success or its fall, no matter how sudden or delayed that fall might be.

A great disaster rarely destroys its people. England, we know, lost a third of her people in the Black Death, and yet her great cultural renaissance followed soon after. Germany in the Thirty Years War lost a half of her population and impoverished the remainder, but her culture still persisted. A hundred years ago, Finland suffered both war and famine but in spite of both, her culture persisted and grew progressively in quality and stature. We know from our history that Rome destroyed Carthage, but we know, too, that Carthage already was a decadent state which had forgotten to safeguard its national protection and heritage—the personal character of its people, both as individuals and as a nation.

Arthur Morgan, the famous founder of Antioch College and its unique program and later the head of the Tennessee Valley Authority, reminds us:

"Suppose atomic warfare! If 50,000,000 should be killed, the population would only be back to World War I. If 100,000,000 should be destroyed we should be back to about 1875, when the historian Turner wrote that America had reached the last frontier, and must now turn to intensive development. We should still be ahead of that period by the telephone, radio, electric power, electronics, highways and modern technology. The findings of biology, genetics and psychology would not be lost. A thousand libraries would remain. The scientific method would abide. Fields won from forests, and many engineering works, would survive. The population might be back to the present number in less than a century. However, if a breakdown should result, not from without but by a decay of character, decline might be as long-lasting as in ancient Egypt.

"If there is a time limit on the issue of the human adventure it probably will be set by men, and not by outward circumstance. Now, during crisis, is the time to learn crisis manners."

Many men now give but a minimum of their potential interest or activity to the thought of such a purposefulness; they seem to prefer to let life slip by with interest centered in trivial activities and unrewarding ways. The person however, who uses a portion of his leisure to the unselfish service of his fellowship finds in his puposefulness that he can influence and change existing circumstances for the better.

If the vast amount of energy, imagination, creativity, interest, prestige and money now invested in the mastery of the physical world could be diverted to the changing and the refining and the informing of men's purposes and incentives, there is the great likelihood that corresponding changes in the ethical and spiritual world, in human progress, and in man's inter-personal relationships and goals would develop—as striking as the scientific and technical advances of which we stand in awe.

"The mastery of both in a well-proportioned world requires and should be given dignity and loyalty." We should not consider repudiating the prevailing regard for the control of the physical world for that of character and purpose. What we need is not to belittle the one, but to give greatly increased emphasis to the development of man's character and purpose. In this conflict we should enroll now.

We must not fail to note the remarkable characteristics of mankind—not only his general uniformity, but also his capacity to regulate himself in ever-changing situations. For instance, the normal temperature of the human body is the same whether man lives in the tropics or the arctic. Whether the calendar shows it to be either summer or winter, man's chemical make-up is uniform in its salinity, both in its alkanoic acid, its calcium balance and in many other ways, varying constantly through environment and the intake of food. But just as great as these amazing uniformities is man's power of adaptation to his long-range purpose of survival and posterity.

While nature seems to be callous as to whether it causes pain or pleasure, man takes desirable experiences to be his chief aim. Every religion seeks for its believers experiences which are advantageous to them—keeping the present good in harmony with the hope of survival. Moreover, no matter how diverse man's religions or philosophic ideas may be, there is general acceptance of the belief that good and evil can be modified by human action.

204

Our Declaration of Independence is not a guarantee. It is merely the statement of an ideal; it is ours only as we defend it. Every day is July 4th, an Independence Day—or it should be. It is important for us to remember that our liberty depends upon our willingness to accept responsibility. Our duty—our obligation—is as far as in us lies the building of a society in which men are able to realize that ideal of free agency and individual liberties.

Jean Jacques Rousseau, French philosopher and theorist, 200 years ago gave the challenge: "As soon as public service ceases to be the chief business of citizens and they would rather serve with their money than with their persons, the state is not far from its fall."

We do not have to look long or hard to see evidence of moral decadence, increase in serious crime, increase in juvenile delinquency, increase in divorce, increase in welfare rolls, increase in civil disobedience. Yet we know these problems do not represent the real America—a decent and a self-respecting people, generous and law-observing. They represent a highly publicized percentage which needs our care and attention with the hope of prevention as well as of cure. But we must not be disheartened—they must be to us a challenge. Laws cannot solve the problems. Only people can.

There are many things that we can do. *First* we should become well acquainted with current affairs. We realize that there are those among us who feel that we can be of little value in helping to build a public policy, and, frankly, does not such a conviction of failure already defeat the achievement of a goal? There are those among us who from force of habit act without thinking and others among us who think without acting.

The answer apparently depends upon what type of persons we happen to be. If we are not concerned about what's going on in the world outside our own daily immediate range of interest, if we are bored at the idea of the average man or woman, such as you and I happen to be, being of national importance, if we couldn't care less about what's happening on Wall Street, in Washington, D.C., London, Moscow, or Peking, then there's not a thing we as individuals will do about it.

But if we want to be alive and are concerned about national and international affairs—if we are genuinely interested in what's going on in the other parts of the world, with other folks in other lands, if we recognize the big stakes we have in what is happening on Wall Street and in the capitals of the world and in the increases which we have noted, then here is our challenge:

To keep ourselves informed about significant national and international trends, form our own opinion, to be alert to the moves being made in the eventful political area, and to be watchful that those who represent us are sincere and forward-thinking, protectively and yet with wide-angled vision.

We are not suggesting that we be starry-eyed idealists. We want, as we view the political scene, to appreciate the practical aspects of politics —the job it has to do—the necessity of representation of local interests—races, faiths, groups, interests and regions.

Second, we can develop a concern for others whom we may help. Let us not be dismayed because we are only ordinary folk. Only actions give to life its strength. Carlyle reminds us that our *prime* business is not to see what lies dimly at a distance but to do what lies clearly at hand. Mahomet teaches: Every good act is charity. Your smiling on your brother's face is charity; an exhortation to your fellow-man to virtuous deeds is equal to alms giving; your putting the wanderer on the right road is charity; your removing stones and thorns and other obstructions from the road is charity; your giving water to the thirsty is charity. A man's true wealth hereafter is the good he does to his fellow-man. When he dies people will say, "What property has he left behind him?" But the angels will ask, "What good deeds has he sent before him?"

Third, be alert to the perpetuation of the free agency of man and the maintenance of liberty, freedom and the rights of the individual. Elect good and wise men to public office and learn for yourself their position on principles that you personally approve and desire to be defended and advanced.

The greatest glory we can have is to pass on, untarnished, our freedom to our children.

This is our call to service. We who are old, Herbert Hoover told us, can care for our heritage—"The practical thing," he said, "we can do if we really want to make the world over again, is to try out the word 'old' for a while. There are some 'old' things that made the country.

"There is the 'old' virtue of religious faith.

"There are the 'old' virtues of complete integrity, loyalty and truthfulness.

"There is the 'old' virtue of incorruptible service and honor in public office.

"There are the 'old' virtues of economy in government, of self-reliance, of thrift, and individual liberty.

"There are the 'old' virtues of patriotism, real love of country and willingness to sacrifice for it.

"These 'old' ideas are very inexpensive. They even would help win hot and cold wars. Some of these 'old' things are slipping badly in American life. And, if they slip too far, the light will go out of America, even if we win the hot and cold wars. Think about it."

As retired folk, we know, with the greater freedom of time allotted us, we can keep abreast of current affairs, and not only help our fellows needing us, but, as citizens, we can accept the challenge to go forth, not to do deeds of valor and endurance, but each of us, in our own walk of life, everywhere—at home, in church, in lodge, in AARP meetings, in shopping, traveling, working, playing, or idling, recognize and respect the values which we as Americans hold dear, and, as individuals, with faith we have in ourselves, in our country and our God, strive to transmit to our children our share of our country not only as great and as grand as it was when we received it but far greater and grander that it was transmitted to us. This could be our secret pledge to America and to ourselves.

"We must strive in all areas of life to strengthen American democracy and demonstrate its moral, its spiritual and its economic superiority over any regime."

Our duty,
our obligation,
our privilege

Riley Buchanan, in "Red Carpet in the White House" tells that when Khrushchev visited New York, many luncheons were held. Just before one of them began, the tension reached an unexpected climax. The national anthems of both countries were played, a standard procedure. But as the first notes of "The Star Spangled Banner" sounded somewhere in the vast gathering a little man started to sing.

People stared at him, amazed, but he went on singing in a reedy, quavering voice. Then, hesitantly, one or two others joined him, then more and more, until the great dining hall was filled with a roar of voices.

It was an astounding thing; the emotional impact was tremendous. All the frustration we had been feeling, all the love and pride we felt for our country, all the things we wanted to say and could not, found release and came crashing through in the words of the song. Some people had tears running down their faces, but everyone was singing.

The Russians looked thunderstruck, almost frightened.

In just such a fashion did America, as represented by that vast audience, bear testimony to the faith they have in America, the pride and love they bear her. And you will note that it needed but one of the people, fearlessly and alone, to "stand up and be counted" to give the momentum for the release of expression by the multitude of that same faith and love and pride.

We know sadly and only too well the faults and failings of America; daily we are forced to recognize and admit them, but, even so, she is the envy and the hope of untold millions of people in other lands. The hopeless, the hungry and the persecuted everywhere see in her Utopia. We, because she is ours by simple birthright, ours to treasure and develop, know her as a priceless heritage and one that we in our generation can help by realizing in actuality some of the ideals of her founding. We can help make the miracle come true, "One nation, under God, indivisible with liberty and justice for all."

But it is that man in the Khrushchev meeting, one of the people, and others like him, who rejoice in the extent to which the American dream has been realized in their own lives whom we must depend upon to resolve to make it come true for every American. It is the people, like ourselves, men of good will, who must make a united and a constructive effort toward the protection of our liberties.

It has become the fashion for many to consider that the source of our rights is the government. Nothing can be less true; it is people—like those at the Khrushchev meeting—that gained these rights *from* the government. To forget that—to ignore the obligation that we share to help build the America of our dreams is to ignore nearly a thousand years of the people's struggle and progress toward human dignity and freedom.

Let us not forget that a government can destroy rights. Our founding fathers knew that the primary threat to the natural rights of man has always been government. Woodrow Wilson once said, "The history of liberty is a history of the limitations of governmental power, not the increase of it. When we resist, therefore, the concentration of power, we are resisting the processes of death, because concentration of power always precedes the destruction of human liberties."

Always the fight for freedom has been waged by the people against their government. It is vitally essential that we realize that we can weaken our country through our individual placidity, our own inertia, our own lack of a sense of individual civic responsibility and obligation, our individual failure to vote at all elections, our personal inattention to the position taken by our state and national legislators on basic issues.

We take so easily for granted the liberties we enjoy. Let us not forget that the Bill of Rights, those ten original amendments to the Constitution added in 1791, is really a Bill of Prohibitions against our own government, stating specifically that the government must not destroy our rights. It begins: "Congress shall make no — — —." It continues, "The rights of the people shall not be violated." It concludes, "The powers not delegated . . . are reserved . . . to the people."

And, if we, the people, are indifferent in the promotion of the safety of our Republic and the strengthening of our democratic traditions for the greater welfare of all our citizens, we unconsciously create a public opinion that will be easily a cloak over the threatening infiltration of communism, fascism or naziism, and other forms of un-Americanism.

When John Adams was defending the American Revolution he referred to the Magna Carta as the fundamental source of our freedoms. This concession, forced from King John in the field of Runnymede in 1215 by his insurgent nobles, is the basis of our present system of trial by jury. "No free man shall be imprisoned . . . except by the legal judgment of his peers (equals);" and further, the Charter states the basis of our concept of "due process of law."

Our representative government came also to us as a part of our English heritage. King James and the Parliament had so restricted trade, had granted so many monopolies and exercised so much control over the commercial enterprises that endeavored to settle America that the directors of the London Company, to make their venture a financial success, approved free trade and competition to the operators and established a system of representative government for the eager colonists. Even the indentured servants were granted voting privileges in the first election held in America in the year 1619.

Even though King James later revoked the charter of the London Company, the Virginia House of Burgesses continued as before and became the model after which were fashioned similar legislative representative assemblies. You may recall it was in just such an assemblage that Patrick Henry made his historic declaration, "Give me Liberty or give me Death." This is another of our prized heritages.

When in 1620 the famed Mayflower Compact recorded the agreement of the Colonists to obey whatever "just and equal laws" that they might enact "to the glory of God," no direct mention was made of the freedom to worship as one's conscience dictated. Yet the consensus that motivated their coming to the strange and rugged land was that desire and purpose. It is still considered that the idea behind the Mayflower compact is the historical basis for our individual right to worship God as we will.

Although on the field of Runnymede in 1215 King John had granted the Knights the "Right of Habeas Corpus," King Charles ignored that legally promised privilege and had the practice of putting persons in prison without stating the alleged cause of their imprisonment, kept them there at his pleasure, and denied them both the granting of bail and the satisfaction of a trial. The House of Commons unanimously protected the violation of the pledge of trial by one's peers, and King Charles only reluctantly yielded to the pressure. And so, the Petition of Rights in 1628 was granted, specifically requiring the reason for the arrests, permitting freedom on bail to be followed promptly by a trial by due process of law. This right, abused today in some lands, insured England and later its colonies legal protection against arbitrary authority.

The Right of Freedom of Speech is American in origin and the product of the thinking and the enacting of the people themselves as to their chosen way of life. The Fundamentals Orders of Connecticut are often called "the first written constitution in America." They definitely state that their duly elected government had the "power to give liberty of speech." From that day to this, no matter whether or not this basic right was violated, the right still remains as one of America's basic inherent and natural rights.

Again we turn to England as our then mother country for the rights of the freedom of judges from replacement if their decision displeased authority and from indefiniteness of tenure. In the year 1688 England deposed her King and invited William of Orange and Mary Stuart, his wife, to share the throne. This change of sovereignty was the occasion of the Parliament's passing of the British Bill of Rights, a series of related documents. The first was the Declaration of Rights and later in 1701 the Act of Settlement. Together they outlawed the old doctrine of "the divine right of kings" and granted to the people the right of selecting judges "according to the law of the land" and their permanency in the tenure of that office.

The Right of the Accused to Counsel and Witnesses had its origin in America and its author was William Penn. The Pennsylvania Charter of Privileges is probably the most famous of the colonial constitutions. It provides for representative government, twice requires that "Liberty of Conscience" (freedom of religion) "shall be kept forever" and states further the right of all persons accused of a crime to know the testimony of the witnesses against him and granted them the "same Privileges of Witnesses and Council as their Prosecutors." Later these same rights were incorporated into the sixth amendment to the Constitution of the United States.

When the British governor of Virginia dissolved the House of Burgesses for "seditious" activities, the members reassembled in a tavern nearby and drew up the famous Virginia Bill of Rights. Among its provisions was the statement that "the freedom of the peers is one of the great bulwarks of liberty, and can never be restrained but by despotic governments." This is another of our fundamental rights, the wording of which was composed by a group consisting of Mason, Madison, Randolph, Jefferson and Patrick Henry. In it you will find much of the actual words of the Declaration of Independence and the Constitution of the United States.

In September of 1774, there was held in Philadelphia a delegate assembly from all the American colonies to decide among themselves the relationship they were willing to accept between themselves and the Mother Country. They "declared and resolved" that the "inhabitants of the English colonies in North America by the immutable laws of nature . . . have the following Rights." Among them were "life, liberty and property." Then they did the unprecedented thing; they resolved that these fundamental rights were theirs, not granted by the enactment

212

of Parliament but were based on natural law. This uniquely American concept of natural rights, found to be most objectionable by the British Parliament, made irrevocable the breach between Britain and the American colonies. The doctrine expressed in this Declaration of the First Continental Congress was the inspiration for the Declaration of Independence.

When years later in 1787, there was held another delegate assembly, again in Philadelphia, this time the representatives came from the thirteen sovereign American states "to form a more perfect union." There they announced the sole, the only, basis and purpose of government. "We the people . . . in order . . . to secure the blessings of liberty to ourselves and our posterity, do ordain . . . this Constitution."

Then they provided for a republican form of government, free and open discussion of national issues, freedom from tax discrimination, no test of a religious nature for holders of public office, three separate branches of the federal government with their limited powers and the system of "check and balance," provisions for the state governments and many other devices and ideas to protect the rights of the people from the possible domination of the government.

Remember the purpose they announced for themselves and their posterity. And we are that posterity.

These are our rights—the rights we enjoy today. It has taken 800 years to secure them one by one, and it is our duty and our privilege to treasure and protect them wholeheartedly—freedom of speech, freedom of assembly and freedom of religion. We must continue to strive for equal justice for all citizens without discrimination of race, color, national origin, faith or creed. We must strive in all areas of life to strengthen American democracy and demonstrate its moral, its spiritual and its economic superiority over any regime, whether it be communistic, fascist or nazi. This is our duty, our obligation, and our privilege.

*"We older folk, as long as life lasts, can tell the
story of America's gift to the world—the first declaration
of man's right to own property, his divinely given
individual freedom to life, liberty and the pursuit
of happiness, his relationship to his government
of which he is the creator, not the servant."*

We still measure
the strongest, vastest light
by candlepower

very one of us probably knows several folk who, in varying
degrees, are examplars of the three character traits of the
unusual man—Curiosity, Creativity, and Comprehensiveness.
　　But all of us know of Benjamin Franklin and his various
inventions of the rocking chair, the bifocal lens, the Franklin stove, of
his interest in his chosen craft of printing, and of his success as statesman, diplomat, and author. We know, too, the versatility of Thomas
Jefferson, his scholarship, his philosophical utterances, his zeal for
education, his sagacious foresight in the purchase of the Louisiana
Territory at three cents per acre, the many clever innovations in his
home at Monticello, and the adaptation of steel to the curved plow that
added materially in the breaking up of the virgin sod of the vast new
empire. But not so many realize that Thomas Paine, the impassioned
orator and patriot, the man who was chosen as spokesman for our liberties and the author of The Age of Reason, has also to his credit that

214

he drew the plans and supervised the construction of the first single-span iron bridge with crisscross struts.

Yet we are told that the average folk, like ourselves, expend in one lifetime only one-tenth of that which we are able to produce, to do, or to be. Only one-tenth of our potential is the output with which we are seemingly content. If that is a true assessment, it holds both an indictment and a challenge. Yet we know in our heart of hearts, when we recall those crises that we have faced in our life's experiences where every part of us was called into play to meet a threatened catastrophe, that we responded with vigor and spirit, with all our heart, with all our soul, and with all our mind, and even now in retrospect we are duly moved and supremely alive and alert.

We know, too, sometimes through the protracted illness of our loved ones—sometimes in the course of our work-a-day experiences—when those calls upon our reserves had become a matter of frequency, that we had gained new and wider dimensions for our efforts and larger scopes for our accomplishments. We know that with an influx of courage and a moral reason for our aid, we generated a strength that even to ourselves was impressive—a higher marshalling of our abilities, a firmer union of our skills and talents that made possible more creative and purposeful activities. And we have seen, too, how this increase of power and skill through the process of contagious enthusiasm affected others to go and do likewise.

Yet seemingly the *usual man* willingly accepts for his performance and production, dull and routine mediocrity instead of striving for excellence. And this in spite of his probable acceptance of certain proven phenomena in which we all believe—a range as wide as the universe itself.

No matter what the ideologies a people hold, they stand in respect in the presence of heroic valor and self-sacrifice.

No "leader" can put courage or meaning or moral standards into our lives. We do that ourselves by *choosing*.

To reach a port, sometimes we sail with the wind, sometimes against it, but to advance we must sail, not drift or lie at anchor.

We realize that it is not *knowing* but is *caring* that will relieve world tensions—else why Dachau when that nation had the finest scientists, the most profound philosophers, and theologians and the great and famous universities?

We often hear expressions of concern for America's future. But there are many Americas. Some are not worth serving; there are the Americas of privilege and of smugness, an America of lethargy and inequality, an America of discrimination, and an America of violence. But there are other Americas, too; of tolerance and generosity, of benevolence and understanding, of curiosity and creativity, an America of dynamism and access to opportunity—the America we finally hope to realize.

Is it not odd to note that society, or any organized group, can easily become an entity that readily permits itself to do, or have done in its name, acts for which any one of that society or group would find offensive to his own individual moral convictions? At those times it would seem that such a society or group ceases to regard people as persons, but only as means to an end. The reason given for their impersonal actions being that in this combination no single individual is being held responsible. You find examples of this sort of reaction everywhere, from the isolating of all older individuals into a group of so-called "Senior Citizens"—the formulating and enforcing of such all-inclusive, stupid regulations as are named "chronologically enforced retirement." The cruel, wanton disregard of individual differences where the school places all youngsters into grooves, from which, if they do not fit, they are ejected and, in proportion to the greatness of their need, are displaced and unserved. You see it, too, in the untold unhappinesses incident to the destruction of homes and social ties, without plans within the means of those displaced, in the enforcement of urban renewal projects. And again, in the ridiculous paradox of the Internal Revenue Service in the taxing of indigents on the one hand and the subsidizing of them on the other. Could the reason be that while society in itself is not wrong, that society often simply does not use the human mind in solving its problems. It does not develop human standards in dealing with human beings and human needs. It devises laws behind which it can hide—but it fails to evolve standards of human measurement by which it can equate its goals and purposes.

This process of depersonalization, so at variance with everything that we call the American tradition of respect for the individual, ignores the basic truth that what has made America great has been man's self-reliance, his personal feeling of liberty and of choice, and the conviction of individual independence. In these many ways the traditions of this heritage of ours are being seriously threatened. We find it in the passive willingness of people to accept of themselves and of others only second- and third-rate standards of behavior and performance.

We uncover apathy and indifference toward civic and associational leadership and responsibility. We note with deep regret the desire on the part of many not to become involved in unpleasant or controversial issues, to be content to be one of the mass—and anonymous. This evasion of personal responsibility is most noticeable in the witnessing of acts of violence and outrage, where no protest is made—no aid is offered. We observe it, too, in the parent's ignoring of his natural obligation to guide and direct the child's behavior. Rather than face stern realities at times, he substitutes the immediate and easy way of yielding and the desire to be loved, not necessarily respected or revered. So he fails his parental obligation to transmit to his offspring the true relationship between rights and responsibilities, between privilege and obligation.

The question now confronts us: How did it happen that so many have substituted, in their thinking, governmental dependence for self-faith and self-reliance, the need of security for a drive toward self-development, the protection of socialized benefits in place of the rewards for individual effort, the escape into anonymity instead of involvement in the unpleasant or the strange?

Can we, without protest, without effort, stand by and see America sold so short?

Should we not rather feel incumbent upon ourselves to

"Hold high the torch
We did not light the glow,
'Twas given us by other hands, you know
Ours is to keep it burning bright
Ours to pass on when we no longer

need the light."

In some regards, we seem to have already passed and missed the turning point that separates us from the adventures of individual independence to an organized control, direction, and security. You may truthfully ask: who are we to hope to stem such a tide, to help hold back the trends toward mediocrity and the exchange of escape from responsibility to a willingness to stand up and be counted? My answer is: we are part of those who stood by and, unmindful and without too violent a protest, did not realize that this could happen to us. We are now contrite; we want now to help. We must do our best and our bit.

I make no pretense that I am speaking for other than myself. I speak only what I myself know. Granted, that I want to see life meeting its current needs; I do not resent adaptations which try to meet those needs. I hope to continue to be flexible, to be adaptable. I want, at the same time, to hold fast to the old principles; to recognize the eternal verities; to respect the individual and to preserve for him his patent of nobility and his right of choice. And so I devoutly pray, as each of us sees the problem, that in our thinking we plan our purposes, the perspective that will have ultimate meaning so that we may build together, we hope, toward a future in which our children may live life wholly and well. I feel anything less would be moral surrender.

Do our people really realize the contribution America has made to the world? Do they really know its story—how our earliest settlements, both in New England and in Virginia, started as communal projects and nearly starved, would have been abandoned as tragic failures, until, in desperation they recognized the need of competitive enterprise without ignoring the necessity, at the same time, of caring for the social welfare of all? Do they realize that, though each man's burden was thus so doubled, failure and discouragement were converted into increased effort and/or correspondingly increased reward? Why? Because, with freedom from coercion, intelligence was put to work. There were no governmental controls to hold them back; no barriers of territorial controls to limit their venturing. They were free—and in the Declaration of Independence they told the world of their discovery; they stated that most revolutionary concept of all concepts—that a free will is the

God-given gift to every individual—that every man is his own master and can choose and follow the dictates of his own conscience. He is not the subject of the State. He is its master, its creator. The State exists to serve him—not be served by him.

At the time of the pronouncement of this invention—for such does the economist, Harry Grady Weaver, call it in his *Mainspring to Human Progress,* (Published by—The Foundation of Economic Freedom, Inc.) —at the time of its pronouncement, the people of our land were like people elsewhere in the Western World. Their limitations were similar —their resources no greater, their privations no different.

"When the American revolution had its beginning, living conditions had scarcely changed since the reign of Nebuchadnezzar. The colonial woman gathered her own firewood and cooked over an open fire, just as women had cooked since the dawn of history, and just as more than two-thirds of the women on earth are cooking today. She spun thread and wove coarse cloth with a spindle and loom handed down from the early Egyptians. Every housewife made her own soap and candles and carried water from a spring or well. A crude millstone, dating back to ancient Babylon, ground the grain that the American farmer cut and threshed with knives and flails that were older than history.

"These were the conditions existing when our forefathers threw off the shackles of Old World tyranny in order that human beings might be in control of their own lives and make full use of their individual initiative."

Within three generations America became the foremost country of the world with the proud record of its achievements. It had learned to exalt its facilities, to become involved in thoughts and in deeds that generate ever-higher motivations. No country has approximated it. And why did it happen? How did it happen? It happened because men put their intelligence to work! It happened because men believed in the search for excellence! It happened because man became *involved!* It happened because men did *not* seek security; they welcomed opportunity and they developed strength and power and vision to meet danger, hardship, and the unknown.

The people of the United States occupy only 6 per cent of the world's land area and represent less than 7 per cent of the world's population, yet they own:

85 per cent of the world's automobiles
60 per cent of the life insurance policies
54 per cent of the telephones
48 per cent of the radio sets
46 per cent of the electric power capacity
15 per cent of the world's railway mileage
30 per cent of the improved highways
92 per cent of the modern bathtubs

As salesmen for America, we can perhaps help our people to become more appreciative of what America has produced and to remind them that every moment is not a time for assessment, not a time for cessation. There is still an opportunity for greatness. There is always time for a call to keep alive the sense of a significant being, a need of being involved in thoughts that are ahead of what we already comprehend, a drive to be involved in deeds that will increase higher motivations, an essential to keep alive a sense of indebtedness to the authenticity of the American traditions of self-reliance, self-development, individual effort, and personal responsibility.

We realize that the America that is to be is being conceived in the minds and the visions of the young folk still in their schools. But we older folk, as long as life lasts, can tell the story of America's gift to the world—the first declaration of man's right to own property, his divinely given individual freedom to life, liberty, and the pursuit of happiness, and his relationship to his government of which he is the creator, not the servant.

Emerson reassures us, "We fancy others greater than ourselves because they light the divine spark given to them, and we do not. It is because we minimize ourselves that we do not accomplish. We do not realize the power of our positions!"

Then, too, we find solace in the scientific fact that even the strongest and the vastest of light is still measured by candlepower.

220

*"A forward strategy for America gives us
an approach to optimism, when it says
'America has the men and the tools wherewith
to fashion the instruments of victory.'"*

What *you* can do
for *your* country

o you recall how you thrilled at the President's statement in his inaugural when he said, "We are unwilling to witness or permit the slow undoing of those human rights to which this nation has always been committed and to which we are committed today. Let every nation know, whether it wish us well or ill, that we shall pay any price, bear any burden, meet any hardship, support any friend or oppose any enemy, in order to assure the survival and success of liberty." You felt the same sense of prideful dedication as did our forefathers in their founding of this nation. At the time of the inauguration, the need to rally to the support of our American principles might not then have seemed urgent, although it was just as real as now, but today the need is a compelling one we cannot ignore.

Perhaps we have been too quiescent, feeling secure in the conviction that the FBI was the shield and buckler against communistic aggression. But actually we learn to our dismay that the function of the FBI is that of "an *investigative* agency, not a *public information* agency. Its job is to gather evidence for court action. At times, the Director of the FBI, J. Edgar Hoover, releases public statements

221

WHAT YOU CAN DO FOR YOUR COUNTRY

about communist activity in the United States, but usually these statements do not attain the wide and detailed dissemination they deserve."

However the FBI is alert and much concerned at the apparent apathy and indifference of the general public to the danger of the insidious spread of communism. J. Edgar Hoover tells us: "It is indeed appalling that some members of society continue to deplore and criticize those who stress the communist danger. What these misguided 'authorities' fail to realize is that the Communist Party, U.S.A., is an integral part of international communism. As the worldwide menace becomes more powerful, the various Communist Parties assume a more dangerous and sinister role in the countries in which they are entrenched. Public indifference to this threat is tantamount to national suicide."

And again: "The defense of the cherished freedoms secured and handed down to us by our forefathers is the responsibility of each American. Knowledge of the enemy, alertness to the danger, and everyday patriotism are the brick and mortar with which we can build an impregnable fortress against communism. Only the intelligent efforts of all Americans can prevent the decay of public apathy from laying open our Nation to the Red menace."

Eugene Lyons, Senior Editor of the *Readers' Digest,* bears the same testimony as your editor of the awakening apprehension of his readers. He states, "The real enigma is why free men submit supinely to the subversion of their schools and their churches, subversion of their trade unions and their youth and their economy; why they allow the domination of some of their industries and waterfronts by the representatives of an alien totalitarian movement. There simply is no answer in logic for it. Even expediency, which might be brought forth as an explanation, is simply illogical. What is expedient in the short term is going to prove fatal in the long term."

"Khrushchev himself, you know, isn't young, and he's a little on the bloated and unhealthy-looking side, but he told a group of Americans in Moscow, when they discussed his questions, 'We are alive only a little while and I would like to see the Red flag flying over the whole world in my life time.' Well, don't dismiss that hope of his as

222

boastful rhetoric. He was referring to a consummation that he considers not only likely but inevitable. And look at the picture! Already one-third of the world is under that Red flag, and that figure doesn't begin to tell the story. The story isn't told by maps because, in addition, maps don't show the lines of Communist power reaching into every other non-Soviet nation. It doesn't show the enclaves of open or disguised Communist control inside every non-Communist nation. Above all, it doesn't show a type of incursion that can be measured statistically, and I am referring to the incursion of our minds and spirits—the extent to which the Communists, through these decades, have managed to reduce our self confidence, to corrode our courage, and to erode our moral stamina."

Again the question comes: Just what can we do, as citizens, to help? Perhaps the best thing we should do is to review our knowledge of just what are the National principles we prize as treasure, the eternal political verities once so dearly won and defended with bloody sacrifice.

Is it not a pity, for instance, that we in America award the Boy Scouts for "getting out the vote"? We are prone to hold so lightly the franchise toward which we are proudly helping the undeveloped nations of Africa.

When we have again informed ourselves, then we can share those convictions and that renewed dedication with our neighbors—those folks too in your community whom we now seek out, with the contagion of enthusiasm, to share our sense of dedication and service.

We quote further: "An informed public is the best defense against subversive propaganda. The premise of the American Way of Life is that everyone will be free to speak his or her opinion, and that in a free market place of ideas, the people as a whole will then choose among these opinions and come to a sound conclusion. This premise is based on the assumption that everyone will express a genuine and a responsible opinion. Unfortunately, the basic rule of Communists is to say *anything* that they think will help the ultimate aim of Communism, which is world domination. They do not sell Communism as such in the marketplace of ideas, because they have found that they *cannot* sell their ideas to any large number of people. So they must deceive, create issues, agitate, and suppress free expression where they can.

"When Communist propaganda is labeled for what it is, the public has a chance to decide whether the ideas expressed have a real validity, or are simply advanced to confuse matters for ulterior purposes. This is why it is so important for the public to keep abreast of the latest Communist 'line' and propaganda techniques.

"How does the idea of 'promoting harmony' fit into this concept?"

"Again a basic Communist technique is to agitate racial issues and create racial frictions. This is contrary to the American ideal, and an informed public can see these attempts for what they are."

A Forward Strategy for America gives us an approach to optimism, when it says "America has the men and the tools wherewith to fashion the instruments of victory. The question is not one of means or ideas or friends. Specifically, the question is asked whether the people of the United States can shake off that chronic apathy which seems to afflict all Western democracies when they think themselves at peace while, in fact, the aggressor moves stealthily to destroy them."

We are told that an essential part of Soviet education is the imparting of the Communistic theory as an idealistic sanction. Are the young people in our schools likewise versed in our interpretations of liberty? Is liberty, in the minds of youth, coupled with responsibility and obligation? What can we, as older people, with free hours and eager hearts, do to help the youth of the community to understand the bases of our national survival? Is there not a call also for youth to feel and to do? Youth, like age—like every one—needs to be needed, needs to stand high in folks' regard. Is there not here an opportunity for them to achieve under our direction? Let's not think of our service to youth only in terms of recreation and indulgence. Let's think of it in terms of challenge.

Think for instance the numerous opportunities offered the community in the observance of the holidays—

Lincoln's Birthday—February 22
Flag Day—June 14

224

Independence Day—July 4
Citizenship Day—September 17
Veterans Day—November 11

Why not begin to plan for a celebration on September 17 of those newly made citizens and the young people casting their first vote? Why not have youth take charge of that celebration? Think of all the preparation it could involve: The leading of youth to appreciate his heritage and awakening in him the urge to do something constructive about it.

Here is a skeleton of the activities you might develop in a community program. They are in your power to promote and to bring to a satisfying conclusion. Give youth the obligation of: alerting the clergy of the community, asking of them the privilege of youth's addressing the various congregations for announcements and invitations; preparing for insertion in the weekly church bulletin a reminder of the celebration and the necessity of participation; writing news-releases; radio 30 seconds and 60 seconds flashes—planning meaty and news-worthy programs and urging their acceptance by the stations; staffing the ceremony; having youth in person invite the civic dignitaries and the leading citizens of the community; planning music—drills and participating in them; securing flags perhaps from the United Nations. The details—and the jobs can be tailored and expanded to your needs so that *"everyone is the act."*

I am mindful of a tale of a group of followers of a great leader of China. Upon his departure they asked him to leave with them a message of inspiration and dedication. The leader paused awhile and then he said, "Oh, God, revitalize our China, but dear God, please, please, begin with me."

"In the Declaration of Independence, here in America, was born a new nation, a mosaic of people from every land and here they found their answer and here they evolved a slogan, E Pluribus Unum, 'Out of many, one.'"

Diversity has its values, too

The nations of Western Europe, unconsciously, in great part, are responsible for arousing the distressed peoples now eagerly seeking their independence. Through their appointive representatives, they presented to their colonized peoples a different culture with its comforts and amenities. They also discovered in their colonies an endless and economical reservoir of man-power in times of war.

When the drafted veterans returned from the wars to their native lands, they brought with them memories of strange and moving sights, and of wonderful death-dealing weapons with which they had been entrusted. They brought with them, also, the growing suspicion that the countries which they had been taught were invulnerable, were perhaps not so powerful, were not necessarily supreme. Convictions of their being always subordinate in status began to fade. Discontent set in; then rebellion. Nationalization was on the march. Within a decade, the map of Africa was changed.

Like Africa, Asia too is also aflame. Concurrent with this surging of new hopes and purpose is likewise in these lands a religious awakening. Buddhism and Mohammedanism are there aggressively militant. Cultures and religions both are being everywhere affected, and these changes concern us all.

Senator McGee of Wyoming, in a sensitive and penetrating report,

226

tells of his recent visit to the Congo. On being flown there by jet, he landed on one of the longest airstrips in the world and found himself welcomed by a group of naked Africans. They promptly and proudly pointed out to him nearby a massive structure, explaining that it housed a nuclear laboratory—vast reactors. The Senator saw in them a bridging of the thousand-year gap between the handtool and the spear and the atom with its potential for untold constructive usefulness or for utterly destructive oblivion.

Interested in the passionate fervor of one of his young receptionists, the Senator asked him the impetus for his inflammatory dedication. Amazed at such a question, the man answered that it was, of course, the precept of Thomas Jefferson. From Jefferson's declarations he learned that man's right to life, liberty and the pursuit of happiness was not a license issued by a state, not a favor granted by an overlord, but a God-given gift to man, man's divine right.

Seemingly, commented the Senator, America has taken so for granted its unique concept of liberty as a divine right, that it now considered it a natural benefit and as commonplace as the air we breathe—or our mother's love—America accepts and depends upon all of these, yes, but does not consciously hold them as an inspiring ideal in its everyday thinking.

Senator McGee summarized his impressions by saying that he had learned much in these emerging nations that America could profit by, that he had seen the germination of this seed which America had propagated and marveled that America could be so forgetfully unaware of its rudimentary share in this nearly-global upheaval.

The idea of democracy 300 years ago as a desirable form of government control would have been considered either a lunacy or a heresy, unreverent or impious. Democracy then was practised, unnoticed, only in the villages of the Old World. There it grew to full stature on its being imported to America which later announced to the world its great "invention."

In the Declaration of Independence, here in America, was born a new nation, a mosaic of people from every land—pioneers, some in search of freedom; some seeking the right to worship as they would, others eager for land ownership, for the right of assembly; and still others impelled simply to act, to think and to speak as they would. And here they found their answer, and here they evolved a slogan, "Out of many, one" and *E Pluribus Unum,* a concept of unity out of a diversity.

Such was the goal. But as the unifying aspect of the American concept became ever stronger, we began to recognize and extol the universality of the "Melting Pot." The concept of "many" grew dim, and faint. From those from near and far, from many diverse lands and cultures, there emerged the standardized American.

Regrettably, but gradually, the stereotype of the typical American emerged and its pattern has become nearly a form of intolerance. Restively we began to want everyone to be alike, not only in appearance and in behavior but to adopt other forms of our culture as well. We grew to discount the values of diversity in favor of those of unity—the stereotype. The pity of it is that we find the stereotype is not one being aimed at or picturing excellence. It seems to be one content with mediocrity. Hence, the person of studious type becomes an "egghead"—and the person of discriminating ethical standards is labeled a "square."

Not only have we wanted to put all America into the "Melting Pot" in our great generosity—we wanted unconsciously to share the values of life as we saw them—with all other people and all other lands. Years ago we used to call this the "American Century." Now we know that, no matter how many billions of American dollars we are pouring into other lands to "do them good," to help them acquire freedom as in the American way of life, we are in that very process finding ourselves not respected but actually feared and hated.

Our fault was that we did not realize that Liberty, far from being an eternal thing, is always identified with and related to a specific need and to the present situations. It can not be offered or shared on our terms, but only as those relevant to the people to be served and in the light of their particular culture and their deprivations as recognized by themselves.

Margaret Mead, the famous anthropologist, stresses that concept. For America intelligently to extend to the women of a certain part of

228

India the gift of an easier cooking device, she prepared a two-page list of specifications geared to their unique needs and customs. Preferably the stove should be a solar one, and on being finished, be no higher than two feet because the Indian woman always sits on the floor in the preparing of a meal. Then too, the stove's arrangements should take into account the recognition of the Indian's concept—a division of function between the right and the left hands. To the right hand is allocated all the clean duties; to the left, those considered unclean. Cooking is essentially a work for the right hand. Much less honorable a status is given to the midwife, who performs her duties with the left hand. The Indian housewife bathes before entering her kitchen and sees that her clothing is newly washed; indeed, Dr. Mead tells us often it is still wet. The midwife, however, does not wash even the left hand with which she performs her duties. So universal is this division of hand status followed, that when a stranger to the culture pats affectionately the arm of the babe hanging loose from its swathing, the mother, recognizing the kindly impulse that prompted the action, immediately protects the stranger from giving either further affront or evidence of his ignorance of the correct procedures; she withdraws the babe's left arm from such contact.

By the East Indian, we, who have made a cult of cleanliness, are adjudged as unclean, because we do not use a fresh twig for caring for our teeth, but a device of bristles made from animals, held to be themselves unclean, and we use the same device over and over again!

Even in lands, less foreign to us than the countries of the Orient, we find many differences that we should regard and respect; even trivial customs differ. In Germany, for instance, we note, in greeting, the custom of hand-shaking. We see the custom followed even among young lads; in many shops, on leaving you are escorted by your salesperson to the door and given a gracious farewell with the handshake as part of the ritual.

We, too, are often, by some act to which we are accustomed, thought strange and lacking. Much more often in Germany than among us, there is followed the thoughtful presentation of a flower; but the flower is often a single rose, sometimes as much as three—to give an even number, the act is considered to offend the standards of good taste.

Indeed, a friend of mine, while engaged in a governmental assignment in Israel, celebrated his 18th wedding anniversary; and in his effort to present his wife with a rose for every year of their wedded life, was met with the shocked consternation and disapproval of the florist who presumably thought such an act a regrettably ostentatious display.

I, myself, remember while being a guest, I expressed a wish to remember a friend who had done for me a thoughtful courtesy with a bouquet of a certain shade of flowers that I thought she would enjoy because it was the same as the decor she had followed in furnishing her home, only to be met with the horrified and incredulous query, had I never been taught the language of flowers?

One story of Dr. Mead's I remember with a surprised amusement. Talking to a group representing many cultures, she questioned the young man who had been detailed to see to her comfort, asking an estimate of Americans that might be there included. The young guide told her that he would soon have the answer. Upon being again questioned, he again said he could soon tell her. Then when the dessert was being served, he escorted her to a balcony overlooking the guests at dinner, and he explained that she could see for herself the answer, because he had arranged, in the serving of pie, that the wedge-shaped point would not be facing the diners, and he added the informative comment, "Only the Americans will turn the tip of the pie toward themselves."

In our relations with folk of other lands, we know ourselves to be kindly and benevolent, generous beyond any other country or people. But we know, too, that our benefactions have not always won us friends or even gratitude or decent courtesy. Often we have gained their suspicion of our motives, sometimes only a crude and demanding insistence, that, the donation of such and more—is our evident duty. We have been met frequently even with hostility and hate.

We wonder why; perhaps the reason is that we have sold them as our treasured concept the magnitude of things—not the glory of an idea— we gave wealth but not ourselves—we had not studied their unique needs that we might help them meet these needs themselves. We may

230

unconsciously have offended because we were using our scale of values, not theirs. The task for us now is still to help; but the challenge is how best to do it.

We know one does not buy friendship; only by perceptive sharing—by the act of giving, do we finally arrive at accord and good will.

If our national purpose is to help men to be free—and I sincerely believe it is—we must earnestly cultivate the skills that make our helpful endorsements of freedom really operational. We should courageously determine to proceed only on the firm basis of information and of considered concern; we should work out each commitment on the basis of individual knowledge of specific situations. Perhaps then their response to us may be different. That is at least our hope.

To do this is a feasible human enterprise well within the scope of our human ability. There are no inseparable barriers in the American human nature, no such rigidity in our values so established as to the value of things that could prevent such an achievement. So as we travel through life we should seek to learn, and learn to respect what constitutes for others, purposeful living. We, too, will grow in flexibility as we note the varied life patterns and values of other folk. I believe that we are on the way, and that this should be our commitment.

The privilege that is ours

he story is told that once upon a time the Emperor demanded of his wise men that, on the pain of death, first they tell the story of the world about them—a story that would be true that day and tomorrow and the day after, world without end; and, second that they phrase it in five words, no more, no less.

The scholars, the logicians, the poets—and the seers toiled hard and long, some in fear and trembling, others confident and assured. Finally they all agreed that this was the universal truth, and so on the prescribed day they unrolled before the Emperor the scroll, illuminated in scarlet and in gold, this legend:

"And this too will change!"

We, more than any other generation that ever lived, know how true this is.

All life, we know, is always in a state of flux. We are well advised today to keep the eyes open, the mind working and flexible, sensitive to changing conditions and especially *before* they change. And so it is amusing to note that the U.S. Commissioner of Patents in 1844 is quoted as predicting that the world at that time had arrived at that stage when human improvement was at an end, and yet not more than a century later William James, the psychologist, exulted "The greatest discovery of my generation is that human beings can alter their lives by altering their state of mind."

232

The members of our two associations, with the same sense of curiosity, and the same urge for comprehension, are eager to keep abreast of the change in our culture. They are restive intellectually. They are seeking opportunity not security, challenges not guarantees. They realize that to enjoy dignity and the rich essence of human living, they must themselves participate intellectually in the changing life of today.

They realize the thought expressed in Sullivan's Psalm against the Darkness:

"There are two majorities, son, though you ask me no questions. . . . The nameless dead, the unborn legions of time—but we are the thin minority, the living who hold God's spectre of light."

A great responsibility that is—when we realize the awesomeness of the opportunity to do God's will, if we choose, to further His plan of peace on earth and good will to men.

At a preliminary conference to the White House Conference on Aging, this comment was made:

It cost Julius Caesar $50 to kill an enemy; it cost Napoleon $5,000 to kill an enemy; it now costs the United States of America in a projected, God-forbid nuclear war $200,000 to kill one person in the enemy camp."

Public opinion has sensed the vital relationship between war and peace. Perhaps the most important need for us is to recover a dynamic faith in the American institutions we are trying to preserve. As a defensive warfare does not bring victory, so a defensive attitude about the goals of America will not bring peace. We must avoid negative attitudes. We must orient ourselves toward positive and fundamental principles.

In that delightful musical comedy, "South Pacific," the comment is made: "I know what you are *against*; what are you *for*?"

We know that we are *against* war. Are we *for peace?* peace and democracy? How can we help gain that peace? How can we renew in our thinking the bases of democratic government? how clarify its principles? how strengthen our faith in the individual and enlarge his opportunities for freedom?

How can we help abandon the sins that have made us weak and

recover the courage that has made us heroic?

To do so, is not the work of the statesman alone, nor of the experts or the specialists. Their contributions are important, but far more essential to the peace of our land are the thoughts and the hopes of the plain people like ourselves, who have made America—men and women with common sense, shrewd judgment and ambitions for themselves and even brighter ones for their children, folks who have not lost their sensitiveness to the concepts of justice and human dignity, persons of moral insight and spiritual stamina.

Democracy is founded upon two fundamental beliefs: (1) that reason governs mankind. As Justice Oliver Wendell Holmes phrased it: "The ultimate good desired is . . . reached by free trade in ideas. . . . That, at any rate is the theory of the Constitution." Ultimately men will do the reasonable thing after deliberation. Edmund Burke, our defender before the English Parliament, at the time of the Stamp Act, summed up the democratic process: "He that wrestles with us strengthens our nerves and sharpens our skill."

The second belief, equally fundamental, is the spiritual worth of the individual. Walt Whitman defines it: "In the center of all, and object of all, stands the Human Being, toward whose heroic and spiritual evolution poems and everything directly or indirectly tend, Old World or New."

We all grant that the essence of democracy is the individual, morally, intellectually, spiritually—living his life with a maximum of freedom and a minimum of restraint.

Do we sometimes sense a loss of faith in the individual, "the only moral being in the universe"? Only as we accept the deep-rooted faith in the individual is democracy possible. Freedom and morals are exclusively the possessions of the individuals. They are not attributes of the state. Muirhead, an Englishman of older days, notes this quality possessed by Americans; he calls it "an almost childlike confidence in human ability and fearlessness of both the present and the future, a wider realization of human brotherhood than has yet existed, a greater theoretical willingness to judge by the individual rather than by the class, a breezy indifference to authority and a positive predilection for

234

innovation, a marked alertness of mind and a manifold variety of interest . . . But below and behind and beyond all of its weakness and evils, there is the grand fact of a noble national theory, founded on reason and conscience."

As Woodrow Wilson said, "The history of Liberty is the history of the limitations of governmental power, not the increase of it. We must resist, therefore, the process of death, because concentration of power is what always precedes the destruction of human liberties." This is what Jefferson had in mind when he said: "Every government degenerates when trusted to the rulers of the people alone. The people alone are the only safe depositions."

We who are old know that it is not things that win men's hearts. It is ideals—the vision of a better world—that invites heartbeat.

The issue is clearly before us. Do we or do we not believe in the dignity of the individual?

We, all of us, cherish for America a body of ideals, practices and values; even when we do not achieve them, we never surrender the dream—never entertain the thought that the quest should be abandoned. "It is better," said Confucius, "to light one small candle than to curse the darkness."

We cannot be content with being for peace and for the survival of our society. We must each do something to prove his pride in his inheritance.

Everything we have of a social nature which has become the accepted part of our life today has grown through just social contributions by folks sharing viewpoints and working with others in the pursuit of goals: the church, the state, the schools, the libraries, the programs for health, citizenship—associations like our own.

J. Wallace Sterling, President of Stanford University, at the school's 1962 Commencement made a remark as a summation of American ideals: "Our government is our creature; it is ours to control. It does what it does by our majority consent. It has no dollars or home of its own except what we provide and permit. When it assumes responsibilities for national defense and the maintenance of law and order, it is acting for us. It extends its provision for public health, for education, for social security, it does so with our approval and with our dollars."

"Any invasion, government legally makes upon our purse, property or person, it does with the warrant we have given it. If you are, indeed, genuinely concerned with the enjoyment and expression of your individualism, I hope you will examine with scrupulous care any warrant that you may give to government. Once given, it is difficult to recover. And, on the chance that your sense of individualism is, in part at least, prompted and nourished by compassion for others less privileged than you, may I commend you for your compassion and, at the same time, ask that you not allow it to make you inattentive to the privilege which helps to make compassion possible."

"Geographic distances, the differences in spoken languages,
the commonly held stereotypes of other lands and peoples,
the love and pride of nationality, the jealous and
suspicious fear of that which is foreign:
these are the hurdles when we think of global peace."

To achieve world peace

What are the obstacles that deter us from attaining our goal of world peace?" The answer seems to me that the deterrents are the same enemies that retard advance everywhere. They are ignorance, fear, injustice and misunderstanding. These evils can be found here at our doorstep as they can be found elsewhere even at the ends of the earth. The geographic distance between good and evil is small; from your home, by the payment of a token fee, the local tramway will take you to an area overrun with the same enemies —conflict, tension, injustice, misunderstanding, fear and often hate. Then when you begin to feel that all is hopeless and the task overwhelming, you recall Milton's saying in *Paradise Lost* and are cheered: "Since good, the more communicated, the more abundant grows." And Whitehead's words: "Each tragedy is the disclosure of an ideal: what might have been and was not, *what can be."*

That is the consolation. In some places small victories are being won; and in the spirit of striving, not to conquer but to redeem, many persons of good will are striving to their utmost to develop here in America common understandings, common concepts, common ideas and common ideals. As Robert Hutchins says, "The chance of success is slight. We take the chance or die."

President Kennedy in commenting on the political education of the

237

American citizen said, "His opinion, his votes and his efforts define the limits of our policy, provide its guideposts and authorize its implementation." And he continued, "Public opinion in a democracy has, on many occasions in this nation and others, been too slow, too selfish, too shortsighted, too provincial, too rigid, too impractical, we as a nation cannot, we dare not—exclude the people or ignore their opinions."

Lincoln, too, noted that the average citizen "makes statutes possible or impossible to execute."

Are not those opinions that are hostile to the attainment of world peace the same as those attitudes we often deplore? Can they not be classified as:

(1) An amused disdain for intellectual effort as typified by the contemptuous epithet of "egghead"?

(2) A distorted sense of proportion exemplified by comparison of funds spent voluntarily on gambling and cosmetics with those voted for the support of and the furthering of education?

(3) A cynical disregard for politics as a profession?

(4) Values placed on economic success of the learned as the standard of high achievement rather than the giving of leadership and the sharing of guidance?

(5) Stereotypes that confuse political idealism with rigidity of thinking, that regard compromise or concession to the conditions of an evolving world as treason and disloyalty?

(6) Labeling of other nations as good, bad, progressive or backward?

(7) Confusions between true economy and the financial support of national security?

Are these not some of the hurdles at home which only patience and the truth may help remove?

Just what we, as mature folks, can do about these domestic challenges rests upon the conscience of each of us. As individuals we are asked today, wherever we are, and as we are, to do whatever we can to advance the cause of peace, first in our own selves and in our immediate environment, to help generate a climate—perhaps a way of life—where the very thought of war, racial violence and conflict will be outmoded, not only in our thinking but in that of our neighbors and friends.

238

Internationally, too, we are challenged to help bring about for our children and our children's children, the age-old dream of a world peace by building with every people a strong bridge of mutual respect and understanding, and undergirding it through the friendly interchange of ideas and traditions and ideals. The Association of Retired Persons International is just such a movement, providing, as it does, a forum for the thinking of older folk the world around and maintaining a showcase for their talents and achievements. It is a world-wide, nonprofit, nongovernmental organization of older persons with the aims and functions of dignifying the years of maturity and challenging older persons to continue to grow and to serve.

Geographic distances, even with travel shrinking them as to quicker availability, the difference in spoken languages, the commonly held stereotypes of other lands and peoples, the love and pride of nationality, the jealous and suspicious fear of that which is foreign to the accepted and the known, various and varying religious values and standards: these are the hurdles when we think of global peace.

The problems that such a world-wide movement hopes to solve are many. The obstacles here are the same as those in our own land: misconceptions and lack of understanding, added to the lack of appreciation of certain phenomena found in the actions of the United States and not paralleled elsewhere, but regrettably held as convictions by many nations throughout the world. Reports state them as:

(1) Lack of appreciation of the basis for the advancement of foreign aid to countries to which the United States owes no financial obligation.

(2) The nations awarded foreign aid from the United States have the perfect right to expect financial aid without any obligation whatever.

(3) The belief that foreign aid is extended solely as a means of buying military advantages.

(4) The United States is responsible for the problems of the world, having created them.

(5) Since the United States is the richest of nations, it is automatically responsible for the poorer ones.

(6) The conviction that the United States is more interested in maintaining nuclear superiority than in the attainment of world peace.

(7) The utter lack of understanding or of appreciation of the influence of the electorate upon the elected, based on the belief that the government of the United States can do as it wishes or what seems expedient for it at any given situation.

Even the most ardent of optimists do not believe that we can succeed in obliterating passion and self-interest or the desire for power and prestige. But they do believe that these barriers and roadblocks are due to the lack of vision and understanding and that, if we can at long last dispel these myths that cloud people's minds, we can, in the words of President Eisenhower, "raise a strong enough chorus of good will, so that governments around the world must listen"; and, "to the will of the people even the most arbitrary of tyrants must yield."

President Johnson, too, pleads that we as individual citizens promote friendship among citizens of every land so that we can come to understand each other and respect each other and want peace. He knows of no other task more important for the people of every country.

Here is our challenge. Never have the nations of the world had so much to lose or so much to gain. "World peace, like community peace, does not require each man to love his neighbor; it requires only that they live together in mutual tolerance, submitting their dispute to a just and peaceful settlement."

General Eisenhower described the movement as follows: "The People to People program should make it possible for the peoples of the earth, the poorest and the richest, the weakest and the strongest, to dedicate all their resources, all their intelligence, to improving man's lot on earth spiritually, intellectually and materially. So doing we shall help the world's people to achieve mutual understanding based on truth proudly and fully exposed."

The job is a monumental one—is it not worth doing? It calls on each of us to help—with all our might and main. As we repeat the Lord's Prayer, we say, "Thy will be done." Do we realize that only we are His means of realizing that will? That we are committed to the task and must strive for its realization?

240

OUR RICH
HERITAGE

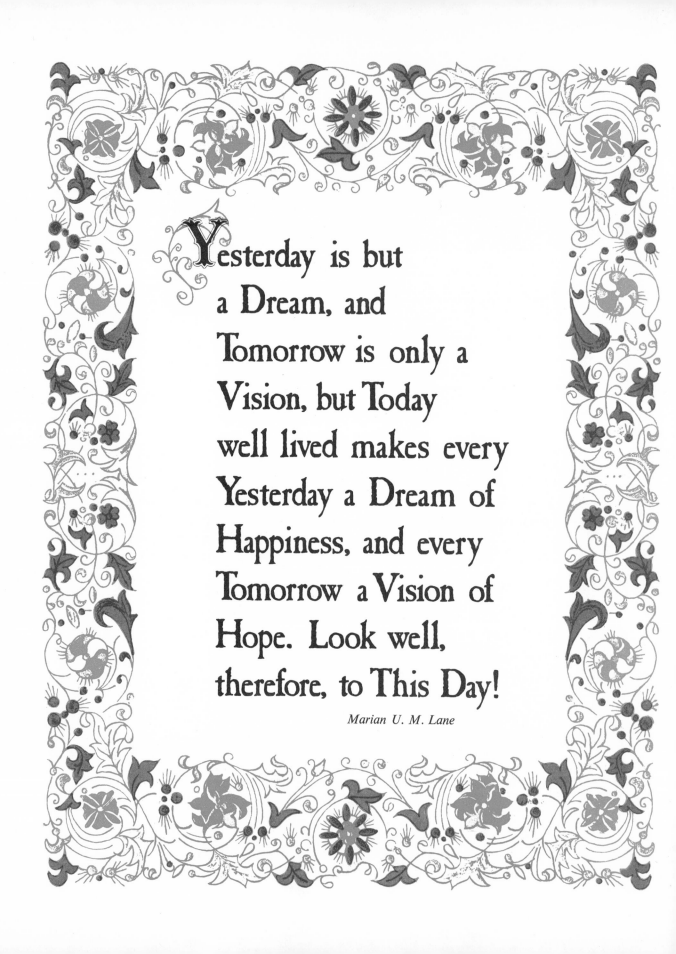

Yesterday is but
a Dream, and
Tomorrow is only a
Vision, but Today
well lived makes every
Yesterday a Dream of
Happiness, and every
Tomorrow a Vision of
Hope. Look well,
therefore, to This Day!

Marian U. M. Lane

*"For the holiday season, here is the picturesque
background of the names of our days and months. It
is a story on ancient days, universal and international
in scope, giving us glimpses of the dynamic activities
of people to whom we are linguistic heirs and of whose
existence we are perhaps unmindful or unaware."*

A New Year's greeting

It's interesting to note how wonderful and how complex are even the simplest things that we normally take for granted. We say, for instance, Anno Domini, the year of our Lord 1964 or 1,964 years after the birth of Christ; yet now the experts tell us that Dionysius Exiguus, the monk who was responsible for the suggestion of so naming the years, made a mistake in his calculation, and the probable birthdate was some four to six years earlier.

However we shall continue to say with the businessmen all over the world A.D. 1964, although some folks in China may call this year 4959. The Jews religiously name it 5724; the Moslems compute it to be 1382, and the Ethiopians mention the date as 1972.

A calendar strangely like the one we use today was evolved by Thoth, an Egyptian mathematician and astronomer who lived about 5000 years ago, and was considered by some to be a god.

From centuries of watching, the priests of the temples could predict the exact time when Sirius, the brightest of the fixed stars, would rise above the horizon. They knew the number to be 365½ days. So accurate was their computation that in five years they were less than an hour incorrect in their estimates.

The history of the calendar is a long and varied one. There are the obvious two recurring cycles in nature, the cycle of the sun and seasons and the cycle of the moon is indicated computing by them, but difficult, for these cycles just won't easily harmonize. The solar year is 365 days 5 hours 48 minutes and 46 seconds long. The moon passes through its phases in about 29½ days, makes the lunar year 354 days 8 hours and 48 minutes long. The Egyptians began with the sun and so devised their calendar.

In the most primitive form the Roman calendar was divided into 10 months of unequal length; March, 31; April, 29; May, 31; June, 29; Quintilis, 31; Sextilis, 29; September, 29; October, 31; November, 29; and December, 29. To fill out the year a blank number of days were added. Later January with 29 days and February with 28 days were added. Often there were found, in a four-year cycle, four days too many. What was worse, the high priest, Pontifex Maximus, was given the power to regulate the calendar and the practice grew of using these extra days for political ends to lengthen or to shorten an official's term of office.

By the time of Julius Caesar the calendar was so abused that January was falling in the autumn. By his authority as Pontifex Maximus, with the advice of the Alexandrian mathematician and astronomer, Sosigenes, Julius Caesar revised the calendar, making the year to consist of 365 days, with 366 days every fourth year. He commenced the year also on January first. Had the solar year consisted of 365 and 6 hours, the Julian calendar would have been perfect, but over the next fifteen centuries, it had deranged the calendar ten days.

Pope Gregory III decreed that the year A.D. 1582 would consist of 365 days only and otherwise adjusted the calendar. Roman Catholic countries at once adopted the reform. Protestant states one after another followed the example, whilst the Russian and Greek Church conserved the old Julian arrangements. When the new style was adopted in England by Act of Parliament in 1752, eleven days were struck out, October 4 being called October 14, 1752. Benjamin

Franklin commented upon the relief for those who loved their ease they would go to bed on the fifth and awake 10 days later. He said it mattered naught to him.

To prevent further derangement the Gregorian plan provided that only one in four of the years ending centuries shall be leap years; thus the years 1700, 1800, and 1900 were not leap years, nor will be the year 2000.

As one reviews the history, one can easily see why the old Roman year beginning in March, that September would be called the seventh month as its name signifies; and October, the eighth; November, the ninth; and December, the tenth. In the revising of the calendar into twelve months, the significance of this nomenclature was ignored.

January, made by Julius Caesar the first month, was named in honor of Janus, guardian deity of gates and doors, the guardian of the past and the foreseer of the future. On his festival, the first of January, the Romans, observing an annual festival, exchanged good wishes with one another. It also became the accepted date of important official beginnings. (Today we use the derivative of this word *janus* in our word *janitor,* the gateguarder.)

February to us recalls the groundhog's day, the second, when—
"Half the coal and half the hay
Must still be left on St. Michaelmas Day."

It also recalls to us that jolly St. Valentine and the birth dates of our great leaders, Washington and Lincoln. In Roman times, The Ides of February (the 15th) was observed as a time of expiation and atonement, presided over by the goddess, Juno. Once upon a time February was the last month of the year but even then the Ides of Februarius were always celebrated as a feast of purification.

March, named *Martius Mensis,* in honor of the god *Mars,* marks the season of the approach of good weather when martial campaigns could again profitably be under way. Mars, the reported father of Romulus and Remus, the founders of Rome, was worshipped in three capacities, as war god, as a rustic divinity, and as guardian and protector of the state. Sacred to him were the wolf, the dog, the raven, the horse, the woodpecker, and the crowing cock. His great festival took place the first three weeks of this month, but we remember the Ides of March because of the warning Caesar heard and brushed aside on that fateful day of his assassination. You may recall that early in Roman history March was the beginning of the calendar year.

April, the month of spring and the opening of flowers, is named for the goddess of love, Venus. Some say its derivation comes from the Latin word *"aperiere"* which means to open, but others state that the name probably comes from aphros, the sea foam, from which Venus Aphrodite is pictured as rising in all her astounding and be-witching beauty.

May, with us a feminine designation, is in this instance the deus maius (magnus, great; maior, greater), named for Jupiter himself, the great god, and the time chosen for his presentation was that con-sidered to be in the prime of the year, its very heyday.

By the way, this same derivation gives us such words as widely varied as *majority, major, magistrate,* and *master.* And oddly enough, from the opposite *minus* comes *minority* and *minister,* the servant of the Lord.

The poet Longfellow prefers the legend that the month is named for Maia, the daughter of Atlas, the world-bearer, and the mother of Hercules by Jupiter.

June, our month of brides, the Romans dedicated to the great family of Junius, of which the patriot Junius Brutus was a member, immortalized by Shakespeare, the very same whom Dante in his *Inferno* consigned to the lowest round of hell not because he had been a murderer but because he had betrayed a beloved friend.

The month of *July* is also tied in our thinking with Marc Anthony, for it is he, who after the death of Caesar, had the month, the fifth month, Quintilis, changed to Julius to honor his friend and patron Julius Caesar.

In the renaming of the next month from *Sextilis* to *Augustus,* we meet a friend from one of Shakespeare's dramas, another Julius Caesar, nephew and adopted son, Octavius, the first of the Roman Emperors. Legend has it that to keep the month honoring him as great in the number of days as that honoring his illustrious adopted father, he took a day from February, leaving it 28 days and making August a month of 31 days.

The remaining months repeat the older names not revised when the calendar was remodeled.

The names of the days of the week are also interesting, first, because the very word *day* originally meant just the hours of sunlight, the span of 24 hours being called *night*.

But perhaps the most revealing fact in recalling the naming of the days of the week is that of its high antiquity. In Sweden, the very same planets and godheads are recognized for the same day in both the lands of the North and in the valleys of India, the Aryan homeland. For instance, if the day in Sweden is Sunday honoring the sun, the same in India is also Aditwar, the day of the sun.

Monday memorializes the moon.

Tuesday, the Teutonic god of war and athletic activities. Tiu (often called tyr) whose name, through the variations of Grimm's sound change has a common percentage with the Latin word *deus* for god and the Greek for Zeus, the sky father. In Latin countries Tuesday was named *martius dies* the day of Mars, we have an echo of this in our Mardi Gras, literally *fat Tuesday,* Shrove Tuesday, the day of feasting before the beginning of Lent.

Wednesday recalls Wodin, the greatest of gods of Norse mythology, the god of war, wisdom, poetry, prophecy, and magic. He kept in touch with the lower world by means of his ravens whom he sent out every day to tell him what was going on in the world of men.

Thursday recalls Thor, the torch bearer, the hammer thrower, a god who brought good luck and whose images were carved on doors, houses, and ships for that reason. With his red beard (symbolic of the lightning) flaming in the wind, he drove to battle in a goat-drawn chariot. His hammer, like a boomerang, returned to his hand after being thrown.

Friday, however, is named for Freya, the goddess of love and the art of healing. She was entitled to receive the souls of half the heroes who fell in battle, the other half going to Wodin. Her name gives us the treasured word "free'—a word of loving and of being beloved.

247

Only such said our forebears are really free.

Saturday carries with it the Latin name of Saturn, the god of fertility, and the builder of that mythical "golden age," of which men told to the hearer's wonder and delight. It was the Chaldeans, we are told, who refined the days into 24 hours and the hours into 60 minutes and the minutes into 60 seconds, but it was probably Moses to whom we must say our thanks for the persistence of a seven day week instead of Thoth's 10 day. However, the decimal system has attractions. Even as late as 1795 a determined effort was made during the French Revolution to resurrect Thoth's ten-day week plan, but the people resisted partly due to the inertia of habit and partly because the work span of nine days was found to be too exhausting; so after twelve years of revolutionary effort the six-day work week and the Sabbath became the accepted method of time measurement even in the turbulent France of that day.

Our word history can open to us intriguing vistas for further study and adventure. It is in truth an exciting racial biography, portraying customs and creeds of forgotten times, bringing to light the creative endeavors of the great ones of past peoples and civilizations, and recalling to us, vividly the vast and thrilling experiences that have gone into the formulating of our language which still is in the process of ever evolving word-study and can be a most rewarding enterprise.

*"The secret of our power over ourselves, over
heredity, over environment, lies in our own viewpoint,
in our choosing that which is active, that which is
intelligent, that which is individual, that which
is a law unto itself and therefore is free."*

Cherished communications
across the centuries

efore the Western Civilization, as we like to call it, had
learned to write there was a vast and varied oral literature. This was in part proverbs compressed into witty or
wise capsules, easily to be stored in memory or take the
form of direct preachments or as illustrative parables. All were focused
on the safeguarding or improving conditions for the younger folk to
come after them. Whatever life had taught the oldster in man's continuing battle against evil in some form or other for manhood, for
honor, integrity or patience; whatever life had taught him as
techniques to be needed or dangers to be shunned, these lessons he passed on, sometime in rhyme, often in fable.

With a people like the early Persians whose lives were a struggle
in a land of great extremes of climate, that counted as affluence
the possession of an ox and a cow and a shepherd dog as an essential
asset and a helper, custodian and friend; this training from a creature
of the wilds became so imperative a needed taming and training
technique, that the instruction comes from Ahura Mazda, the Divine
One, himself.

The Zoroastrian religion and its literary treasures fell victim to the invader, Alexander of Macedon, but some of its proverbs and some of its preachments we can still enjoy. Some tell us the important place the dog holds in that society, but they also give us pleasant and not-so-pleasant glimpses of life as it was then lived.

"Whoever shall smite either a shepherd's dog, or a house dog, or a trained dog, his soul, when passing to the other world, shall fly howling louder and more sorely grieved than the sheep in the lofty forest where the wolf ranges." (Vd. XIII:8)

> (Then follows praise for every kind of dog, and the punishment for every hurt inflicted upon any of them.)

"O Maker of the material world, if a man gives bad food to a shepherd's dog, of what sin does he make himself guilty?" "He makes himself guilty of the same guilt as though he had served bad food to a master of the house of the first rank." (Vd. XIII:20)

"The dog, I, Ahura Mazda, have made self-clothed and self-shod; watchful and wakeful, sharp-toothed; born to take his food from man, and to watch over man's goods. I have made him strong of body against the evil-doer. And whoever shall awake at his voice, neither shall the thief nor the wolf carry anything from his house without being warned." (Vd. XIII:39-40)

Unfortunately the faith of these Persian folk with their early acceptance of a monotheistic god is still practiced now only by the Parsen (Persians) in India and is one of the faiths with a dwindling following. Its preachment is still challenging, "On three excellent things be ever intent; good thoughts, good words and good deeds."

Universal thoughts in their broadest sense we find stressed in nearly all the living faiths—peace, charity, brotherhood, justice, truth, wisdom, love and loyalty. There are, too, various basic concepts to which some faiths object—such as monasticism, definitely tabooed by Mohammed.

Buddha's list of Ten Perfection's paint, in part, a different picture:

1. *Giving*—without reserve as a full jar overflowing keeps back nothing.

2. *Duty*—your duty you will pursue with the same zeal as the yak-cow which would rather suffer death than have her tail come to injury.
3. *Renunciation*—as a man in prison suffers awaiting ultimate release—so man looks upon his life here on earth and waits release from it.
4. *Insight*—you will get by questioning all, the wise and the great also.
5. *Courage*—you will hold fast to each of your individual existences.
6. *Patience*—you will exercise, if you accept alike with indifference both rebuffs and favors.
7. *Truth*—will find you as firmly fixed as the Star of Healing in the Heavens which does swerve not from its affixed time and path.
8. *Resolution*—shall abide in you even as the stone fountain, firmly built, does not quail before the tempest.
9. *Lovingkindness*—you will show to friend and foe alike, just as water quenches the thirst of both good and bad regardless of their nature.
10. *Serenity*—you may attain if you will feel and display it always in meeting what may come of either joy or sorrow.

These are the essentials of making wisdom perfect. There are no others. Buddhism, a religion of introspection, of renunciation and compassion is essentially an elaboration of these fundamental teachings.

The sayings of Confucius are profound in a different fashion. Upon his being asked: "Is there one word that sums up the basis of all good conduct?" And he replied, "Is not 'reciprocity' that word? What you yourself do not desire, do not put before others."

Confucius was asked, "What say you are the essentials of good government?" He answered, "The ruler should esteem the five excellences and avoid the four evils. The five excellences are: plentitude without extravagance; taxation without exciting discontent; desire without covetousness; dignity without haughtiness; majesty without fierceness. The four evils to be avoided are: without instruction in the law, to inflict punishment—that is tyranny; without proper warning to expect perfect adherence—that is oppression; late in giving orders and expecting early obedience—that is robbery; to tax and to spend in a stingy manner—that is a misuse of government function."

The greatest of the Rabbis, Hillel, repeats for us in the Sayings of Judaism this profound nearly universal preachment, "Do not unto others that which is hateful to you. This is the whole of the law; all the rest is commentary."

Among the Maxims from The Sayings of the Fathers are these treasures:

67a. Seven traits mark the wise man and seven, the foolish: The wise man does not speak before his superior in wisdom; he does not interrupt his friend's speech; he is not hasty to answer; he questions to the point and answers to the point; he speaks on first things first and on the last, last; regarding that which he does not understand he says, "I do not understand it"; and he always acknowledges the truth. The foolish have the opposite traits.

69a. There are four characters among men: He who says, "What is mine is mine and what is yours is yours"—his is a neutral character. (Some say this is the character of the men of Sodom.) He who says, "What is mine is yours, and what is yours is mine"—he is a boor. He who says, "What is mine is yours and what is yours is yours" —he is a saint. And he who says, "What is mine is mine and what is yours is mine"—he is a wicked man.

72a. There are four types of students: the sponge, the funnel, the strainer and the sieve. The sponge, which soaks up everything; the funnel, which takes in at one end and lets out at the other; the strainer which permits the wine to pass out and retains the lees; and the sieve which separates the bran from the fine flour.

We are born into this world with clenched fists, we leave it with fingers apart—preaching the lesson that you take nothing with you.

The Parables, background of the New Testament, are a part of our great cultural background as well as for many of us a part of our religion's tradition. There are some so apt and so lucid that we remember not only the Parable but even its very wording. Always a comparison, the Parables emphasize the preachment by its vivid illustration. Their number is a matter of debate. Some place it in the fifties, others in the thirties, but who among us do not know the story of The Good Samaritan? And the lawyer, who wishing to justify his doubt, asked, "And who is my neighbor?"

The angry brother of the Prodigal Son for whom the father had killed the fatted calf saw life in its broader aspect when his father said to him, "Son, you are ever with me and all that I have is yours. But it was fitting that we should make merry and be glad for your brother was dead and is alive again, was lost and is found."

And who among us do not recall the joy of recovering the lost sheep, who had strayed away from the ninety and nine, that safely lay in the shadow of the fold?

Such simple stories, so simply told, so close to the heart of all mankind. And the mustard seed which is the least of all seeds but can grow a plant so stalwart that the birds of the air can lodge in the branches.

And the House That Was Built On Sand, and the winds blew and beat upon that house and it fell, and great was the fall thereof.

And the Story of the Pounds and the Talents—and the verdict on the wicked and slothful servant who hid the one talent entrusted to him. "Take the talent away from him and give it to him who has ten. For to every one who has it shall be given and he shall have abundance, but from him who has not it shall be taken away from which he has."

The Parable of the Sower whose seeds when they fell on good ground brought forth fruit, some a hundred fold, some sixty fold, some thirty fold, but when he sowed by the wayside the birds came and devoured them and when he sowed among the thorns the thorns choked them. And the other parable of The Tares and the Wheat tells the same story.

Many of the others you will be disappointed not to have recalled; they may be favorites of yours. So that you may find them easily, here they are listed with gospel chapter and verse:

Wedding Guest (Matt 9:14-18) (Mark 2:18-20) (Luke 5:33-35);

New Patches for Old Tears (Matt 9:16) (Mark 2:21) (Luke 9:16); Children in the Bazaars (Matt 11:16-19) (Luke 7:31-35); The Leaven (Matt 13:33) (Luke 8:20-22); Hidden Treasure (Matt 13:44); Pearl of Great Price (Matt 13:45-46); The Dragnet (Matt 13:47-48); New and Old Treasures (Matt 13:51-52); The Unjust Steward (Matt 18:23-35); Laborers in the Vineyard (Matt 20:1-16); The Test of Deeds (Matt 21: 28-32); The Unfaithful Tenants (Matt 21:33-45) (Mark 12:1-11) (Luke 20:9-18); The Marriage of the King's Son (Matt 22:2-14); The Ten Virgins (Matt 25:1-13); The Last Judgment (Matt 25:31-46); Those Who Need the Physician (Mark 2:15-17); The Two Debtors (Luke 7:36-50); Friends at Midnight (Luke 11:5-13); The Rich Fool (Luke 12: 16-21); The Barren Fig Tree (Luke 13:6-9); The King's Rash Warfare (Luke 14:31-33); The Lost Coin (Luke 15:8-10); The Rich Man and Lazarus (Luke 16:19-31); The Unjust Judge (Luke 18:2-8); Two Men Who Prayed (Luke 18:10-14).

The secret of our power over ourself, over heredity, over environment, lies in our own viewpoint, in our choosing that which is active, that which is intelligent, that which is individual, that which is a law unto itself and therefore is free.

A legend from the Raja Yoga tells this same story: A great God-sage, travelling everywhere, found a man who had been meditating until an ant-hill had been built up around his body. The man begged the sage to ask God to give him his ultimate freedom. Further on the traveler saw another man who was dancing and singing, and who begged him to ask the same boon. Later, the sage, returning, met the first petitioner, to whom he brought the message from heaven: "The Lord told me that you would attain freedom in four more births." And then the man began to mourn. But the sage met the second petitioner, to whom he said: "I have to tell you that as many leaves as there are on that Tamarind tree, so many times you will be born, and then you will attain your freedom." And the second man shouted: "I will have freedom after so short a time!" But a voice came, "My child, you will have freedom this minute."

Our mother tongue

The little twins were talking together with animation and gestures. "What are they saying?" I asked, for I could not identify the language they were using. To my utter amazement I was told, "Oh, that's their own invention. They've lived so long away from where there were other children, and their parents are migrant workers; so for their own private intercourse, the twins talk to one another in the language they have themselves developed; while here at school, we're trying to teach them English."

Language is an amazing example of an answer to the social need to communicate with others. Language is thus in a continuing state of development, borrowing words from other tongues and cultures, and is therefore both imaginative and inventive as well as imitative and adaptive, in English the borrowed word taking on a phonetic form peculiar to the English language. We are told that there are at least 3,000 other major tongues and dialects spoken somewhere in the world today.

A most interesting hobby would be the study of our language. There are many theories, among the most intriguing of which is that advanced by the German philologists, Johann Jacob and Wilhelm Grimm. You and I know them as tellers of fairy tales, but the fairy tales they told were not publicized for the pleasure of children but to report the folk lore they discovered in the European and Asian language they had studied. In these delightful tales are told the stories probably repeated about the family hearth where Sanskrit was the spoken tongue. From them we learned the English language is closely connected with Dutch and Frisian, more remotely with German, more remotely still with Latin, Greek, Welsh and Russian, and very remotely with Sanskrit and Iranian. Noting the relationship of forms like the English *brother,* the Dutch *broeder,* the German *bruder,* the old Saxon *brothar,* the Lithuanian *broter,* the Greek *phretsa,* the Roman *frater,* the Irish *brothair* and the Sanskrit *barathar* gives a hint of the relationships by which such a pronouncement has been made.

English, however, prevalent in the United States, Canada, Australia and New Zealand and in much of South Africa is probably the native tongue of more people with the exception of the North Chinese. It is also used as an auxiliary language.

The origin of the English language lies in the emigration of certain groups to England with the consequent breaking down of communication between them and their continental relatives in Europe. The Angles and the Saxons invaded England in the fifth century, bringing with them their spoken language. Here begins the history alike of England and the English language. As you know they named their tongue and the people Engles—the Angles of Angilian. Then 1066, when the Norsemen conquest brought in foreign rulers, the English language was eclipsed by the French as the official language. When English again came to be the language of the upper classes, in about 1450, the tongue spoken was the dialect of London, the capital.

Like other languages, English has changed greatly, albeit so imperceptibly that an Englishman of 1500 would not be able to understand the Englishman of 500 nor the Englishman of today.

Many of our common words came from our Anglo-Saxon forebears, such as home, hearth, father, mother, brother, sister, good, shower; from the Scandinavian settlers we have such words as egg, knife and take; from the Norman Conquest with French as the language of the Court, we acquired such words as judge, jury, tort, assault, and such words denoting rank, as duke, baron, parliament; indirectly classical in origin. The later direct influence in the classical languages came with the Renaissance and has continued even till today, when it is the chief source of naming new inventions, such as the telephone (*tele*—Greek for afar off), bicycle, etc.

There are many interesting examples of how Americans living on a frontier adopted words to adjust to their new environment. The Colonists of early days invented such words as alewife, basswood, clearing and chickadee. Likewise the later frontier of the west gave us adobe, alcalde, canyon, arroyo, mañana. Still later they developed colloquial terms such as crowbait (a sickly horse), on the anxious seat, and bandwagon. When these frontiersmen borrowed a word existent in another language they often adjusted it to their use, and sometimes it became a word with a different meaning, such as succotash, bayou, calaboose, bass and prairie. Under the pressure of necessity they combined words to denote their meaning, so we have selectman, mass meeting, alarmist, lightning rod, windfall, drugstore, office holder, cross town, haul, ground hog and legislate.

Adjustment such as this often changes the meanings of words common to both British and American folk. American coal-oil and bills become in England parofin and bank notes, a dry goods store becomes a draper's shop, then a shoulder of the road becomes beside a verge; crackers become biscuits, a business suit, a lounge suit, and a sidewalk, a foot path. You may know of many others.

Every American belongs to one speech minority or another, but these differences do not seriously hamper us from communicating with one another. No matter how one pronounces a *calf* or a *vase,* we can still recognize the calf or the vase. In America alone there is a country where one can travel 3,000 miles without encountering serious difficulty in oral communication.

It's fun to see how many words shine with a brighter brilliance when we know their history. Even the study of Greek or Latin prefixes adds to one's appreciation. Take for instance such as we all know:

> *a* (meaning not) as in amoral, atypical
> *bene* (good) in benefactor, benefit
> *con* (with) contribute, convention
> *circus*—curriculum, circular, circumference

de (down) degrade, depression
eu (well) eulogy, eugenics
fac (make) facsimile, factory
geron (old man) gerontology, geriatrics
hemi (half) hemisphere
hydro (water) hydroelectricity, hydrogen
intra (within) introduction, introspective
jus (justice) justice, jury, jurisprudence
kinema (motion) kinetics, kinescope
logos (word) philology, philogistics
manus (hand) manuscript, manufacture
non (not) nonpartisan, nonessential
ora (speak or pray) oratory, oratorical
poena (punishment) penal, penology
quo (where) quotient, quandry
re (again) refill, renew
scope (see) telescope, microscope
uno (one) uniform, universal
verbum (word) verbal, verbatim
x (eks, letter chi) X, initial letter of Greek word *Christ*
zest (piece of orange peel) to add pungency to drink

By and large our calendar tells us much of the diversity of our tongue. Monday and Sunday is the same in thought and derivation in the German language. Tuesday, Wednesday, Thursday and Friday, and their variants in German, lead us back to the days when our Teutonic ancestors worshipped the gods they had created to represent for them their ideals of beauty, the godhead, war and love. The names of our months remind us both of our linguistic Roman heritage and also of the change over the years in the calendar. The two-faced Janus commemorates the god of gates, bridges, beginnings, he who looks both forward and backward. February dates the celebrations of that time; March honors the God of War; April the fourth month of the Gregorian calendar; May for the Roman goddess Maia and a time of blooming; June for Juno, Queen of Heaven in Roman mythology;

July immortalizes the great Julius Caesar and August, his nephew and successor. All the other months are numbers, September the 7th month to December, the 10th, since in the earlier days the calendar counted March as the first month of the year.

It's fun to note how our tongue has grown.

Then there are many interesting stories behind many words. These are a few; you can find many.

A-1 (the very best) Comes from Lloyds of London's rating of ships and shipping for insurance. Letters were used to rate ships; numbers to rate cargo. A-1—excellent.

abracadabra—a cabalistic word used by Assyrians in naming the supreme God and later as a charm to be worn about the neck.

```
a b r a c a d a b r a
  b r a c a d a b r r
    r a c a d a b r b
      a c a d a b r a
        c a d a b r d
          a d a b r a
            d a b r c
              a b r a
                b r r
                  r b
                    a
```

Acre—once a field, but later determined in the reign of Edward I to be that portion of land a team of oxen could plow in one day— 4840 square yards.

Alcohol is oddly "eye paint," a black powder so named and so used by the Egyptians and later by the Arabs as a paint for the eyelids. The Arabs called it *al kohl*. The extract that was withdrawn by a charcoal fibre came to be given the name.

Alimony comes from the Latin word meaning nourishment *alimania*.

Amen, the last word in the Bible is the Hebrew word *truly*. When we use it, we attest to our sincerity in the belief stated.

April Fool—New Year's Day in France fell so often in Holy Week, up to 1564, that when it, New Year's Day, was changed to January 1st, people often called out the former greeting and so were called "April Fools."

Bachelor was a soldier who was not rich enough to go to war under his own banner; hence the word meant "of inferior rank." In academic work, it meant one lower in rank than a doctor.

Bankrupt was an Italian money-lender who was required to place the money he wished to loan on a bench—*banca*—and when he was no longer able to offer money, his bench was broken, *banca rotta*.

Bell, book and candle alludes to a ceremony of excommunication introduced into the Catholic Church in the 8th century. After reading the sentence, a bell was rung, the Book was closed and a candle extinguished.

Benefit of Clergy was the privilege of exemption from bail by a secular court if accused of a felony. Later the other persons were extended this same freedom, if the accused could read the first verse of the 51st Psalm—called because of this "the neck verse."

Budget comes from the French word for bag. When the Chancellor of the Exchequer presented the papers on the financial situation of England to Parliament, he brought them in a leather portfolio or bag, which he placed on the table before him. Then he literally "opened the budget."

Carte Blanche, literally "white card" or white paper, refers to the custom of signing a blank paper for the trusted subordinate to fill in the details above the signature. It is a "white paper" because of the absence of any writing upon it.

Corn was the word used to describe any small object, even salt. Hence we have the expression "corned beef." When the time came to differentiate the cereal, the word was transferred to the prevailing type of grain in the locality. Hence corn in England refers to wheat; in Ireland and Scotland to oats, and in America to maize.

There are hundreds of others. Perhaps, if you are interested, we can at times tell you the genealogy of other words or phrases that have an interesting heritage; words like eavesdropper, leisure, saunter.

260

*"Let's take time this blessed day to give thanks for the
things we take for granted, for freedom, for security,
for life, for the opportunity to work and plan for peace and
a happier, safer life for our country and our children."*

November offers
many challenges

he month November, meaning ninth because of its Roman
heritage with the year starting in March, directs our attention to many causes that would help enable us to build a
world characterized by justice and peace and human well-
being.

Despite the poet's description of its bleak and blustering nature:

"No warmth, no cheerfulness, no healthful ease,
No comfortable feel in any member—
No shade, no shine, no butterflies, no bees;
No fruits, no flowers, no leaves, no bride—November!"

its thirty days bring to us days of remembrance of loved ones gone
before, days of election where the leader is chosen, days of celebration of victories thought won, days of thanksgiving—happiness and the
enjoyment of living—of faith and inner calm, of courage and confidence and achievement, days of love and family life and hope for
the future.

All Saints' Day

The month begins in an auspicious way. The first day—All Saints'

261

Day in many lands—is the great memorial day in which the living in many Christian lands turn back for guidance and inspiration to the men and women who, though gone forever, are still ever anew teaching through our love for them how to live and how to die. On this day we feel ourselves truly the heirs of the ages. Then we keenly feel our linkage with the past.

Like many other religious holy days, All Saints' Day is ushered in by a folk festival of fun and frolic. All Halloween Eve is the time when witches walk abroad and the future is supposed to be forecast, when in one's youth can one learn the secret of who is to be one's love; it is the time, too, when "the goblins will ketch you if you don't watch out."

Election Day

Then comes the third of November, the day of privilege to choose, to instruct and to empower those of our choice to act for us as we would have them act.

This, sad to confess, is the day when the Boy Scout urges his older neighbors to be sure to exercise their right of suffrage—to remind those who are eligible to be participating members of the commonwealth, to remind them of a duty which millions of men and women in other parts of the world are giving their lives to win—and we pray, having won, will continue to treasure and to use.

In the presidential election of 1900, however, 75 per cent of the electorate voted. In 1944, only 55 per cent voted. In the 1946 Congressional election only 30 per cent cast a ballot.

When you consider this figure of a 30 per cent vote for Congressional posts, we can infer that a majority of as little as one over the 15 per cent of the eligible voters could select the spokesmen whom we have elected to guide the nation. Thus, 85 per cent of the people were being governed by leaders chosen by 15 per cent. Now this 15 per cent can certainly be justified in supposing that democracy is not the real pride and achievement of our people, and yet we know that this is not the truth.

However, we know, too, the truth in this case of the old French

262

expression, "The absent are always wrong."

Nevertheless, we know that this country of 180 million people, which criticizes itself and is criticized around the world, for 17 years, really for more than that, for almost 20 years, has been the great means of defending first the world against the Nazi threat, and since then against the Communist threat. If it were not for us, the Communists would be dominant in the world today, and because of us, the free world is in a strong position. That is a pretty good record for a country with 6% of the world's population, which is very reluctant to take on these burdens.

On this day of November we are privileged to exercise our freedom of choice, the obligation of every eligible citizen to register his convictions on matters of public policy, so helping share in the realization of making the American dream a reality. Our concerted action on this day is vital and meaningful.

Election Days grant us as persons the right to help establish that climate of opinion that we, the people, want our land to hold and be guided by. It is the day when we choose representatives to serve us, not officials to manipulate us or rule over us. It is the time when we, the people, in each hamlet, town, or city, can determine whether or not, in every type of elective office from that of sheriff and mayor, from assessor to legislator, or from school trustee to national administrator, the man or woman we choose is a fitting officer pledged to respect and observe the American tradition of freedom and justice.

Woodrow Wilson emphasized the role that we must play:

"When I look back on the processes of history, when I survey the genesis of America, I see this written over every page: that the nations are renewed from the bottom, not from the top; that the genius which springs up from the ranks of unknown men is the genius which renews the youth and energy of the people. Everything I know about history, every bit of experience and observation that has contributed to my thought, has confirmed me to the conviction that the real wisdom of human life is compounded out of the experiences of ordinary men. The utility, the vitality, the fruitage of life does not come from the top to the bottom; it comes, like the natural growth of a great

263

tree, from the soil, up through the trunk into the branches to the foliage and the fruit. The great struggling unknown masses of the men who are at the base of everything are the dynamic force that is lifting the levels of society. A nation is as great, and only as great, as her rank and file . . ."

Armistice Day

Who among us can ever forget the eleventh hour of the eleventh day of the eleventh month and what it meant in our own personal lives—and how its promise has been dissipated until today the Armistice Day that was to have ended all wars for all time*s* has now become Veterans' Day in commemoration of those who gave their lives in the cause hoping their dream of peace might be realized?

On this day we must ponder the warning of General Omar Bradley, Chief of Staff of the United States Army, given in his address in Boston on November 10, 1948:

"With the monstrous weapons man already has, humanity is in danger of being trapped in this world by its moral adolescents. Our knowledge of science has clearly outstripped our capacity to control it. We have many men of science, but too few men of God. We have grasped the mystery of the atom and rejected the Sermon on the Mount. Man is stumbling blindly through a spiritual darkness while toying with the precarious secrets of life and death.

"The world has achieved brilliance without wisdom, power without conscience. Ours is a world of nuclear giants and ethical infants. We know more about war than we know about peace, more about killing than we know about living. This is our twentieth century's claim to distinction and to progress."

Soon after the atomic bombs had wrought their havoc on Nagasaki and Hiroshima, Einstein reviewed our situation:

"The time has come now, when man must give up war. It is no longer rational to solve international problems by resorting to war. Now that an atomic bomb, such as the bombs exploded at Hiroshima and Nagasaki, can destroy a city, kill all the people in a city, a small city, the size of Minneapolis, say, we can see that we *must* now make

264

use of man's powers of reason, in order to settle disputes between nations."

And years later, while research and development of biological and chemical warfare were being pushed forward not only in our land, Einstein, two days before his death, joined with other scientists in the plea for peace:

"There lies before us, if we choose, continual progress in happiness, knowledge, and wisdom. Shall we, instead, choose death, because we cannot forget our quarrels? We appeal, as human beings, to human beings: Remember your humanity, and forget the rest. If you can do so, the way lies open to a new Paradise; if you cannot, there lies before you the risk of universal death."

The problem faces each and every one of us—how can we build the climate where peace may survive.

Know Your America Week

"Know Your America Week" is now an established institution thirteen years old. Presidents of the United States, governors of states and mayors of many cities have annually so proclaimed the week that includes Thanksgiving Day, realizing that democracy's surest safeguard is the devotion of citizens to their heritage of freedom.

In promoting the impressive observance of this week, you may meet apathy, indifference and even the conviction that one individual's count doesn't matter. That attitude is one of a parasite living upon and enjoying the largess of the land but not making any contribution toward it; such indifference is basic to the failure of tens of thousands of eligible voters either to cast their ballot on Election Day, or to avoid if possible serving on a jury. Yet, if you would be a free citizen of a republic and not a helpless subject of an all-powerful state, in no other way can you be a participating partner in our great national enterprise.

Thanksgiving Day

This one day is uniquely American. It is ours. As *The Pendulum* tells us, "This is one day when all we Americans who are not self-made

265

go back to the old home to eat saleratus biscuits and marvel how much nearer to the porch the old pump looks than it used . . . Thanksgiving Day is the one day purely American."

Whittier, too, paints a similar picture of an earlier day:

> *"Ah! on Thanksgiving day, when from East and from West,*
> *From North and South, come the pilgrim and guest,*
> *When the gray-haired New Englander sees round his board*
> *The old broken links of affection restored,*
> *When the care-wearied man seeks his mother once more,*
> *And the worn matron smiles where the girl smiled before.*
> *What moistens the lips and what brightens the eye?*
> *What calls back the past, like the rich pumpkin pie?"*

Sometimes in the joy of family reunion and the pleasant gaiety of the festive dinner the Thanksgiving part is often ignored; not so was it in the older days, for no matter how grand were the preparations for the feast, plans were made for attendance at one's service of thanksgiving.

Let's take time this blessed day to give thanks for the things we take for granted, for freedom, for security, for life, the opportunity to work and plan for peace and a happier, safer life for all.

Abraham Lincoln voiced this need both of gratitude to God and of concerning ourselves with the welfare of others:

"We have been the recipients of the choicest bounties of heaven; we have been preserved these many years in peace and prosperity; we have grown in numbers, wealth and power as no other nation has ever grown.

"But we have forgotten God. We have forgotten the gracious hand which preserved us in peace and multiplied and enriched and strengthened us, and we have vainly imagined, in the deceitfulness of our hearts, that all these things were produced by some superior wisdom and virtue of our own.

"Intoxicated with unbroken success, we have become too self-sufficient to feel the necessity of redeeming and preserving grace, too proud to pray to the God that made us."

Fittingly the last day of our month is the first of *Hanukkah,* the

266

season of joy and of thanksgiving in the Jewish calendar. Celebrated more in the home than in the synagogue, it memorializes the victory of the Maccabees over the Syrian tyrant, Antiochus.

Antiochus had captured the Jewish temple in Jerusalem and converted it into an edifice for his own gods, defiling among the sacred objects the oil used in the religious sacraments. The charming legend told us in *The Talmud* relates how the Jews upon overthrowing their enemies found only enough oil undefiled to burn in the Temple lamp for one night, but miraculously the same amount was renewed for eight days until more could be had.

Hanukkah, which means dedication, recalls to the Jews the rededication of the temple. During the eight days of the festival the *Hanukkah* lights are lighted on the *Hanukkah menorah,* the eight-armed candelabra, to celebrate the miracle, an additonal one for each of the eight evenings of the ceremony.

Usually, the *Hanukkah* comes later, nearer to our Christmas, but come when it may, it, like the Christian Christmas, celebrates the victory of God and carries with it messages of peace among men of good will.

So ends happily this month, and may we end this recital of its special days with this parable left us by Dr. Lyman Abbott:

"I picked an acorn from the ground, and held it to my ear, and this is what it said to me, 'By and by the birds will come and build their nests in me. By and by the cattle will rest under my shade. By and by I will furnish warmth for the home in the pleasant fire. By and by I will be shelter from the storm to those who have come under my roof. By and by I will be strong ribs of the great vessel, and the tempest will beat against me in vain, while I carry men across the sea.' 'Oh, foolish little acorn,' said I, 'wilt thou do all this?' And the acorn replied, 'Yes, God and I.' "

"Winston Churchill — he was us as we would like to know us. We enjoyed him."

He enlightened our minds and stirred our hearts

he flag opposite my window this morning was as usual flying high, whipped by a brisk wind, and then, as I watched, it slowly descended until it rested at half mast. In such a dramatic fashion the world about me learned that the noblest Englishman of the century—a man wholly English, half Amreican, one of the irreplaceable men of all time—has gone from among us. America and men and women who love liberty all around the globe mourn for him in a way that the world reserves for immortals.

His death has been long expected, but when it really came we realized what we had lost—not a father figure. No, we had lost instead a titan, so towering, so magnificent, so simple, and so explosive that we are swept along in the astonishing survey of his life as if it were a part of a moving pageant that portrays in vigorous continuity this climactic, stirring era of our century. These large, world-shaking events are in motion and these great, powerful men—an unparalleled cast—bestride the state, and he, the leader, always with a flair, unequalled among them, the vortex, the epitome of zeal and devotion, of enthusiasm, gaiety, and attractive exuberances.

Soldier, painter, politician, parliamentarian, orator, prime minister, war leader and prophet—and most of all a maker of history. Now he is history.

How shall we remember him?

268

Perhaps for his love of freedom. In his History, he is telling of the story of the birth of liberty. He writes:

"Back in the mists of time on that little Anglo-Saxon island there was kindled the flame of *freedom and equality* for the individual. This idea grew and was spread over the earth by the English-speaking peoples, and has now brought democracy to the whole free world and becomes the shining hope for the future of mankind."

The tribute we would pay him is that in which as a master story-teller of our time he paints the picture of Alfred the Great; "We discern across the centuries a commanding and versatile intelligence, wielding with equal force the sword of war and of justice; using in defense arms and policy; cherishing religion, learning, and art in the midst of adversity and danger; welding together a nation, and seeking always across the feuds and hatreds of the age a peace that would smile upon the land."

We will remember him best as he forged our common tongue into the greatest weapon of World War II. Embodying the British spirit of resistance, he gave England its finest hour when he became prime minister and led his people through "blood, sweat and tears" to victory.

"It was the nation and the race—all around the world that had the lion's heart," Churchill said in a rare moment of modesty. "I had the luck to be called upon to give the roar."

During England's darkest days Churchill made his famous defiant speech in Parliament, he said: "We shall go on to the end. We shall fight on the seas—We shall fight with growing confidence and growing strength in the air. We shall defend our island whatever the cost shall be. We shall fight on the beaches. We shall fight on the landing grounds. We shall fight in the streets and in the hills.

"We shall never surrender and, even if, which I do not for a moment believe, this island or even a part of it is subjugated and starving, then our empire across the seas, armed and guarded by the British fleet, will carry on the struggle until in God's good time the new world in all its strength and might sets forth, to the rescue and liberation of the old."

While repeating the speech to a radio audience, Churchill is reported to have said in an aside. "And we'll hit them over the head with beer bottles, which is about all we have got to work with."

He went ont: "You ask, what is our policy? It is to wage war by land, sea and air, war with all our strength that God has given us— You ask, what is our aim? I can answer you in one word, it is victory. Victory at all costs—Victory however long and hard the road may be, for without victory there is no survival—"

An indomitable man, on the verge of disaster he was confident that England would survive so that "the world may move forward into bright, sunlit uplands" free of tyranny. How could they win, almost unarmed? He told the defeated French generals the plan for stopping a cross channel invasion—"drown as many as possible on the way over and knock the others on the head when they crawl ashore."

Within a few weeks after he was called to the prime ministry came Dunkirk. The Belgian army surrendered. That exposed the flank of the British and French defenders to the Nazi armored columns.

"Fight to the channel ports," Churchill ordered. The battered and exhausted armies reached the beaches under the pounding of the German planes and ranks. The oddest fleet in history then sailed from the British ports. Naval vessels, sailing ships, fishing boats, pleasure yachts headed for France. In nine days this strange armada had rescued 338,000 men—the navy had fondly hoped for 45,000.

A grand achievement we called it, but Churchill described it as a "colossal military disaster," pointing out that 1,000 guns and all the armor Britain had were lost. "Wars," he warned, "are not won by evacuations."

It was at Fulton, Missouri, that Churchill etched the term "iron curtain" on the pages of history.

With President Truman on the platform, he said: "From Stettin in the Baltic to Trieste in the Adriatic, an iron curtain has descended across the continent. Behind that line lie all the capitals of the ancient states of central and eastern Europe, Warsaw, Belgrade, Prague, Vienna, Budapest, Bucharest and Sofia—all lie in the Soviet sphere —all are subject to a very high and increasing control from Moscow."

270

Had the western world heeded Churchill's warning, as far back as those days before Munich, millions might today be living who were sacrificed in that war. His messages, ignored, he warned us of the folly of unconcern, of permitting ruthless power to erode away the boundaries of the free world. He thundered out the imperative need to prepare, to withstand the steady sweeping away of free lands, free peoples and freedom itself. He foresaw the threat of Soviet communism and its growing hunger through success. And so a war came that never should have happened and drew us all "into the awful whirlpool."

Remember? That glorious contempt of "this whipped jackal, Mussolini, the Italian jackanapes." And of Hitler, "this wicked man, this repository of many forms of soul destroying hatred, this blood-thirsty guttersnipe. We will have no truck with you or the grisly gang that works your wicked will—you do your worst and we will do our best."

He mourned the failure to throttle Bolshevism "at its birth and to bring Russia, then prostrate, by one means or another into the general democratic system." He knew that "a thousand years scarce served to form a state" and yet, with refusal to foresee danger and keep guards posted, "an hour may lay it in the dust."

Of course we knew he was great, we knew he was English, and yet in some mysterious fashion, he seemed to be of us, and with Churchill's passing, something has gone from us. But something is left, too, of great value. It is the memory of his integrity—his faith in the common people—telling them the truth as he knew it—never glossing over the dangers, the tragedies, the threatened defeats. So sincere he was that when he told us all was well, we did not question the policy behind his statements. We knew he trusted us and what he said we could rely on. With all his other virtues, his integrity endears him and so he goes down to posterity as a leader who did not fear his people, did not seek their loyalty. Fearlessly and unafraid he led them.

He was us as we would like the world to know us—we enjoyed him. Often we chuckled over his tyrannical, his impish and petulant ways. Even while we marveled at him and were dazzled by his grandeur, he became dearer and nearer to us because of his rip-roaring zest for living, his kindly humanity, his boyish and infectious joy of adventure and his genuine simplicity. We forgave him when he was outrageously unfair, even when he was manifestly in the wrong, but we were vastly thrilled and strengthened by his steadfast fortitude and courage, his devotion to liberty and the fierce vigilance against the menace of the holocaust he foresaw and vainly tried to gird us against. He was one of Nature's great: "In war: resolution. In defeat: defiance. In victory: magnanimity. In peace: good will."

He dominated the history of our era and our thinking. At times he seemed, in the tragic intensity of that awful war, to be our only hope. We took courage at the eloquent cadence of his inspiring and defiant speeches: the "V" for Victory of his pudgy hand, his forthrightness and his other trademark, his ever-present cigar.

He was so human; he loved life, and he shared that love with us all. We even came to know his Clemmie and to love her as he loved her, for he shared somehow with us all the verve and the elan of a courtier, the painstaking exactitude of a skilled bricklayer, the joy and appreciation of a brilliant painter and the pugnacity and persistence of a bull dog.

"He had written great books," says Patrick O'Donovan in the *London Observer,* "and relished great adventures that others knew only in fantasy. He had wielded unimaginable power. He was a man who could weep at a school song, or bow before his sovereign with the awe of a courtier, or walk in procession to the Garter Chapel muffled in a great cloak, buried under a preposterous Tudor hat, looking like a giant blue mushroom."

As an inspiration for the mature, he is a storybook picture. He had his ups and downs; his friends frequently wrote him off as finished. A failure at 65, at ninety the world stands at salute. A great one has gone. We shall not in our lifetime see his like again. He was one of the world's titans; he was also our hope—and our dear friend whom we knew intimately as we do all those who have shared their lives and their astonishing vigor for us and with us.

When he was 75, he had observed genially, "I am prepared to meet my Maker. But whether my Maker is prepared for the ordeal of meeting me is another matter." He laughed easily, and he wept easily. His emotions were never far below the surface. He was vastly simple; he was singularly himself.

As a friend once said of him ,"He was easily satisfied; all he wanted was the best." With President Roosevelt we can say it was fun to be living in the same eon as Winston Churchill.

*"These are the freedoms we prize; these are the
freedoms we will keep, provided we become vigilant
in our nation's responsibility — realizing that
every privilege entails an equal obligation —
that we become politically awake, alive and alert —
that we elect worthy folk to represent us —
and that we confine government to its justifiable role."*

Our American heritage

It may have been in *Appleton's Reader,* I'm not sure; but in the album of my memories I can still see the picture—King Canute with royal crown seated in an armchair throne, and pointing with his staff on the ocean sands. He had just ordered the tide to come no further; yet you saw the little ripples had already advanced to surround his seat.

In these days when our heroes are customarily stripped of their glamour, it is a comfort to report that this same Canute gave another startling command that makes us begin to wonder if the King, in his wisdom, had not been teaching his nobles a lesson on that seagirt coast, and not learning one himself, for the command Canute gave his counselors in 1027 was that "henceforth they neither commit nor suffer to prevail any sort of injustice either from fear of me or from favor to any powerful person." This Dane; as a Monarch of England, ordered his magistrates to administer the law fairly and equally to rich and poor, to high and low.

England's earlier Kings, Alfred the Great and Edward the Confessor, had given charters which were cherished and guarded. Canute gave mandates but no charter; yet, his expression of man's equality

274

before the law is part of our legal great tradition.

A hundred years later, when the Normans now ruled the land, the next great English lawgiver was a woman and a Scot. Princess Edytha, the daughter of King Malcolm of Scotland, changed her name to Matilda in deferential courtesy to the King's mother, but the people who loved her, mindful of the terrors of the Norman's Doomsday Book, called her "Good Queen Maud"—She loved freedom and wanted it for others; before she would consent to marry Henry I, she forced from him a promise that he would sign a charter guaranteeing the rights of individuals and a return to constitutional rule. As a safeguard, 100 copies of this new charter commitment were sent throughout England to be held for safe keeping, together with the laws of Alfred and of Edward.

These three, the charters of Alfred and of Henry, were the foundation for the Magna Carta, which Lord Macaulay, the historian, said "commences the history of England and the English-speaking people around the world."

The fusion of Norman and Saxon blood created in England a new feeling of nationalism, but all was not well. King John, by his continual extortions of money and his violations of custom, had not only aroused the barons but also many of the lower gentry, the townspeople and the artisans as well. Compelled to enter into parley with the barons on the field of Runnymede, on June 15, 1215, the King set his seal on the charter "willingly" it stated, although truthfully under extreme coercion.

There were few provisions in the Magna Carta that were new, but there is definitely set forth the theory that the power of the King was not supreme. Most important were the vaguely worded general grants against oppression, which later came to be interpreted as guarantees of trial by jury and of habeas corpus. The important underlying principle, it declared, for all time—that government should be conducted in accordance with law.

The list of civil liberties was further extended by the Petition of Right, forced from King Charles I by the Parliament in 1628. Based upon the earlier charters, the Petition of Right secured to the people recognition of four principles: no taxes may be levied without legislative consent; no person may be imprisoned without cause being shown; no soldiers may be quartered on the citizenry; martial law may not be used in time of peace.

A third great instrument in the history of civil liberties grew sixty years later out of the revolution which resulted in the dethroning of King James and the calling to the throne of William III (of Orange) and Mary II, King James's daughter. By its provisions, this English Bill of Rights, in 1689, gave political supremacy to Parliament, although the monarch still remained formally the head of the British state.

When Englishmen came to the New World, they brought with them, a concept which they had learned highly to value (1) the recognition of the human being as an individual before the law and (2) a fervent love of freedom. They brought with them the prize of civil liberties won. As in the motherland at home, it was taken for granted that when English people would settle a new colony, they would at once establish representative government. In 1619, in Jamestown the royal colony of Virginia, the House of Burgesses was convened. In 1620, the next year, the Mayflower brought the Pilgrims from England to New England. After a two months' voyage, the ship sighted land on Nov. 9 or 10, but, before seeking a place on the unknown shores, where they could live according to their beliefs, free and unurged, they drew up an agreement which is regarded as one of the most memorable documents in modern history. They called it the Mayflower Compact. It began "In the name of God" and it continued, "We . . . solemnly and mutually in covenant combine ourselves together into a body politic."

Echoes of the rights gained by Magna Carta were heard in the early constitutions of Virginia and Massachusetts and in the greatest and most important of all American documents, "The Declaration of Independence." Familiar to all Americans, it states the theory of *Natural Rights*. It begins, in its engrossed form:

"When in the course of human events, it becomes necessary for one people to dissolve the political bonds that have connected

276

them with another, and to assume among the powers of the earth, the separate and equal station to which the Laws of Nature and of Nature's God entitle them, a decent respect to the opinions of mankind require that they should declare the causes which compel them to the separation. . . . We hold these truths to be self-evident, that all men are created equal, that they are endowed by their Creator with certain inalienable Rights, that among these are Life, Liberty and the Pursuit of Happiness. That to insure these rights, Governments are instituted among Men, deriving their just powers from the consent of the governed" . . . and it ends: "And for the support of this *Declaration,* with a firm reliance on the protection of divine Providence, we mutually pledge to each other our Lives, our Fortunes and our sacred Honor." All the signatures except three, were signed August 2, 1776.

Second only to the Declaration of Independence in the high regard with which it is held is the United States Constitution. It has the superior sanction to the ordinary laws of the land and is subject to a gradual process of amendment.

The Constitution is concise, and its very brevity and its statement of principles have made possible a latitude of interpretations, which have fostered growth.

In our constitution, there are but seven articles and a Preamble; in all *21* amendments have been adopted.

The Preamble does not confer power but it has been of great importance because of the weight that has been placed on its first words, "We, the people of the United States." Another phrase, "to promote the General Welfare" has been used to uphold much recent social legislation, for which no warrant could be found in the powers of Congress.

Within two years of its adoption, nine amendments to the Constitution were added. These are called the U.S. Bill of Rights. They developed from the widespread feeling that, unlike the majority of State constitutions, the Federal Constitution did not specifically note and sufficiently guarantee individual liberties. These are not rights granted by the government to the individual, but rights of the individual protected against possible encroachments by the government. They guarantee:

First Amendment: The freedom of worship, of speech, of the press, of assembly, and petition to the government for redress of grievances.

Second Amendment: The right to bear arms—adopted with reference to State Militias.

Third Amendment: Freedom from the quartering of soldiers without the consent of the owner of the house.

Fourth Amendment: Freedom from search except with warrant.

Fifth Amendment: Guarantees: no person shall be held for an infamous crime without indictment; be twice put in "jeopardy of life or limb" for the same offense; be compelled to testify against himself, be "deprived of life, liberty or property," without due process of law; private property may not be taken for public use, without just compensation.

Sixth Amendment: Guarantees the right of a speedy and public trial by an impartial jury in all criminal prosecutions.

Seventh Amendment: Guarantees the right of trial by jury in all common-law suits "where the value in controversy shall exceed twenty dollars."

Eighth Amendment: Prohibits excessive bail and fines and "cruel and unusual" punishments.

Ninth Amendment: "The enumeration in the constitution of certain rights shall not be construed to deny or disparage others retained by the people."

Such is our Bill of Rights, so liberal in provisions that, the newsprint tells us, it was recently withdrawn from a public bulletin board, because of its highly controversial contents and was permitted to be replaced only upon proof that it is the law of the land! (Had the Founding Fathers known to what base purposes these safeguards have been converted, they would have perhaps added, also a Bill of Commensurate Responsibilities.)

Such is the heritage we enjoy! No matter what may have been our family background of other nationalities, our ancestors, for the most part, came here and helped build the U.S.A. because they valued freedom and with a disciplined courage and high purpose safeguarded their liberty and gave respect to the rule of law.

And what is this freedom? It is a personal thing. It recognizes the inherent worth of every individual. It is man above State. It is a man's right to be himself, to make of himself creatively what he will. It's what makes life worthwhile. It is the goal toward which peoples and countries around the world have learned to treasure, sometimes even value above life itself.

The pity is that our work-a-day world has grown so great, so complex and our relationships so involved and impersonal that we may have grown passively to hold this precious trust put into our hands to cherish. We accept it proudly and in a reserved sort of fashion, actually we value it; safeguarded we feel because of their protection and its permanence.

But here's the rub!—Is freedom a protection and a permanence? Can it be a gift? Must it not always be a prize to be won and defended and its permanence guaranteed only while it alertly is guarded?

And yet we are disturbed—perhaps not yet alarmed—at the political apathy of our day, the crushing indifference of the average citizen who seems not to realize that the more of our personal burdens we encourage our government to assume, the closer we bring the day when the ruler will be stronger than the ruled and self government will have faded away.

Generally we seem only objectively to view the sensitive area of race relations, to read with interest, in a detached sort of fashion, the frightening problems of urban life with its apparently diminishing water supply, its problems of transportation facilities, its lack of housing accommodations, its crime statistics, its mounting welfare rolls and its school drop-outs—we seem to think "they" *should* do something about them.

Is it not time for us to realize that there is no mythical "they" in this land where these freedoms and rights exist and seemingly are forgotten—that "we" are the "they" whom so many talk about as being responsible and corrective?

We realize, of course, that there are many millions who every day use their freedoms, well and wisely, to work and grow along healthy, constructive lines, but we know, too, that hundreds of radical young people, with the eyes of the world focused upon them, without provocation, denounce the policies of their government and shout insults at persons in elected authority, decry and defy the laws of the land, and build a false image of American youth in the eyes of our nation and the world. As John Edgar Hoover has stated, "The American college student today is being subjected to a bewildering and dangerous conspiracy perhaps unlike any social challenge ever before encountered by our youth. On many campuses he faces a turbulence built on unrestrained individualism, repulsive dress and speech, outright obscenity, disdain for moral and spiritual values, and disrespect for law and order. This movement, commonly referred to as the 'New Left,' is complex in its deceitful absurdity and characterized by its lack of common sense.

"Fortunately, a high percentage of the more than three million full-time college students are dedicated, hardworking, and serious-minded young people; however, their good deeds and achievements are greatly overshadowed by those who are doing a tremendous amount of talking but very little thinking."

Here is the problem we face. What is our recourse? As I imagine, the answers will be as many and varied as those answering. As for myself, I do not scoff at the significance of the collegians' flare-ups as being partly communist motivated, and, if so, we are rightly alerted and should be on guard. Oliver Wendell Holmes wrote of "freedom leaning on a spear." It is well that "the world knows that freedom has a spear."

If, however, our young revolutionary idealists are proclaiming their indignation at the lack of fidelity we show to the concepts we hold of freedom: equal access to opportunity; of the respect due the individual, of the ideals of justice, of one's sense of brotherhood and responsibility, then we can understand and share in part their indignation, as we share the values to which we have proven ourselves so faithless. And we know, too, that given time, these young Patrick Henrys will develop in their maturity into either practical idealists or just embittered critics and faultfinders. For, after all, don't we, as older people, realize that it is common habit to think that young people should always be more pliant, more controlled, more dedicated? That the distant past is the golden age, and the present is one that tries men's souls? As one of the Hebrew prophets, Hesiod in the 7th Century, B.C., stated, "There will be no end to anxiety and suffering, no end to family strife, broken promises, unjust men prospering, might prevailing over right. . . . I wish I had been born before this time or after it." For thousands of years it has been so—we, too, may in the future be considered as living now in a golden age.

Some people react to this situation facing us in terms of apathy— we can do nothing about it, so we'll just be on our way. But most of us share in the apprehensions and anxieties of our time. While I do not want to dwell upon our fears, I do want to stress our reasonable hopes.

Walter Kerr, the dramatic critic, recently wrote that the trouble with the plays today being presented on Broadway is that they no longer have heroes. Instead, their leading characters are neurotic and mentally ill. Audiences leave theaters depressed and perhaps confused. No longer have they been inspired, informed, exalted or grown in stature.

Our theaters need the return of heroes. We all need them. Our young people, although they do not know it, need them too, for they learn their moral or social values, not as concepts, not as words or definitions; they learn them by a kind of osmosis, in living and contact, in interpersonal relationships. They learn not through the process of transmitting but through the conversion of transmuting; they learn them through songs and stories, festivals and drama, games and sports, and stories and deeds of heroes. In our passion for debunking our heroes and overlooking the human drama in their deeds, we are stripping history of its glamorous personalities, its thrilling events and its "hoary legends," and that is one of the ways we are selling our young people short; they are not being given the models whom formerly we learned to admire, to love and shape our lives after.

Believe it or not, in spite of their bumptiousness, they are, for the most part, thoughtful and sensitive folk. They are facing a world vastly more complicated and enormous than ours—before them the mastery of outer space is challenging, but the mastery of inner human relationships even more demanding and perhaps more imperative for our survival.

The American spirit is still vital and vibrant in them as in us. It is our faith that, in their applying religious liberty, political liberty and civil liberty to their problems, in their own time and way, they may keep sensitive to the forces that are about them—that they may seek only that which is good for all men's happiness—and that they will always recognize that every right *entails* a responsibility. . . . We want them to realize that participation in life is not given to the separate individual. It is given to all in unity with mankind and everything that lives.

The position of the U.S.A. as an example of a free land, is strong —not because we are a rich nation, not because our standards of living are high, but because, young and old, we bear witness in our daily lives to our pride in self, our respect for our fellows, our observance of the law, our right to worship as we will, vote as we think proper, to assemble and to speak and to volunteer as we will.

These are the freedoms we prize; these are the freedoms we will keep, provided that we become vigilant in our nation's responsibility —realizing that every privilege entails an equal obligation—that we become politically awake, alive and alert; that we elect worthy folk to represent us; and that we confine government to its justifiable role.

While there is deeply rooted in the minds and hearts of young and old alike the pride we feel in our civil liberties, we can take comfort in the fact that here in our land Jews, Moslems and Christians are living side by side, neighbors and well-wishers—that as the years roll by, we find, an even greater number of men and women with serious and constructive thinking, sharing interests and sympathies as wide as the world is wide, and seeking understanding even when we feel ourselves most misunderstood. These are our encouragements; this is the faith we have, by which we live.

NATIONAL RETIRED
TEACHERS ASSOCIATION

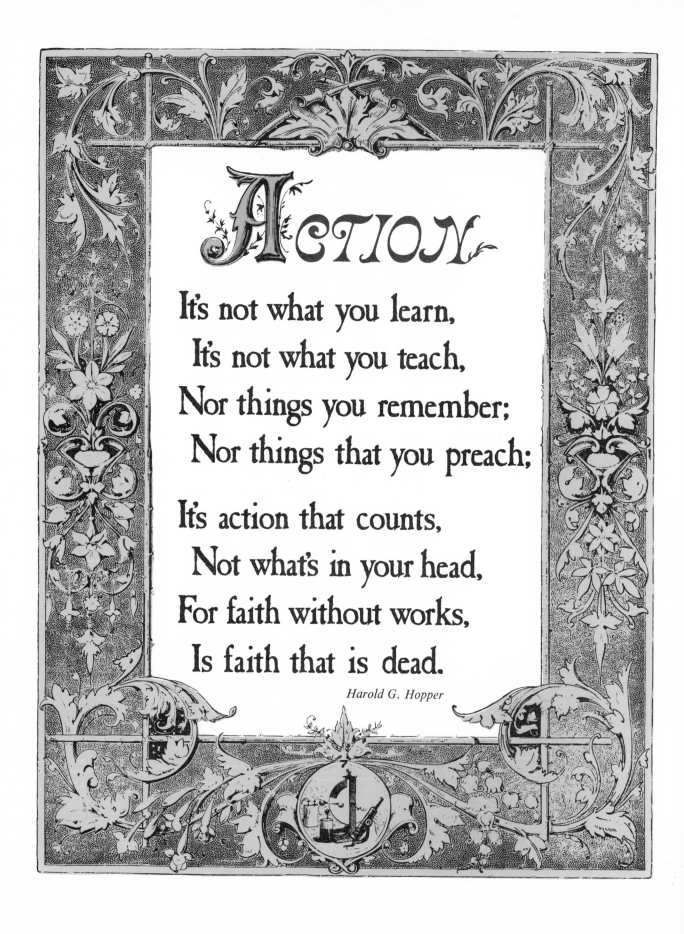

ACTION

It's not what you learn,
  It's not what you teach,
Nor things you remember;
  Nor things that you preach;

It's action that counts,
  Not what's in your head,
For faith without works,
  Is faith that is dead.

Harold G. Hopper

"Such to me is the new image of aging:
growth in itself and service for all mankind."

We know that adversity
is a fine whetstone

In the 40 years following the beginning of this century, technology shortened the working man's day from 60 to 40 hours, tripling at the same time the Nation's per capita income and raising ever higher the standard of living. Technology's greatest achievement of that period, as regards those of mature years, lay in the production of time: freed time, idle time, leisure time—call it what you will. For the first time, as the individual advanced into maturity, he found himself enshrouded in time for the use of which he had not yet evolved a purpose or a plan. To some, this freedom from routine came as a boon, a relief. To others it loomed as a menace and a dread. But to all, a shock and a surprise. And the end is not yet.

Statisticians report with the increasing impetus of automation in the next 40 years it is entirely conceivable that the routine production for the material support of the world need not call upon more than 3% of the available manpower. For 97%, no work!

We now know, in our heart of hearts, that we are in the throes of an industrial revolution and a social—and, perchance, even a spiritual—revolution with *time—free time* being the vortex about which all other matters will revolve.

We are in the incipient stages now of that revolution. As automation advances, the untrained man of routine skills will undoubtedly

285

be the first affected—the untrained man, who is *least able,* profitably and worthily to use free time. It may even end up that the more competent individual will be working longer and harder, for *automation* is not *automatic;* it still needs man's direction and intelligent control. Granted that mistakes may be less frequent with automation—that may be true—it may be true also that there will be eliminated the correction of mistakes that now absorb, they say, 80% of operational time. Yet we know that when automation does make a mistake, it surely is a whopper! Who has not recently heard of a person being deluged one morning by the delivery to him at his home of 3000 copies of his favorite monthly. And you have read of that happily-unhappy individual who was sent by the U. S. Department of Internal Revenue a check upon the government for $1,000,000 odd dollars as a tax refund.

The problem ahead for all to decide in the 1980s will be the same as that which struck us who were engulfed in free time in the middle 1940s and unprepared to profit by it effectively. This will be the real crux in the days to come—a man whose life no longer holds, as a core, the sustaining qualities of work and production, a satisfying sense of need and of effort.

Man, if no longer he will need to support himself and his mate and offspring by the sweat of his brow, still will need challenges —for we have thought the meeting and the solving of obstacles to be an essential need in the seeking of a satisfactory life. The orientals tell the same story in their trenchant saying, "All sunshine makes a desert."

We know that adversity is a fine whetstone. We know, too, that it need not be a deterrent and an obstacle. Indeed, there is nothing that we as teachers better know than where there is no obstacle to be surmounted, there is no spur to heroic and generous effort.

This is the great paradox of the future: no work and more time to do it in.

Jeremy Taylor, the adventurous son of a barber, who became chaplain to King James I and later a bishop, stated bluntly, "No man is more miserable than he who has no adversity." Working has always been a necessary part of life and has been basic to our belief in ourselves.

Because of this, men of vision foresee the inherent danger of so much unemployed free time. Many devices are being sought to lengthen the period of man's productive years: the shorter workday; the shorter work week; longer vacation periods, even the American collegiate plan of sabbatical years; retirement at 60 and 55; all are being considered for industry. And still the major problem stands: a growing block of freed time, of open time, as yet unrestricted and unprogrammed. What to do with it? Yet we must hold to the fundamental thesis that without exercise you may expect atrophy! Without effort and use you will soon meet death.

That will be the problem of the 1980s.

It was also the same problem we met in the mid 1940s. Then this free time came out of the blue, without preparation, dispossessing us of many of the supports needed for the consummation of a happy life: a conviction that the work of our hands was important and needed; our share significant, best done by ourselves; the earning of a wage that helped provide us our means of livelihood; the close and comfortable companionship of fellow workers; the community's regard for our being part of its working members; the dignity of the regard of relatives and friends as being the provider of the home; and the sense of one's vast importance within the area of his responsibilities and commitments.

These were the losses of the 40s. These benefits the man of a problematical 1980 or 2000 may never be able even to imagine. But in the 1940s we lost much more than that: we lost often our faith in ourselves, in our need of survival in a world that seemed no longer either to need or to want us, that regarded us no longer as valued fellow citizens but statistics that threatened the financial security of the United States itself.

Even today the first question in the summer's program of gerontological study at the University of Michigan asks, "Can the Nation afford to support its older citizens?" surely not a consoling or heartwarming thought for an oldster forcibly severed from his job, his livelihood, his circle of friends, and his sense of security and self-esteem.

This, then, was the time, 1947, when the NRTA came into being. This was the time when the men and women who found adjustment tragically needed the steadying hand of friendly fellow workers who, though also caught in this strange and disturbing confusion, did not feel themselves unoriented or at a loss.

The first problem concerned itself with these adjusted folks themselves. This deplorable situation, which we saw with mounting disbelief and a growing sense of horror, was this situation one of their concern? The answer, of course, was YES, emphatically, YES. But was this situation something we could do something about, other than by the expression of sentimental indignation or vituperative verbal attacks on forces that seemed powerless to rescind decisions but had to limit themselves to expressions of concern and regret?

Could we be realistic and study the situation objectively and then do that, which we could do now under our own power, with everything within our power? We decided that that was our mission and we chose for our guidance and consolation that passage from Daniel Webster that reads:

> *"If we work upon marble, it will perish*
> *If we work upon brass, time will efface it*
> *If we rear temples, they will crumble in the dust*
> *But, if we work upon man's immortal minds,*
> *We engrave on those tablets something which time*
>   *will not efface*
> *And which will brighten and brighten to all eternity."*

Setting to work seriously upon this tragic plight, we thought we had delineated three major causes for deep consideration. The first was occasioned by three seemingly impossible hurdles, any one of which seemed to preclude any possible future happiness and all of which, in one fashion or another, seemed to be inextricably enmeshed with the other two.

The first was definitely financial.

The second concern was emotional, purely subjective: they no longer felt contented and at peace with the world; they no longer felt worthy and noble; they no longer esteemed themselves to be effective, adequate and equal to events. Indeed, they felt themselves to be insignificant and a bit of flotsam and jetsam cast aside from the mainstream of life. They were utterly discouraged and heartsick.

The third great sorrow voiced was the loss of companionship, the withdrawal of respect and regard: sometimes expressed, perhaps, and sometimes only implied. Often family loyalties and ties were broken or strained, when the need of finances distorted the picture.

Now we had the worksheet. What could we do about it? Perhaps we had better say, just what did our NRTA *REALLY* do about it?

We noted the financial obstacles. Well, first, since the retirement salary was a state affair, liberalization campaigns were soon underway at the state level. Exemption legislation on the federal level was helped by discriminatory measures gradually evolving into more equitable patterns. Money-stretching devices were initiated by NRTA services, in pioneering hospital coverages, making available drugs at substantial savings, etc.

The emotional blockings were attacked in conferences, in NRTA publications, in conventions such as this, and by the fine comradely spirit of the group.

> *"Isn't it strange that princes and kings*
> *And clowns that gather in sawdust rings*
> *And common folks, like you and me,*
> *Are builders of eternity?*
> *To each is given a bag of tools*
> *A shapeless mass and a set of rules*
> *And each must build, ere life has flown,*
> *A stumbling block or a stepping stone."*
> *—Anonymous*

We recall the tale of how the Devil one day announced that he was going out of business and that he would sell the tools of his trade to anyone who would pay the price. These tools were an ill-assorted and sorry-looking lot. Hatred, fear, and lots of others, each carried their own price tag. Among the others was a harmless-looking wedge-shaped tool that was priced higher than any of the others. Some one asked the Devil what that tool was. "That's discouragement," was the reply.

"And why do you have it priced so high?"

"Because," replied the Devil, "it is the most useful tool of any of the others. I can pry open and get inside a man's consciousness with that when I couldn't get near him with any of the vices. And, when once inside, I can use him in whatever way suits me best. It is so much worn because I use this tool, *discouragement,* with everybody, as few people yet know it belongs to me." It is needless to say that the high price prevented its sale and *discouragement* is still in the possession of the Devil and is still his most useful tool.

The need for work, for the overcoming of obstacles, so essential to the firm building of a happy maturity, generated services and aids and projects innumerable and worthy, delightfully solving the problem of effort and the satisfaction of accomplishment. The withdrawing were being wooed back into the charmed circle of former friends. Neighborliness bloomed and people began to delight in sharing their benefits acquired for themselves alone. AARP was sponsored, the New York World's Fair pavilion was opened.

This is the story of the achievements—to me this story makes a tale of wonder and cooperative effort but the significance of what NRTA has done is the real story—the story behind the story.

NRTA, not knowing that it was involved in the nationwide industrial and social revolution, had, instinctively, helped in the solving of some of their inherent problems.

We think that NRTA has solved:

First, the need of continuing the productive skills in a *no-work* world. Its answer is found, not in theory, but in realistic action. Production goes on at an increasing pace, but the shifting is from a production of goods to the production of services, intangible, elusive, heart-warming services; endless, for man's appetite for such is insatiable.

Second, the required shift in goals in a *no-work* world from the concept of *happiness through comfort* and the collection of status

290

symbols to the concept of *happiness through self-fulfillment.*

To me, this is the story of NRTA's dedicated effort. It stands high along the measuring arc of *service to self* in the giving of self to the *service of others.* Like Schweitzer, NRTA in its growing maturity, has grown *socially, intellectually,* and *spiritually,* in line with the hoped-for program of the world of peace and good will, for which we all pray and work. It forgets its age in years and its physical shortages in the challenge of growth and services of a happier world because of our stay in it. Such to me is the new image of aging: *growth in self and service for all mankind.*

*"If we truly seek a perspective and hope for
the future, we must accept the responsibility, thought
and decision of contributing our share to the enlargement
of life under our free system of government
and to the establishment of a peaceful world."*

Our imperatives

Recently I had the happy privilege of returning to the university from which I received my first degree and speaking to the older alumni gathered there. Proudly I said my loyalty and my love to our Alma Mater—and our debt. There we were privileged to meet great teachers, distinguished scholars, men and women of "moral splendor," folk who pushed our horizon wider, gave us a greater openness of mind and a more flexible way of thinking. They challenged us to see the star and follow the gleam.

We may not remember anything which they taught us, but we remember them. They taught themselves—their vigor, their zest for learning, their faith in us, in themselves, in the university, in life. They awoke in us something that we didn't know we had— a greater sensitivity of the human spirit and a greater perceptivity! How?—because they had it themselves. They transmitted really the goals of our culture. It was a great joy to recall these vibrant leaders and to say years later our lasting debt and gratitude.

In the informal get-together before, I was often asked what was my line of work before retirement, and when I answered, "Teaching," invariably, I was than asked, "What did you teach?" And I began to wonder—what did I teach? What did we all teach? Youth certainly—some subject matter—but probably ourselves most of all.

We know we taught *confidently*, for we believed in our ourselves and in our mission. We were conscious of the great trust placed in us by the fathers and the mothers of the young people who shared with us the richest treasure they possessed.

We know we taught *hopefully*, for we believed in the worth of every child and youth, believed in his capacity to grow and develop; believed that we could help him find himself.

We know too that we taught *reverently*, for we realized the significance of our responsibility to guide the young to high ideals and great achievement. We acknowledged conscientiously the far-reaching, never-ending influence that the teacher—for good or for bad—can exert upon the lives of men.

We taught *prayerfully*, because of us would they be more humane, more tolerant, have wider interests and understanding, be more sympathetic and have kinder hearts.

This is how we felt about teaching and here is what we did about it. With our students—active and passive, perfect and imperfect, we accepted the charge to help them meet life *as it really is* and to help them to bravely and persistently condition themselves to full and wholesome living. The instinct of *curiosity* we sought to satisfy and to stimulate. We planned to find answers for the craving for *companionship*. We provided for the joys of shared experiences, promoted conditions calculated to yield at once gratifying *social approval,* the satisfaction of purposeful activity and the *self-assurance* of individual worth; security of all sorts and conditions—we planned for intellectual, spiritual, physical, yes—even economic fulfillment. We felt we had done a good job!

Now we are faced with the need of the same imperatives of how to grow and how to find happiness and fulfillment. The result of our *self appraisal* and self communion was our decision that we as individuals would be responsible for a fine and a comparable accounting of ourselves. We would *estimate our own resources* with a frank acceptance of the physical changes age brings with it. In so doing we developed a deeper understanding of our society, a fuller appreciation of the moral and aesthetic values of our civilization.

We convinced ourselves of the need of participating with others, and of sharing pleasant and exhilarating experiences with others. We studied our need and the question of the future—how to fill it, how to build a well-rounded life.

The NRTA was our answer. In it we found unity in diversity. In it we learned that we could look forward to tomorrow because we had lived today.

The National Retired Teachers Association is unique in that it is run *for* and *by* older Americans. The story of its genesis is a fascinating one. Twenty years ago compulsory retirement, because of age, was a new idea: its enforcement, without due warning, and, with no opportunity given for economic preparation, demoralized many who felt themselves of no further value to society—unwanted, unneeded; they became humiliated and embittered.

The demoralizing effect of this psychological affront of sudden change we saw particularly in the case of those whose utter absorption and devotion to their work had left no time or provisions for other interests. With the tap roots of their life severed, many had quickly withered and died. To still others retirement meant an unhappy *finale*.

Some of us believed that we could help them help themselves realize that this new and unplanned for leisure might make retirement an *overture:* We recalled the motto of Nova Scotia—"God helps those who help themselves and each other." The founding of the National Retired Teachers Association was the outcome.

It is true in our thinking and in our planning we were considering a homogeneous group, with the social cohesiveness of similar training, dedication and service; but we reasoned: "Is there not here the creative minority, the spearheaded society, the aristocracy of intelligence and virtue which Thomas Jefferson said was essential to the preservation of a democracy?"

First, we studied why this man-made tragedy had robbed these teachers of their pride in self, their economic security and their concern for others than themselves.

In the light of the life-goals often we found in the culture of today—success, power, the search for status, in the constant emphasis on youth, fun, happiness and recreation—we could easily realize the need of the alternative goals of identity, independence and involvement.

First Goal, Identity:

Identity implies a feeling of who we are, what are the values we esteem, and the goals we really seek in life. In our search for identity, we tried so to re-establish the faith we had in ourselves—to ignore the age-old stereotype of decadence, disability and indigence. We needed to reactivate the zest for living and to establish again the pride of belonging. Instead of searching for success, we stressed excellence in thought and deed. Happiness we interpreted as our capacity to give love and our gracious willingness to receive it. We sought to substitute for fun the joy of external realities about us and the enjoyment of that joy. We explored the possibility of elevating play to the intellectual pleasure of handling ideas and the creativeness of our imaginings.

Second Goal, Independence:

Identity was our first goal. Second came independence. As regards the shock to one's economic status, we knew we could do something. We vowed never to offend the pride of independence; *that* we knew was one of the pillars of one's faith in self. As basic to our actions, we knew that we would not petition the government for subsidy; we would see what we could do about economic independence ourselves—and we did.

We developed a health insurance plan—the first voluntary plan ever made available to older people, to be revised as need arose and lately to coordinate with Medicare. Our lower priced, top-quality drug service we established to take care of several thousands of prescriptions a day through locations in Washington, D.C., Long Beach, California, and St. Petersburg, Florida. We organized a travel service. Each year thousands of our members are enjoying budget-priced tours especially arranged for them—tours to Europe and the world, with guides trained to the service of elderly folk.

Many other tangible services are dollar stretching, but there are also those of extending cultural interests too. The Institute of Life-time Learning helps expand the older person's vision, and challenges adventures in the creative arts and crafts, philosophy, psychology, and religion.

Third Goal, Involvement:

Third, our goal of purpose and of involvement—action placed at the service of liberty, of tolerance and of universal brotherhood. Involvement with others implies the gospel of work, the sacrifice of devotion and the inner mastery of spirit. We realized to live fully, we must be conscious of living—of laughing—of having an easy smile and a heart lit with joy. Here no apathy could live— no loneliness, no self-pity.

NRTA was established in 1947, It now has 215,000 members. There are state retirement associations in every state and some 800 local RTAs. It is important to bear in mind that the local groups are established, not to provide a recreational program for the mem-bers—a need that is being met by hundreds of senior citizen cen-ters around the country—but to provide for the involvement of thousands of members in projects of a constructive nature, locally and Federally.

In addition to the money-saving services, there are other services devised that benefit millions of others in the upper age bracket.

At the Federal level, we serve as consultants to every depart-ment and agency that has an announced program for older citi-zens. We also serve in a consultant capacity for many of the state Commissions on Aging. We have registered lobbyists in the nation's capital; and we are consulted by both political parties. In our legis-lative work we are nonpartisan, supporting or opposing legislation rather than candidates or parties. We are the only retiree organi-zation which has been asked to testify before both the Democratic and the Republican convention committees in 1960 and 1964.

Offshoots to these major groups are the Retirement Research and

296

Welfare Association, a philanthropic association which receives gifts, conducts research and offers free of charge its findings on Retirement Housing. We are also working with church groups of all denominations, helping them develop services and programs under their own auspices. We presented at the New York World's Fair a pavilion showing the world our intensive effort to expand the international side of our program.

Such is the story of NRTA, organized to grow and to serve. We believe age is an achievement, not a tragedy. The latter years, we contend, have much meaning and great promise. Activity, we contend, is life, and work is our salvation. We are living proof that the elderly can proudly go on serving as an integral, serviceable and respected part of their communities.

The story is told us by Fritz Kreisler, that once upon a time he was playing a joint recital with Rachmaninoff in New York City. At a certain point he suffered a momentary lapse of memory about the score. Leaning toward the pianist, he whispered, "Where are we?" The dextrous fingers never paused in their exciting flight over the keyboard, as his fellow artist answered, "In Carnegie Hall."

Perhaps no question do we more often ask in these troubled days, "Where are we?" We older folk realize that this is no time for laxness and slackness in our concern for our country's welfare.

When Carl Sandburg was presented with a gold medal by the Academy of Arts and Letters, he said, "We find it momentous that Lincoln used the word 'responsibility' nearly as often as he used the word 'freedom.'" Note the word "momentous"—a fitting word for our obligation.

If our nation is to be as great morally and spiritually as it is materially, it might be well for us to recall and to ponder that quotation of Tennyson's that we recited so glibly in our youthful days, "Self-reverence, self-knowledge, self-control. These three alone lead life to sovereign power."

If we truly seek a perspective and hope for the future, we must accept the responsibility, thought and decision of contributing our share to the enlargement of life under our free system of government and to the establishment of a peaceful world.

Partisan temperatures will be raised; so much the better for us. Walt Whitman said, "I know nothing grander, better exercise, better digestion, more positive, proud of the past, the triumphal result of faith to humankind, than a well-conducted American national election."

It is through such diligence that with continued zeal and purpose, our principles can prevail, can be effective and give purpose to our lives and bring about at long-last the gleam of peace and goodwill among nations. We must interest ourselves in the men and women who offer themselves as candidates for those posts of honor and responsibility; what is their program for their positions if it is entrusted to them?

These candidates must be our concern. We must make it our duty to study the situation we and they face, and, to the best of our considered judgment, decide for ourselves what we want their desired post to be and to achieve, and next to choose that candidate whose past activities seem to be similarly motivated.

We teachers, dedicated as we were, know, that there is no panacea for any problem, no preachment, political or otherwise that will transform fear and hate into respect and goodwill.

As St. Francis of Assisi taught us in his great prayer, that has over the centuries inspired people of all faiths:

> *"Where there is hatred, let me sow love,*
> *Where there is injury, pardon,*
> *Where there is doubt, faith,*
> *Where there is despair, hope,*
> *Where there is darkness, light,*
> *And where there is sadness, joy."*

AMERICAN ASSOCIATION
OF RETIRED PERSONS

Faith is the progeny of belief and trust; Hope is the child of expectancy and confidence; and Love is the progenitor of all good things. The greatest of these is love, for without love nothing has worthiness. Our most precious possession, life, would be intolerable without it. As for future existence, who would desire it if it were devoid of love?

Harold G. Hopper

"AARP believes that aging enhances the worth of the individual."

American Association of Retired Persons — its pros and cons

he American Association of Retired Persons is an independent and unique organization—it has been called the fastest growing association in America today—composed of older folk—men and women who at the time when they might be considered shelved are vital, progressive and serviceable.

To paint the picture of AARP we must show you a colorful progress of self-assurance, dedication, effort and purpose. To understand its uniqueness and its strength, you must realize that AARP is not interested in only improving the status of its members, but also in developing and sharing this information with older people everywhere.

To present clearly to the world the picture of AARP and its accomplishments, you must first realize what AARP is; then, what it does; and last, what are the goals it seeks. You must also know the reverse, what AARP is not, what it does not do, and what goals it does not seek. To tell you the story is the purpose of these columns:

WHAT AARP IS	WHAT AARP IS NOT
AARP is a nongovernmental organization, nonpartisan and	AARP is not sponsored by or connected with either any

---

nonprofit, accepting all who qualify by age, regardless of sex, color, creed or previous state or country, an organization of mature men and women who voluntarily associate themselves in the interest of self-development and of giving service not only to themselves and to each other but also to all whom they, through their skills and abilities, might benefit.

AARP is an all-inclusive, self-respecting organization of congenial men and women aged 55 or over, wherever they may be and whether employed or not. Associate membership is open to any interested person under 55.

AARP is unique among organizations of older people in that its members believe that aging is a normal and dignified segment of living with potentiality for growth and service, for maintaining one's independence and earning dignity and respect.

AARP hold conferences biennially in nine areas, and alternating, a biennial nationwide convention; also workshops and leadership training courses to

governmental agency or any political party or trade union, or religious group. Its finances cannot be expended to the advantage of any individual or group of individuals but only to the improvement or the expansion of the AARP itself and its membership. It does not exploit its members for either political or partisan profit.

AARP is not confined to only those who are retired from a business or profession. Perhaps a better word for the retired in AARP is *refired,* not *retired.*

AARP is an organization of persons who do not regard aging as a pitiful and decadent part of life, with illness, penury and helplessness as its salient features.

AARP holds no meeting to bewail the hardships of old age, nor to formulate pressure programs or stress potential political strength of older folk nor exchange inspirational information and operational ideas and programs.

AARP is a self-motivating group of older folk who voluntarily are bonded together to help stretch the purchasing power of their retirement income.

AARP consists of three allied units: first, the membership at large; second, the officers, elected or volunteer, (none of whom receive either a salary or a stipend) who plot policy; and third, a staff employed at the going rate, to administer those functions too continuous or specialized for the members or officers to perform.

AARP presents in dignified fashion the nonpartisan viewpoint of its membership to Congress and the legislatures of its respective states for their evaluation and action.

to urge governmental subsidy.

AARP is not unmindful of those older persons who do need help from a governmental source and we have been diligent in our efforts to bring about improvements in these programs, but we know that most older persons are able to live in independence and dignity. AARP does not welcome the welfare state as the way of life for all older persons.

AARP is not an organization either manned or promoted by persons or agencies which exploit it for the advancement of either partisan or personal or group profit. AARP pays for services rendered not for propaganda broadcasting.

AARP is not a pressure group, petitioning for special privileges and exemptions because of age and numbers.

AARP has many laurels to which it may lay claim—a mail-order nonprofit drug service, travel service, a group health insurance plan geared to Medicare, hospitality centers and an Institute of Lifetime Learning both in Washington, D.C. and Long Beach, California and by radio on the air.

AARP has promoted the initiation and the development of local volunteer chapters of AARP for those members who favor the goals of individual growth and service to self, to fellow members and to the community in general.

AARP is definitely nonpartisan in both policy and practice. It works with both political parties in matters of legislation which affect older people generally whether or not they are members of AARP or any of its kindred affiliated organizations

AARP is an organization of older folk who believe in keeping alive their interests, in broadening their horizons and

AARP is not an organization of discussion or resentment, of talking over the problems of the aging but a doing organization successfully and constantly seeking how to better conditions. Its philosophy is not negative and defeatism. It is positive and dynamic.

AARP chapters are a unique features of AARP in that they are service centers and do not stress or promote activities of an entertainment, social or recreational nature.

AARP definitely does not favor or approve the program or platform of either political party or of any candidate. Also it does not limit its legislative activity to the general welfare of only its own group membership. It accepts no favors or support from any political party or group.

AARP is not an organization of older folk who mainly desire, for their aging years, play-type amusements and rec-

maintaining an image of aging for themselves as one of growth and service.

reation. It is not organized to seek governmental relief and direction nor is it a welcome recipient for playground activities.

The membership of AARP is now over a million strong. It is all-inclusive—an interesting cross section of America—city folk, town folk, rural folk; bankers, lawyers, doctors, farmers, salesmen and artisans; all of them, like you and me, immigrants or the children of immigrants, all.

Naturally more are to be found in California, Florida and New York and fewer in Alaska, Nevada and the Dakotas, but all of them seasoned and matured with years of living, bringing to the Association gifts of greater insight and understanding.

From the membership come our officers, volunteer and elective, usually men and women of broad and successful administrative experience in a situation sufficiently complex to require a mature executive. They are skilled in communicating with their fellow members and are capable of giving leadership and interpreting the AARP program to the world at large. They demonstrate their capacity for decisive leadership by helping develop policy, maintaining sound financial and community relationships and understandings. They have associated with them other officers who have ability to arrange priorities, practice teamwork and accept graciously delegated authority.

The directors are the determiners of AARP's associational policy. They have demonstrated personally that each is committed to an all-inclusive unified organization and able to develop balance and coordination among the various sections and services of AARP, to make use of judgments of competent executives and to delineate effective courses of action.

The elected National Officers are chosen because of their vision of what AARP can be and do and because they have the ability to inspire the Association to move toward these ideals.

The unit of employed AARP staff is selected for his or her type of service, because of the individual fitness and qualifications possessed by the person. The staff is also all-inclusive, ranging in rank and responsibility from that of the Executive Director to a helper in one of our various services. Among them we proudly number men and women who are strong leaders, knowledgeable persons who have before them a clear insight, each of his particular field and its potentialities and a strong sense of direction and needed strategies and techniques to realize them. Outstanding and dedicated, the salaried personnel serve wholeheartedly the rapidly growing AARP family.

Still another unit in the AARP structure is that of our counselors and consultants who are the very finest to be found in their respective areas, men and women with wide academic background and expertise, and constructive, protective and inventive in the particular zone of their interest. They cover various fields—*health protection; legal matters, finance, CPA accounting, various services.*

Such is the AARP, an organization that realizes that our civilization regrettably tends to think in terms of statistics. Retired folk so cease to be any longer persons. They become pin-points on a chart that focuses our attention on classifications, on categories, so many sick, so many unemployed, so many indigent and despondent, etc. The trend is for the individual spirit to be forgotten or ignored.

AARP believes quite differently, that aging enhances the worth of the individual, each and every one, giving the individual impetus and insight and purpose to continue building the good life not only for himself but to help build it for others, in both body and in soul.

AARP humbly, but proudly, pledges itself to help build a kind of public opinion that will give for all older persons not only greater access to opportunity but will dignify their selfless efforts and their zeal with the corresponding esteem and respect they deserve. AARP is building toward the kind of world that can make possible a full and fruitful life for all mankind.

The price of life

Upon the wall of our Union Station is the foregoing truth—an epitome of the messages that come to us of the creative enterprises that AARP folks are involved in over the nation. The challenge to contribute to the welfare of those both near and far is itself a call to the nobility in us and as the mural notes it also, when answered by us whole-heartedly, becomes a like call to those about us. The world is the better off for there being AARP.

These members have applied the preachments that life has taught into the daily practice of the art of responsible living. Theirs are realizable ideals, within the reach of every one, living each day a little more fully than yesterday, observing happenings about them with sensitivity and an urge to understand and to help, to relieve when relief is indicated, but sharing humor and the upward and outward look. They are practicing idealists.

Simple or far-reaching, the projects undertaken are voluntary expressions of the urge of neighborly concern, testimony to the belief that each of us is truly his brother's keeper. Sometimes the contribution is made in one's own home, sometimes by one bed-bound; sometimes by the cooperative enterprise of vitally dynamic men, but no matter what the dimensions of the project may be, it is still humanity transmuting into action those ethics of social living they have inherited

307

from their forebears. They don't try the impossible but they do have the fealty to a lofty ideal and the courage and drive to realize that ideal in practice. And they have a good time doing it! You remember that Wesley is quoted as saying that we were not going to leave all the good times to the devil!

They have learned that the simple duties are the most important. They know, too, that in service it is possible to realize the truest and the highest of happiness.

A recent survey report from our members reveals 1161 separate and distinct types of retirement activities practiced by our membership. They range from such an ambitious communal activity as at Atascadero, California, in erecting an AARP Building on its own piece of land donated by a member, to the daily custom of many members using the telephone on a schedule to contact invalids and other disabled folk and check upon their well-being and report possible needs and tensions. The pride we feel in their initiative and drive and the public respect they have earned are in accordance with the fact ·that they realize that "no man is an island" as Donne has written, but "a piece of the continent, a part of the whole."—that they are in truth assuming a vital share in today's gravely needed renaissance of humanism.

Deepened insights are sought by those who have retained the zest for living creatively. Some are studying a second or a third foreign language, some are eagerly striving to understand the world-encompassing problems and the changing cultural patterns that we, who care, must help to form what could affect not only our welfare but our very existence, and so are developing latent talents in the arts and crafts.

Then there are those interested in the cultural phase of our living, giving of themselves in personal growth to others in teaching and tutoring in all the ramifications that such service covers, in scope from nursery to post graduate, from the formal institutional to the home variety of service, in all media from the arts and the sciences and technology. Many report helping young and old alike in speech correction, in both braille understanding and transcriptions, in lip reading and children story telling. Library and museum work on a voluntary basis are frequently mentioned as are also the processing of recording books and the talking books for the bind.

Many are expressing themselves creatively in the writing of stoires, books, articles. Many are helping the sick and the shut-ins by writing letters for them, doing for institutions and individuals alike secretarial and clerical work, local press reporting and research both genealogical and historical.

Along somewhat the same lines are the counciling and advisory services offered by men and women of varying backgrounds, helping in technical problems of occupational interest, often guidance, sometimes placement and its essential follow-up.

Many services for the welfare of others reported include volunteer work in hospitals, rest homes and nursing institutions—ranging from reception service, data taking, library distribution to ward visitation, individual and group technical guidance in various arts, crafts and small construction, also in various types of recreational skills, ranging from such sedentary activities as cards and chess, to the more active and stimulating square dancing and dramatic presentations.

Still others of our members we find working in civic and political groups of their own selection. These activities range from membership solicitation to participation on boards of school trustees, of libraries, of chambers of commerce, of local and state historical societies, civil defense, participation in community programs including such as welcoming services, general safety, and responsible membership in municipal or town councils.

The same type of comprehenisve service is being generously given to the various religious institutions of the individual's choice—decorating the building, distributing literature, servicing the program in musical contributions, reception, friendly visiting, financial arrangements, planning an ever-expanding area of helpfulness, etc.

For social clubs, alumni, professional, trade or fraternal associations, the membership does much in organization, solicitation, and administrative duties and in recreational and entertainment activities. They show travel pictures, take part in drama readings, give book reviews, and share their musical talent, and organize and assist in games and programs.

Individual activities that add much to the happiness and comforts of the recipients are those to others in need of such services—preparing food for sales or meals for shut-in's; acting as mother's helper, doing laundry work for ill or handicapped neighbors, donating carpentry and plumbing services, transporting others to and from church, the cinema, the hospital clinic, the doctor's offices, or just for "the joy of a ride to see things." Others deliver meals on wheels, raise and contribute flowers for the pleasure of others, etc., etc., etc.

Last but far from least is the untiring service given AARP. Santa Barbara, California, Chapter donates time, skill and infinite resources to the improvement of conditions round about. The tale is endless but electric in its details and its potential inspiration and encouragement. in opening exciting doors for exploration by others.

In the world of today this dedication of the countless men and women of AARP devoting their talents and energies to the building of a better world is heart-warming. Here in a land where daily we hear tales of apathy and callous indifference and stories of man's hand raised against man, we are comforted in seeing AARP's philosophy being realized in practice. They teach the world that one's personal growth, mental and spiritual, is an integral part of life's adventure and that a concern for one's fellow man, when realized in constructive acts of remedy, repair or improvement, are richly rewarding and a source of happiness.

This is a story of respect and strength and principles and intelligence. It is a simple recital of thousands and thousands of folks who would be amazed to be thought of as crusaders in the cause of responsible and honorable living, in a time of crowded excitement and social adventuring. In a time of great self-indulgence and easy morals, the achievements and the spirit that prompts their accomplishment are wholesome trends to a return of self-control and the temperate and worthy dignity of life, so tragically needed. Thousands of AARP members are perhaps unconscious of either the nobility of their actions or of the possible contagious influence elsewhere. Yet they are perhaps solving for others what is the true secret of retirement happiness—the gift of unselfish neighborly sharing!

Carlyle with earnest vigor states the case: "My brother, the grave man has to give his Life away. Give it, I advise thee—thou dost not expect to *sell* thy Life in an adequate manner? What price, for example, would content thee?

"The just price of thy Life to thee—why, God's entire Creation to thyself, the whole Universe of Space, the whole Eternity of Time, and what they hold; that is the price that would content thee; that, and if thou wilt be candid, nothing short of that! It is thy all; and for it thou wouldst have all . . .

"Thou wilt never sell Life, or any part of thy Life, in a satisfactory manner. Give it, like a royal heart; let the price be *nothing;* thou *hast* then, in a certain sense, got *all* for it."

"We cannot stress too strongly the problem that older people, on losing their dear ones, often face stark loneliness in our restless urban America. I have seen men and women housed in those pigeon crofts that we city folk call apartments find in the meeting of other AARP folk a fortunate relief, a new home-life."

A tale of adventure, courage, faith

The full story of the American Association of Retired Persons is really a tale of adventure, courage, and faith. To rehearse its dramatic growth in a few pages requires much simplification and the touching of only the high points, for AARP is like the proverbial iceberg, much of its foundation is not apparent at first sight to the casual observer.

It is nevertheless a pleasure to review its story. A nongovernmental organization, nonprofit and nonpartisan, AARP has a paid-up membership of over one million mature persons, described by Reader's Digest as the youngest, fastest growing and most energetic organization in the United States.

Actually these AARP folk see in their mature years of retirement a greater opportunity for self-expression and self-fulfillment. Definitely they are not "on the shelf"; they are seeking and finding a greater amplification of life; they are exhibiting a larger capacity for joyous living and a broadening interest in community and world affairs.

The question is often asked, just what are the unique features of

312

AARP? How does it differ from the golden age or senior citizen clubs that are recreationally oriented? The difference lies in its underlying philosophy!

1. AARP believes that older people, like all people, have as their primary responsibility, the material, intellectual and spiritual ordering of their own lives.

2. AARP engages itself, with deep concern and conviction, in a practical fashion, to increase for its members the purchasing power of the retirement dollars in direct contrast to seeking welfare subsidies and benefits from the Federal Government.

3. AARP recognizes that creeping inflation with the subsequent fluctuations in both the cost of living and the general standard of life is the greatest potential and actual enemy of the purchasing power of persons with fixed incomes.

4. AARP believes it to be essential that the system of the compulsory retirement at 65 be revised to be more flexible, not only for the benefit of the elderly but for that of the nation as a whole.

5. AARP holds, as a high purpose, the involvement of its members in the affairs and the life of their respective communities, to the limit of their capacities.

6. AARP appreciates recreation when it is planned, but not as a device provided for the elderly alone, with the thought of their social nonparticipation with the community and their social isolation from the community; neither does it consider it on its agenda as a priority number one. AARP considers recreation as a wholesome and delightful means of cultural and social expression of older folk integrated into the life of the community as a whole.

7. AARP designs its program to realize the goals described in its seal—independence, dignity and purpose.

In summary, AARP Chapters maintain that they offer the finest insurance against loneliness, for the development of a mental elasticity, the cultivation of community commitments and enterprises, the adoption of wider interests making of an active and committed retirement

313

a matter of real delight.

The growth and the development of AARP has been closely related to that of its sponsoring organization, the National Retired Teachers Association, which, at its inception in 1947, pledged itself pridefully: (1) to find positive and practical answers to the needs of its members in their wish to lead a self-sustaining independent life; and (2) to encourage their members to maintain their dignity by a life of continuing growth and service, never asking for themselves something they would not share with others of like age and need.

The high intentions of NRTA, its sincere effort, intelligent direction and skillful execution gave vitality to its program. Its two-fold victories—first, the pioneering break-through in insurance history, by establishing a group policy of hopeful protection for persons 65 years and older, without the necessity of a physical examination, with the acceptance of the present physical conditions, enrolling all ages 65 or over, and without the right of cancellation; and second, the winning of the Federal allowance of tax credit under the rulings of the Internal Federal Revenue Service.

These two were the material gifts with which NRTA endowed AARP upon its inception. Other advantages, together they have gained, because of the additional memberships the two associations can offer in securing increases in other services or initiation of new benefits.

Another one of the intangible gifts of NRTA is the sharing with AARP the legislative know-how and expertness earned through eleven years of dignified Congressional lobbying. The prestige and recognition gained is due to NRTA never having been a pressure group seeking selfish interests, but always an active and alert non-partisan informational service agency, guarding the interests of all older Americans. The respect of Congressional members as to NRTA's own integrity and its frank and honest and effective presentations of matters affecting the aged has had and will continue to have a profound influence which is assuredly a valuable asset.

Not only did NRTA share with AARP the benefits it had secured in its 11 years of endeavor, it voted to help in AARP's organization by underwriting all its initial costs in associational material, its incor-

314

poration, counsel fees, and the expenses of publications. Many of the NRTA's best workers became the founding members of AARP and have since its inception worked for its growth and development.

Among the intangible gifts that NRTA gave to AARP, just as vital in its way, was the changing of the stereotype of old age through eleven earnest years of crusading, not by talk—that is left to the theorists—but by precept and example, that these older folk, practical idealists as they were, displayed confidently, proving first to themselves and so to the world:

1. Old age is a figment of the imagination. It is a concept, just as youth is a concept. There is no old age as such; there are old persons, millions of them, everyone uniquely different physically, intellectually, and spiritually, their only similarity being in the number of years of life.

2. Segregating them by labeling them "senior citizens" is a disservice to them and to the youthful sponsors who so named them, forgetting that they, too, if fortunate enough to live long, at last might also be so classified—and so segregated and so belittled.

AARP makes possible for some the making of strangers into friends, and the added happy companionship of old friends with these new ones, with wider interests for all.

To some, AARP is mainly a voluntary association of older people which, through its happy union with its sponsoring affiliate, NRTA, is able to make available to its membership such benefits as hospital-surgical-medical-nursing home protection in coordination with Medicare; group travel at home and around-the-world, with headquarters in Switzerland, London, Rome, Paris and Germany; a nation-wide drug service with mail order facilities and reduced rates; publications geared to their interest and reaching the members monthly; on request, counseling and referral services.

The quality and the variety of services made available do create in AARP a unique organization. However there are many other benefits, highly prized. Among these are the two bimonthly periodicals, *Modern Maturity* and the AARP Bulletin; 500 AARP Chapters, situated in many states and already enrolling about eight percent of the AARP membership; in three centers a Hospitality Lounge; and in two cities our Institute of Lifetime Learning and the Every Wednesday morning lecture series. Plans for the extension of similar facilities elsewhere are under study; you will hear of them soon.

To others, AARP means much more. To them it is the agency that helps supply the motive power or the occasion for the giving of service, not for its receipt.

Among the finest services an AARP member of a chapter does is to help the member at a loss as to a motivating purpose through activity to attest this truth that goodwill service to others is the elixir of life. What our deepest self craves is not mere enjoyment, but some supreme purpose that will enlist all our powers and will give unity and direction to our life. We can never know the profoundest joy without a conviction that our life is significant—not a meaningless episode. The loftiest aim of human life is unselfish service to others.

AARP makes easily possible the making of strangers into friends. The added happy companionship of old friends with these new ones make for wider interests for all.

The AARP brotherhood is magic medicine for the lonely.

I often wonder, if we who have a rich home life realize the cruel and crippling sense of loneliness that seems to rob its victim of a compelling purpose for life and even the sense of personal identity. I believe that we cannot stress too strongly this problem that older people, on losing their dear ones, often face stark loneliness in our restless urban America. I have seen men and women housed in these pigeon crofts that we city folk call apartments find in the meeting of other AARP folk a fortunate relief, a new home life. I have been even told by them that *Modern Maturity* has become for some the nearest substitute they have for "a letter from home" and a view toward the future.

To those suffering from boredom AARP gives many challenges. There may be a project on hand; if not, there can be one uncovered and enthusiasm engendered to supply that need. Dr. Minot Simons tells us that, "We know the world has never been so rich in helpers as it is today, and consequently never have there been people so happy and so

316

blessed in their lives. Volunteers for human service seem to be there when needed. It would be difficult to point out a more encouraging fact for the world's future."

AARP Chapters, too, make possible men getting together with men and enjoying a man's pow-wow, a frank give-and-take on what's new in the world about the community, the UN, the countries beyond from Arabia to Zanzibar—and to decide how each would find the answer of the part our nation should play, taking into consideration the significance of our vast affluent nation in relationship with the uneasy and nonaffluent world. Such contacts can help recreate the "man world" of active workdays.

For those offerings of AARP annual dues of $2.00 are charged; there are no assessments. The $2.00 membership dues, with thrifty management, is able to pay for the maintenance of membership records, the printing and distribution of the publications and the expenses of Conferences and Conventions.

We have chosen to safeguard and to expand our present strengths and special opportunities rather than to try to respond to all the enterprises our members suggest. In initiating a new venture, first we have to see how much income from our operations it might require. At the same time we must show a workable budget representing considered estimates of the facilities being planned for and the staff necessary to support them.

Here is the point when we find it necessary to review our plans, using all the financial prudence available to us. Of course we realize that we must have the courage to make some assumptions. We must do this knowing that our Associational income from dues would not permit any such expansion and that we must count upon the income that is allotted us by our various services for the express purpose of administering these same services. Through the policy, adopted at our inception, of paying no emolument to any of our elected officers, we have been able, without any aid from any membership dues paid to the Association, to finance the initiation of our various services, always with the expectation that these new facilities may in time become self-supporting and repay, so that other desirable facilities might be opened. This plan, of course, would not be always true, such as in the case of helping to defray such convention costs as the transportation and housing expenses of our elected delegates.

With the wholehearted and understanding support of our services by our members and through their patronage, we face the future with the firm conviction that we can hopefully look forward to the expansion of many services we are considering now only in thought.

There are so many other interesting facets of AARP's growth and extended influences. There is the new pre-retirement program and its enabling publication, *Dynamic Maturity,* which already has a subscription list in the thousands with a cooperative working arrangement of over 150 large companies enrolling their older employees; there is the ARP International, an association and a journal affiliated with AARP and an eager and enthusiastic personnel from Asia, Africa, Australia, Latin America and, of course, Canada and the U.S.A. Also, though not officially a member of AARP, there's another organization of which AARP is proud, and that is the Retirement Research and Welfare Association.

Gladly we would report AARP's participation in the supplying of hundreds of candidates for the Peace Corps, its involvement with VISTA (Volunteers in the Service of America); in identifying the elderly personnel needed for the realization of the plans and projects of The Older Americans Act; and the establishment of our information and referral service in connection with National Department of Consumer Affairs.

In brief then may we say that AARP has a real and an abiding concern for the individual; that it will employ every avenue, fact and figure, with every iota of imagination, ingenuity, resourcefulness and experience to create for its members a prideful and a happy situation so that they may live victoriously up to their last breath, realizing that life is a living, not an aging process, and that happiness comes through the realization of its goals, Independence, Dignity and Purpose.

318

I shall pass through
this world but once.
Any good therefore
that I can do or any
kindness that I can show
to any human being,
let me do it now.
Let me not
defer or neglect it,
for I shall not pass
this way again.

Henry Drummond

HIGHSMITH 45-220